Z974080

PENGUIN BOOKS

THE ROAD TO CHARACTER

David
broadca   ocial
Anima   imes columns reach
over 80   globe.

D1428472

DAVID BROOKS

The Road to Character

PENGUIN BOOKS

PENGUIN BOOKS

UK | USA | Canada | Ireland | Australia
India | New Zealand | South Africa

Penguin Books is part of the Penguin Random House group of companies
whose addresses can be found at global.penguinrandomhouse.com.

First published in the United States of America by Random House 2015
First published in Great Britain by Allen Lane 2015
Published in Penguin Books 2016
001

Text copyright © David Brooks, 2015

The moral right of the author has been asserted

Printed in Great Britain by Clays Ltd, St Ives plc

A CIP catalogue record for this book is available from the British Library

ISBN: 978-0-141-98036-2

www.greenpenguin.co.uk

MIX
Paper from
responsible sources
FSC® C018179

Penguin Random House is committed to a
sustainable future for our business, our readers
and our planet. This book is made from Forest
Stewardship Council® certified paper.

To my parents,
Lois and Michael Brooks

CONTENTS

———

INTRODUCTION: ADAM II

Recently I've been thinking about the difference between the résumé virtues and the eulogy virtues. The résumé virtues are the ones you list on your résumé, the skills that you bring to the job market and that contribute to external success. The eulogy virtues are deeper. They're the virtues that get talked about at your funeral, the ones that exist at the core of your being—whether you are kind, brave, honest or faithful; what kind of relationships you formed.

Most of us would say that the eulogy virtues are more important than the résumé virtues, but I confess that for long stretches of my life I've spent more time thinking about the latter than the former. Our education system is certainly oriented around the résumé virtues more than the eulogy ones. Public conversation is, too—the self-help tips in magazines, the nonfiction bestsellers. Most of us have clearer strategies for how to achieve career success than we do for how to develop a profound character.

One book that has helped me think about these two sets of virtues is *Lonely Man of Faith,* which was written by Rabbi Joseph Soloveitchik in 1965. Soloveitchik noted that there are two accounts of creation in Genesis and argued that these represent the two opposing sides of our nature, which he called Adam I and Adam II.

Modernizing Soloveitchik's categories a bit, we could say that Adam I is the career-oriented, ambitious side of our nature. Adam I is the external, résumé Adam. Adam I wants to build, create, produce, and discover things. He wants to have high status and win victories.

Adam II is the internal Adam. Adam II wants to embody certain moral qualities. Adam II wants to have a serene inner character, a quiet but solid sense of right and wrong—not only to do good, but to be good. Adam II wants to love intimately, to sacrifice self in the service of others, to live in obedience to some transcendent truth, to have a cohesive inner soul that honors creation and one's own possibilities.

While Adam I wants to conquer the world, Adam II wants to obey a calling to serve the world. While Adam I is creative and savors his own accomplishments, Adam II sometimes renounces worldly success and status for the sake of some sacred purpose. While Adam I asks how things work, Adam II asks why things exist, and what ultimately we are here for. While Adam I wants to venture forth, Adam II wants to return to his roots and savor the warmth of a family meal. While Adam I's motto is "Success," Adam II experiences life as a moral drama. His motto is "Charity, love, and redemption."

Soloveitchik argued that we live in the contradiction between these two Adams. The outer, majestic Adam and the inner, humble Adam are not fully reconcilable. We are forever caught in self-confrontation. We are called to fulfill both personae, and must master the art of living forever within the tension between these two natures.

The hard part of this confrontation, I'd add, is that Adams I and II live by different logics. Adam I—the creating, building, and discovering Adam—lives by a straightforward utilitarian logic. It's the logic of economics. Input leads to output. Effort leads to reward. Practice makes perfect. Pursue self-interest. Maximize your utility. Impress the world.

Adam II lives by an inverse logic. It's a moral logic, not an economic one. You have to give to receive. You have to surrender to something outside yourself to gain strength within yourself. You have to conquer your desire to get what you crave. Success leads to the greatest failure, which is pride. Failure leads to the greatest success, which is humility and learning. In order to fulfill yourself, you have to forget yourself. In order to find yourself, you have to lose yourself.

To nurture your Adam I career, it makes sense to cultivate your strengths. To nurture your Adam II moral core, it is necessary to confront your weaknesses.

The Shrewd Animal

WE LIVE IN A CULTURE THAT NURTURES ADAM I, THE EXTERNAL ADAM, AND neglects Adam II. We live in a society that encourages us to think about how to have a great career but leaves many of us inarticulate about how to cultivate the inner life. The competition to succeed and win admiration is so fierce that it becomes all-consuming. The consumer marketplace encourages us to live by a utilitarian calculus, to satisfy our desires and lose sight of the moral stakes involved in everyday decisions. The noise of fast and shallow communications makes it harder to hear the quieter sounds that emanate from the depths. We live in a culture that teaches us to promote and advertise ourselves and to master the skills required for success, but that gives little encouragement to humility, sympathy, and honest self-confrontation, which are necessary for building character.

If you are only Adam I, you turn into a shrewd animal, a crafty, self-preserving creature who is adept at playing the game and who turns everything into a game. If that's all you have, you spend a lot of time cultivating professional skills, but you don't have a clear idea of the sources of meaning in life, so you don't know where you should devote your skills, which career path will be highest and best. Years pass and the deepest parts of yourself go unexplored and unstructured. You are busy, but you have a vague anxiety that your life has not achieved its ultimate meaning and significance. You live with an unconscious boredom, not really loving, not really attached to the moral purposes that give life its worth. You lack the internal criteria to make unshakable commitments. You never develop inner constancy, the integrity that can withstand popular disapproval or a serious blow. You find yourself doing things that other people approve of, whether these things are right for you or not. You foolishly judge other people by their abilities, not by their worth. You do not have a strategy to build character, and without that, not only your inner life but also your external life will eventually fall to pieces.

This book is about Adam II. It's about how some people have cultivated strong character. It's about one mindset that people through the centuries have adopted to put iron in their core and to cultivate a wise heart. I wrote it, to be honest, to save my own soul.

I was born with a natural disposition toward shallowness. I now work as a pundit and columnist. I'm paid to be a narcissistic blowhard, to volley my opinions, to appear more confident about them than I really am, to appear smarter than I really am, to appear better and more authoritative than I really am. I have to work harder than most people to avoid a life of smug superficiality. I've also become more aware that, like many people these days, I have lived a life of vague moral aspiration—vaguely wanting to be good, vaguely wanting to serve some larger purpose, while lacking a concrete moral vocabulary, a clear understanding of how to live a rich inner life, or even a clear knowledge of how character is developed and depth is achieved.

I've discovered that without a rigorous focus on the Adam II side of our nature, it is easy to slip into a self-satisfied moral mediocrity. You grade yourself on a forgiving curve. You follow your desires wherever they take you, and you approve of yourself so long as you are not obviously hurting anyone else. You figure that if the people around you seem to like you, you must be good enough. In the process you end up slowly turning yourself into something a little less impressive than you had originally hoped. A humiliating gap opens up between your actual self and your desired self. You realize that the voice of your Adam I is loud but the voice of your Adam II is muffled; the life plan of Adam I is clear, but the life plan of Adam II is fuzzy; Adam I is alert, Adam II is sleepwalking.

I wrote this book not sure I could follow the road to character, but I wanted at least to know what the road looks like and how other people have trodden it.

The Plan

THE PLAN OF THIS BOOK IS SIMPLE. IN THE NEXT CHAPTER I WILL DESCRIBE an older moral ecology. It was a cultural and intellectual tradition, the "crooked timber" tradition, that emphasized our own brokenness. It was a tradition that demanded humility in the face of our own limitations. But it was also a tradition that held that each of us has the power to confront our own weaknesses, tackle our own sins, and that in the course of this confrontation with ourselves we build character. By successfully confronting sin and weakness we have the chance to play our role in a great moral drama. We can shoot for something higher than happiness. We have a chance to take advantage of everyday occasions to build virtue in ourselves and be of service to the world.

Then I will describe what this character-building method looks like in real life. I'm going to do this through biographical essays, which are also moral essays. Since Plutarch, moralists have tried to communicate certain standards by holding up exemplars. You can't build rich Adam II lives simply by reading sermons or following abstract rules. Example is the best teacher. Moral improvement occurs most reliably when the heart is warmed, when we come into contact with people we admire and love and we consciously and unconsciously bend our lives to mimic theirs.

This truth was hammered home to me after I wrote a column expressing frustration with how hard it is to use the classroom experience to learn how to be good. A veterinarian named Dave Jolly sent me an email that cut to the chase:

> The heart cannot be taught in a classroom intellectually, to students mechanically taking notes. . . . Good, wise hearts are obtained through lifetimes of diligent effort to dig deeply within and heal lifetimes of scars. . . . You can't teach it or email it or tweet it. It has to be discovered within the depths of one's own heart when a person is finally ready to go looking for it, and not before.
>
> The job of the wise person is to swallow the frustration and just go on setting an example of caring and digging and diligence in their own lives. What a wise person teaches is the smallest part of what they give. The totality of their life, of the way they go about it in the smallest details, is what gets transmitted.
>
> Never forget that. The message is the person, perfected over lifetimes of effort that was set in motion by yet another wise person now hidden from the recipient by the dim mists of time. Life is much bigger than we think, cause and effect intertwined in a vast moral structure that keeps pushing us to do better, become better, even when we dwell in the most painful confused darkness.

Those words explain the methodology of this book. The subjects of the portraits that follow in chapters 2 through 10 are a diverse set, white and black, male and female, religious and secular, literary and nonliterary. None of them is even close to perfect. But they practiced a mode of living that is less common now. They were acutely aware of their own weaknesses. They waged an internal struggle against their sins and emerged with some measure of self-respect. And when we think of them, it is not primarily what they accomplished that we remember—great though that may have been—it is who they were. I'm hoping their examples will fire this fearful longing we all have to be better, to follow their course.

In the final chapter I wrap these themes up. I describe how our culture has made it harder to be good, and I summarize this "crooked timber" approach to life in a series of specific points. If you're impatient for the condensed message of this book, skip to the end.

Occasionally, even today, you come across certain people who seem to possess an impressive inner cohesion. They are not leading fragmented, scattershot lives. They have achieved inner integration. They are calm, settled, and rooted. They are not blown off course by storms. They don't crumble in adversity. Their minds are consistent and their hearts are dependable. Their virtues are not the blooming virtues you see in smart college students; they are the ripening virtues you see in people who have lived a little and have learned from joy and pain.

Sometimes you don't even notice these people, because while they seem kind and cheerful, they are also reserved. They possess the self-effacing virtues of people who are inclined to be useful but don't need to prove anything to the world: humility, restraint, reticence, temperance, respect, and soft self-discipline.

They radiate a sort of moral joy. They answer softly when challenged harshly. They are silent when unfairly abused. They are dignified when others try to humiliate them, restrained when others try to provoke them. But they get things done. They perform acts of sacrificial service with the same modest everyday spirit they would display if they were just getting the groceries. They are not thinking about what impressive work they are doing. They are not thinking about themselves at all. They just seem delighted by the flawed people around them. They just recognize what needs doing and they do it.

They make you feel funnier and smarter when you speak with them. They move through different social classes not even aware, it seems, that they are doing so. After you've known them for a while it occurs to you that you've never heard them boast, you've never seen them self-righteous or doggedly certain. They aren't dropping little hints of their own distinctiveness and accomplishments.

They have not led lives of conflict-free tranquillity, but have struggled toward maturity. They have gone some way toward solving life's essential problem, which is that, as Aleksandr Solzhenitsyn put it, "the line separating good and evil passes not through states, nor between classes, nor between political parties either—but right through every human heart."

These are the people who have built a strong inner character, who have achieved a certain depth. In these people, at the end of this struggle, the climb to success has surrendered to the struggle to deepen the soul. After a life of seeking balance, Adam I bows down before Adam II. These are the people we are looking for.

THE ROAD TO CHARACTER

CHAPTER 1

THE SHIFT

O N SUNDAY EVENINGS MY LOCAL NPR STATION REBROADCASTS OLD radio programs. A few years ago I was driving home and heard a program called *Command Performance,* which was a variety show that went out to the troops during World War II. The episode I happened to hear was broadcast the day after V-J Day, on August 15, 1945.

The episode featured some of the era's biggest celebrities: Frank Sinatra, Marlene Dietrich, Cary Grant, Bette Davis, and many others. But the most striking feature of the show was its tone of self-effacement and humility. The Allies had just completed one of the noblest military victories in human history. And yet there was no chest beating. Nobody was erecting triumphal arches.

"Well, it looks like this is it," the host, Bing Crosby, opened. "What can you say at a time like this? You can't throw your skimmer in the air. That's for run-of-the mill holidays. I guess all anybody can do is thank God it's over." The mezzo-soprano Risë Stevens came on and sang a solemn version of "Ave Maria," and then Crosby came back on to summarize the mood: "Today, though, our deep-down feeling is one of humility."

That sentiment was repeated throughout the broadcast. The actor Burgess Meredith read a passage written by Ernie Pyle, the war correspondent. Pyle had been killed just a few months before, but he had written an article anticipating what victory would mean: "We won this war because our men are brave and because of many other things—

because of Russia, England, and China and the passage of time and the gift of nature's materials. We did not win it because destiny created us better than all other people. I hope that in victory we are more grateful than proud."

The show mirrored the reaction of the nation at large. There were rapturous celebrations, certainly. Sailors in San Francisco commandeered cable cars and looted liquor stores. The streets of New York's garment district were five inches deep in confetti.[1] But the mood was divided. Joy gave way to solemnity and self-doubt.

This was in part because the war had been such an epochal event, and had produced such rivers of blood, that individuals felt small in comparison. There was also the manner in which the war in the Pacific had ended—with the atomic bomb. People around the world had just seen the savagery human beings are capable of. Now here was a weapon that could make that savagery apocalyptic. "The knowledge of victory was as charged with sorrow and doubt as with joy and gratitude," James Agee wrote in an editorial that week for *Time* magazine.

But the modest tone of *Command Performance* wasn't just a matter of mood or style. The people on that broadcast had been part of one of the most historic victories ever known. But they didn't go around telling themselves how great they were. They didn't print up bumper stickers commemorating their own awesomeness. Their first instinct was to remind themselves they were not morally superior to anyone else. Their collective impulse was to warn themselves against pride and self-glorification. They intuitively resisted the natural human tendency toward excessive self-love.

I arrived home before the program was over and listened to that radio show in my driveway for a time. Then I went inside and turned on a football game. A quarterback threw a short pass to a wide receiver, who was tackled almost immediately for a two-yard gain. The defensive player did what all professional athletes do these days in moments of personal accomplishment. He did a self-puffing victory dance, as the camera lingered.

It occurred to me that I had just watched more self-celebration after a two-yard gain than I had heard after the United States won World War II.

This little contrast set off a chain of thoughts in my mind. It occurred to me that this shift might symbolize a shift in culture, a shift from a culture of self-effacement that says "Nobody's better than me, but I'm no better than anyone else" to a culture of self-promotion that says "Recognize my accomplishments, I'm pretty special." That contrast, while nothing much in itself, was like a doorway into the different ways it is possible to live in this world.

Little Me

IN THE YEARS FOLLOWING THAT *COMMAND PERFORMANCE* EPISODE, I WENT back and studied that time and the people who were prominent then. The research reminded me first of all that none of us should ever wish to go back to the culture of the mid-twentieth century. It was a more racist, sexist, and anti-Semitic culture. Most of us would not have had the opportunities we enjoy if we had lived back then. It was also a more boring culture, with bland food and homogeneous living arrangements. It was an emotionally cold culture. Fathers, in particular, frequently were unable to express their love for their own children. Husbands were unable to see the depth in their own wives. In so many ways, life is better now than it was then.

But it did occur to me that there was perhaps a strain of humility that was more common then than now, that there was a moral ecology, stretching back centuries but less prominent now, encouraging people to be more skeptical of their desires, more aware of their own weaknesses, more intent on combatting the flaws in their own natures and turning weakness into strength. People in this tradition, I thought, are less likely to feel that every thought, feeling, and achievement should be immediately shared with the world at large.

The popular culture seemed more reticent in the era of *Command Performance*. There were no message T-shirts back then, no exclamation points on the typewriter keyboards, no sympathy ribbons for various diseases, no vanity license plates, no bumper stickers with personal or moral declarations. People didn't brag about their college affiliations or their vacation spots with little stickers on the rear windows of their cars. There was stronger social sanction against (as they would have put it) blowing your own trumpet, getting above yourself, being too big for your britches.

The social code was embodied in the self-effacing style of actors like Gregory Peck or Gary Cooper, or the character Joe Friday on *Dragnet*. When Franklin Roosevelt's aide Harry Hopkins lost a son in World War II, the military brass wanted to put his other sons out of harm's way. Hopkins rejected this idea, writing, with the understatement more common in that era, that his other sons shouldn't be given safe assignments just because their brother "had some bad luck in the Pacific."[2]

Of the twenty-three men and women who served in Dwight Eisenhower's cabinets, only one, the secretary of agriculture, published a memoir afterward, and it was so discreet as to be soporific. By the time the Reagan administration rolled around, twelve of his thirty cabinet members published memoirs, almost all of them self-advertising.[3]

When the elder George Bush, who was raised in that era, was running for president, he, having inculcated the values of his childhood, resisted speaking about himself. If a speechwriter put the word "I" in one of his speeches, he'd instinctively cross it out. The staff would beg him: You're running for president. You've got to talk about yourself. Eventually they'd cow him into doing so. But the next day he'd get a call from his mother. "George, you're talking about yourself again," she'd say. And Bush would revert to form. No more I's in the speeches. No more self-promotion.

The Big Me

OVER THE NEXT FEW YEARS I COLLECTED DATA TO SUGGEST THAT WE HAVE seen a broad shift from a culture of humility to the culture of what you might call the Big Me, from a culture that encouraged people to think humbly of themselves to a culture that encouraged people to see themselves as the center of the universe.

It wasn't hard to find such data. For example, between 1948 and 1954, the Gallup Organization asked high school seniors if they considered themselves to be a very important person. At that point, 12 percent said yes. The same question was revisited in 1989, and this time it wasn't 12 percent who considered themselves very important, it was 80 percent of boys and 77 percent of girls.

Psychologists have a thing called the narcissism test. They read people statements and ask if the statements apply to them. Statements such as "I like to be the center of attention . . . I show off if I get the chance because I am extraordinary . . . Somebody should write a biography about me." The median narcissism score has risen 30 percent in the last two decades. Ninety-three percent of young people score higher than the middle score just twenty years ago.[4] The largest gains have been in the number of people who agree with the statements "I am an extraordinary person" and "I like to look at my body."

Along with this apparent rise in self-esteem, there has been a tremendous increase in the desire for fame. Fame used to rank low as a life's ambition for most people. In a 1976 survey that asked people to list their life goals, fame ranked fifteenth out of sixteen. By 2007, 51 percent of young people reported that being famous was one of their top personal goals.[5] In one study, middle school girls were asked who they would most like to have dinner with. Jennifer Lopez came in first, Jesus Christ came in second, and Paris Hilton third. The girls were then asked which of the following jobs they would like to have. Nearly twice as many said they'd rather be a celebrity's personal assistant—for example, Justin Bieber's—than president of Harvard. (Though, to be fair, I'm pretty sure the president of Harvard would also rather be Justin Bieber's personal assistant.)

As I looked around the popular culture I kept finding the same messages everywhere: You are special. Trust yourself. Be true to yourself. Movies from Pixar and Disney are constantly telling children how wonderful they are. Commencement speeches are larded with the same clichés: Follow your passion. Don't accept limits. Chart your own course. You have a responsibility to do great things because you are so great. This is the gospel of self-trust.

As Ellen DeGeneres put it in a 2009 commencement address, "My advice to you is to be true to yourself and everything will be fine." Celebrity chef Mario Batali advised graduates to follow "your own truth, expressed consistently by you." Anna Quindlen urged another audience to have the courage to "honor your character, your intellect, your inclinations, and, yes, your soul by listening to its clean clear voice instead of following the muddied messages of a timid world."

In her mega-selling book *Eat, Pray, Love* (I am the only man ever to finish this book), Elizabeth Gilbert wrote that God manifests himself through "my own voice from within my own self. . . . God dwells within you as you yourself, exactly the way you are."[6]

I began looking at the way we raise our children and found signs of this moral shift. For example, the early Girl Scout handbooks preached an ethic of self-sacrifice and self-effacement. The chief obstacle to happiness, the handbook exhorted, comes from the overeager desire to have people think about you.

By 1980, as James Davison Hunter has pointed out, the tone was very different. *You Make the Difference: The Handbook for Cadette and Senior Girl Scouts* was telling girls to pay *more* attention to themselves: "How can you get more in touch with *you*? What are *you* feeling? . . . Every option available to you through Senior Scouting can, in some way, help you to a better understanding of yourself. . . . Put yourself in the 'center stage' of your thoughts to gain perspective on your own ways of feeling, thinking and acting."[7]

The shift can even be seen in the words that flow from the pulpit. Joel Osteen, one of the most popular megachurch leaders today, writes from Houston, Texas. "God didn't create you to be average," Osteen says in his book *Become a Better You*. "You were made to excel. You were made to leave a mark on this generation. . . . Start [believing] 'I've been chosen, set apart, destined to live in victory.'"[8]

The Humble Path

AS YEARS WENT BY AND WORK ON THIS BOOK CONTINUED, MY THOUGHTS returned to that episode of *Command Performance*. I was haunted by the quality of humility I heard in those voices.

There was something aesthetically beautiful about the self-effacement the people on that program displayed. The self-effacing person is soothing and gracious, while the self-promoting person is fragile and jarring. Humility is freedom from the need to prove you are superior all the time, but egotism is a ravenous hunger in a small space—self-concerned, competitive, and distinction-hungry. Humility is infused with lovely emotions like admiration, companionship, and gratitude. "Thankfulness," the Archbishop of Canterbury, Michael Ramsey, said, "is a soil in which pride does not easily grow."[9]

There is something intellectually impressive about that sort of humility, too. We have, the psychologist Daniel Kahneman writes, an "almost unlimited ability to ignore our ignorance."[10] Humility is the awareness that there's a lot you don't know and that a lot of what you think you know is distorted or wrong.

This is the way humility leads to wisdom. Montaigne once wrote, "We can be knowledgeable with other men's knowledge, but we can't be wise with other men's wisdom." That's because wisdom isn't a body of information. It's the moral quality of knowing what you don't know and figuring out a way to handle your ignorance, uncertainty, and limitation.

The people we think are wise have, to some degree, overcome the biases and overconfident tendencies that are infused in our nature. In its most complete meaning, intellectual humility is accurate self-awareness from a distance. It is moving over the course of one's life from the adolescent's close-up view of yourself, in which you fill the whole canvas, to a landscape view in which you see, from a wider perspective, your strengths and weaknesses, your connections and dependencies, and the role you play in a larger story.

Finally, there is something morally impressive about humility. Every epoch has its own preferred methods of self-cultivation, its own ways to build character and depth. The people on that *Command Performance* broadcast were guarding themselves against some of their least attractive tendencies, to be prideful, self-congratulatory, hubristic.

Today, many of us see our life through the metaphor of a journey—a journey through the external world and up the ladder of success. When we think about making a difference or leading a life with purpose, we often think of achieving something external—performing some service that will have an impact on the world, creating a successful company, or doing something for the community.

Truly humble people also use that journey metaphor to describe their own lives. But they also use, alongside that, a different metaphor, which has more to do with the internal life. This is the metaphor of self-confrontation. They are more likely to assume that we are all deeply divided selves, both splendidly endowed and deeply flawed—that we each have certain talents but also certain weaknesses. And if we habitually fall for those temptations and do not struggle against the weaknesses in ourselves, then we will gradually spoil some core piece of ourselves. We will not be as good, internally, as we want to be. We will fail in some profound way.

For people of this sort, the external drama up the ladder of success is important, but the inner struggle against one's own weaknesses is the central drama of life. As the popular minister Harry Emerson Fosdick put it in his 1943 book *On Being a Real Person,* "The beginning of worth-while living is thus the confrontation with ourselves."[11]

Truly humble people are engaged in a great effort to magnify what is best in themselves and defeat what is worst, to become strong in the weak places. They start with an acute awareness of the bugs in their own nature. Our basic problem is that we are self-centered, a plight beautifully captured in the famous commencement address David Foster Wallace gave at Kenyon College in 2005:

> Everything in my own immediate experience supports my deep belief that I am the absolute center of the universe; the realest, most vivid and important person in existence. We rarely think about this sort of natural, basic self-centeredness because it's so socially repulsive. But it's pretty much the same for all of us. It is our default setting, hard-wired into our boards at birth. Think about it: there is no experience you have had that you are not the absolute center of. The world as you experience it is there in front of YOU or behind YOU, to the left or right of YOU, on YOUR TV or YOUR monitor. And so on. Other people's thoughts and feelings have to be communicated to you somehow, but your own are so immediate, urgent, real.

This self-centeredness leads in several unfortunate directions. It leads to selfishness, the desire to use other people as means to get things for yourself. It also leads to pride, the desire to see yourself as superior to everybody else. It leads to a capacity to ignore and rationalize your own imperfections and inflate your virtues. As we go through life, most of us are constantly comparing and constantly finding ourselves slightly better than other people—more virtuous, with better judgment, with better taste. We're constantly seeking recognition, and painfully sensitive to any snub or insult to the status we believe we have earned for ourselves.

Some perversity in our nature leads us to put lower loves above higher ones. We all love and desire a multitude of things: friendship, family, popularity, country, money, and so on. And we all have a sense that some loves are higher or more important than other loves. I suspect we all rank those loves in pretty much the same way. We all know that the love you feel for your children or parents should be higher than the love you have for money. We all know the love you have for the truth should be higher than the love you have for popularity. Even in this age of relativism and pluralism, the moral hierarchy of the heart is one thing we generally share, at least most of the time.

But we often put our loves out of order. If someone tells you something in confidence and then you blab it as good gossip at a dinner party, you are putting your love of popularity above your love of friendship. If you talk more at a meeting than you listen, you may be putting your ardor to outshine above learning and companionship. We do this all the time.

People who are humble about their own nature are moral realists. Moral realists are aware that we are all built from "crooked timber"— from Immanuel Kant's famous line, "Out of the crooked timber of humanity, no straight thing was ever made." People in this "crooked-timber" school of humanity have an acute awareness of their own flaws and believe that character is built in the struggle against their own weaknesses. As Thomas Merton wrote, "Souls are like athletes that need opponents worthy of them, if they are to be tried and extended and pushed to the full use of their powers."[12]

You can see evidence of the inner struggle in such people's journals. They are exultant on days when they win some small victory over selfishness and hard-heartedness. They are despondent on days when they let themselves down, when they avoid some charitable task because they were lazy or tired, or fail to attend to a person who wanted to be heard. They are more likely to see their life as a moral adventure story. As the British writer Henry Fairlie put it, "If we acknowledge that our inclination to sin is part of our natures, and that we will never wholly eradicate it, there is at least something for us to do in our lives that will not in the end seem just futile and absurd."

I have a friend who spends a few moments in bed at night reviewing the mistakes of his day. His central sin, from which many of his other sins branch out, is a certain hardness of heart. He's a busy guy with many people making demands on his time. Sometimes he is not fully present for people who are asking his advice or revealing some vulnerability. Sometimes he is more interested in making a good impression than in listening to other people in depth. Maybe he spent more time at a meeting thinking about how he might seem impressive than about what others were actually saying. Maybe he flattered people too unctuously.

Each night, he catalogs the errors. He tallies his recurring core sins and the other mistakes that might have branched off from them. Then he develops strategies for how he might do better tomorrow. Tomorrow he'll try to look differently at people, pause more before people. He'll put care above prestige, the higher thing above the lower thing. We all have a moral responsibility to be more moral every day, and he will struggle to inch ahead each day in this most important sphere.

People who live this way believe that character is not innate or automatic. You have to build it with effort and artistry. You can't be the good person you want to be unless you wage this campaign. You won't even achieve enduring external success unless you build a solid moral core. If you don't have some inner integrity, eventually your Watergate, your scandal, your betrayal, will happen. Adam I ultimately depends upon Adam II.

Now, I have used the word "struggle" and "fight" in the previous passages. But it's a mistake to think that the moral struggle against internal weakness is a struggle the way a war is a struggle or the way a boxing match is a struggle—filled with clash of arms and violence and aggression. Moral realists sometimes do hard things, like standing firm against evil and imposing intense self-discipline on their desires. But character is built not only through austerity and hardship. It is also built sweetly through love and pleasure. When you have deep friendships with good people, you copy and then absorb some of their best traits. When you love a person deeply, you want to serve them and earn their regard. When you experience great art, you widen your repertoire of emotions. Through devotion to some cause, you elevate your desires and organize your energies.

Moreover, the struggle against the weaknesses in yourself is never a solitary struggle. No person can achieve self-mastery on his or her own. Individual will, reason, compassion, and character are not strong enough to consistently defeat selfishness, pride, greed, and self-deception. Everybody needs redemptive assistance from outside—from family, friends, ancestors, rules, traditions, institutions, exemplars, and, for believers, God. We all need people to tell us when we are wrong, to advise us on how to do right, and to encourage, support, arouse, cooperate, and inspire us along the way.

There's something democratic about life viewed in this way. It doesn't matter if you work on Wall Street or at a charity distributing medicine to the poor. It doesn't matter if you are at the top of the income scale or at the bottom. There are heroes and schmucks in all worlds. The most important thing is whether you are willing to engage in moral struggle against yourself. The most important thing is whether you are willing to engage this struggle well—joyfully and compassionately. Fairlie writes, "At least if we recognize that we sin, know that we are individually at war, we may go to war as warriors do, with something of valor and zest and even mirth."[13] Adam I achieves success by winning victories over others. But Adam II builds character by winning victories over the weaknesses in himself.

The U-Curve

THE PEOPLE IN THIS BOOK LED DIVERSE LIVES. EACH ONE OF THEM EXEMPLifies one of the activities that lead to character. But there is one pattern that recurs: They had to go down to go up. They had to descend into the valley of humility to climb to the heights of character.

The road to character often involves moments of moral crisis, confrontation, and recovery. When they were in a crucible moment, they suddenly had a greater ability to see their own nature. The everyday self-deceptions and illusions of self-mastery were shattered. They had to humble themselves in self-awareness if they had any hope of rising up transformed. Alice had to be small to enter Wonderland. Or, as Kierkegaard put it, "Only the one who descends into the underworld rescues the beloved."

But then the beauty began. In the valley of humility they learned to quiet the self. Only by quieting the self could they see the world clearly. Only by quieting the self could they understand other people and accept what they are offering.

When they had quieted themselves, they had opened up space for grace to flood in. They found themselves helped by people they did not expect would help them. They found themselves understood and cared for by others in ways they did not imagine beforehand. They found themselves loved in ways they did not deserve. They didn't have to flail about, because hands were holding them up.

Before long, people who have entered the valley of humility feel themselves back in the uplands of joy and commitment. They've thrown themselves into work, made new friends, and cultivated new loves. They realize, with a shock, that they've traveled a long way since the first days of their crucible. They turn around and see how much ground they have left behind. Such people don't come out healed; they come out different. They find a vocation or calling. They commit themselves to some long obedience and dedicate themselves to some desperate lark that gives life purpose.

Each phase of this experience has left a residue on such a person's soul. The experience has reshaped their inner core and given it great coherence, solidity, and weight. People with character may be loud or quiet, but they do tend to have a certain level of self-respect. Self-respect is not the same as self-confidence or self-esteem. Self-respect is not based on IQ or any of the mental or physical gifts that help get you into a competitive college. It is not comparative. It is not earned by being better than other people at something. It is earned by being better than you used to be, by being dependable in times of testing, straight in times of temptation. It emerges in one who is morally dependable. Self-respect is produced by inner triumphs, not external ones. It can only be earned by a person who has endured some internal temptation, who has confronted their own weaknesses and who knows, "Well, if worse comes to worst, I can endure that. I can overcome that."

The sort of process I've just described can happen in big ways. In every life there are huge crucible moments, altering ordeals, that either make you or break you. But this process can also happen in daily, gradual ways. Every day it's possible to recognize small flaws, to reach out to others, to try to correct errors. Character is built both through drama and through the everyday.

What was on display in *Command Performance* was more than just an aesthetic or a style. The more I looked into that period, the more I realized I was looking into a different moral country. I began to see a different view of human nature, a different attitude about what is important in life, a different formula for how to live a life of character and depth. I don't know how many people in those days hewed to this different moral ecology, but some people did, and I found that I admired them immensely.

My general belief is that we've accidentally left this moral tradition behind. Over the last several decades, we've lost this language, this way of organizing life. We're not bad. But we are morally inarticulate. We're not more selfish or venal than people in other times, but we've lost the understanding of how character is built. The "crooked timber" moral tradition—based on the awareness of sin and the confrontation with sin—was an inheritance passed down from generation to generation. It gave people a clearer sense of how to cultivate the eulogy virtues, how to develop the Adam II side of their nature. Without it, there is a certain superficiality to modern culture, especially in the moral sphere.

The central fallacy of modern life is the belief that accomplishments of the Adam I realm can produce deep satisfaction. That's false. Adam I's desires are infinite and always leap out ahead of whatever has just been achieved. Only Adam II can experience deep satisfaction. Adam I aims for happiness, but Adam II knows that happiness is insufficient. The ultimate joys are moral joys. In the pages ahead, I will try to offer some real-life examples of how this sort of life was lived. We can't and shouldn't want to return to the past. But we can rediscover this moral tradition, relearn this vocabulary of character, and incorporate it into our own lives.

You can't build Adam II out of a recipe book. There is no seven-point program. But we can immerse ourselves in the lives of outstanding people and try to understand the wisdom of the way they lived. I'm hoping you'll be able to pick out a few lessons that are important to you in the pages ahead, even if they are not the same ones that seem important to me. I'm hoping you and I will both emerge from the next nine chapters slightly different and slightly better.

CHAPTER 2

THE SUMMONED SELF

TODAY, THE AREA AROUND WASHINGTON SQUARE PARK IN LOWER MANhattan is surrounded by New York University, expensive apartments, and upscale stores. But back in 1911, there were nice brownstones on the northern side of the park and factories on its eastern and southern sides, drawing young and mostly Jewish and Italian immigrant workers. One of the nice homes was owned by Mrs. Gordon Norrie, a society matron descended from two of the men who signed the Declaration of Independence.

On March 25, Mrs. Norrie was just sitting down to tea with a group of friends when they heard a commotion outside. One of her guests, Frances Perkins, then thirty-one, was from an old but middle-class Maine family, which could also trace its lineage back to the time of the Revolution. She had attended Mount Holyoke College and was working at the Consumers' League of New York, lobbying to end child labor. Perkins spoke in the upper-crust tones befitting her upbringing—like Margaret Dumont in the old Marx Brothers movies or Mrs. Thurston Howell III—with long flat *a*'s, dropped *r*'s, and rounded vowels, "tom*aahhh*to" for "tomato."

A butler rushed in and announced that there was a fire near the square. The ladies ran out. Perkins lifted up her skirts and sprinted toward it. They had stumbled upon the Triangle Shirtwaist Factory, one of the most famous fires in American history. Perkins could see the eighth, ninth, and tenth floors of the building ablaze and dozens of workers crowding around the open windows. She joined the throng of horrified onlookers on the sidewalk below.

Some saw what they thought were bundles of fabric falling from the windows. They thought the factory owners were saving their best material. As the bundles continued to fall, the onlookers realized they were not bundles at all. They were people, hurling themselves to their death. "People had just begun to jump as we got there," Perkins would later remember. "They had been holding on until that time, standing in the windowsills, being crowded by others behind them, the fire pressing closer and closer, the smoke closer and closer.[1]

"They began to jump. The window was too crowded and they would jump and they hit the sidewalk," she recalled. "Every one of them was killed, everybody who jumped was killed. It was a horrifying spectacle."[2]

The firemen held out nets, but the weight of the bodies from that great height either yanked the nets from the firemen's hands or the bodies ripped right through. One woman grandly emptied her purse over the onlookers below and then hurled herself off.

Perkins and the others screamed up to them, "Don't jump! Help is coming." It wasn't. The flames were roasting them from behind. Forty-seven people ended up jumping. One young woman gave a speech before diving, gesticulating passionately, but no one could hear her. One young man tenderly helped a young woman onto the windowsill. Then he held her out, away from the building, like a ballet dancer, and let her drop. He did the same for a second and a third. Finally, a fourth girl stood on the windowsill; she embraced him and they shared a long kiss. Then he held her out and dropped her, too. Then he himself was in the air. As he fell, people noticed, as his pants ballooned out, that he wore smart tan shoes. One reporter wrote, "I saw his face before they covered it. You could see in it that he was a real man. He had done his best."[3]

The fire had started at about 4:40 that afternoon, when somebody on the eighth floor threw a cigarette or a match into one of the great scrapheaps of cotton left over from the tailoring process. The pile quickly burst into flames.

Somebody alerted the factory manager, Samuel Bernstein, who grabbed some nearby buckets of water and dumped them on the fire. They did little good. The cotton scraps were explosively flammable, more so than paper, and there was roughly a ton of the stuff piled on the eighth floor alone.[4]

Bernstein dumped more buckets of water on the growing fire, but by this point they had no effect whatsoever, and the flames were spreading to the tissue paper patterns hanging above the wooden work desks. He ordered workers to drag a fire hose from a nearby stairwell. They opened the valve, but there was no pressure. As a historian of the fire, David Von Drehle, has argued, Bernstein made a fatal decision in those first three minutes. He could have spent the time fighting the fire or evacuating the nearly five hundred workers. Instead, he battled the exploding fire, to no effect. If he had spent the time evacuating, it is possible that nobody would have died that day.[5]

When Bernstein finally did take his eyes off the wall of fire, he was astonished by what he saw. Many of the women on the eighth floor were taking the time to go to the dressing room to retrieve their coats and belongings. Some were looking for their time cards so they could punch out.

Eventually, the two factory owners up on the tenth floor were alerted to the fire, which had already consumed the eighth floor and was spreading quickly to their own. One of them, Isaac Harris, gathered a group of workers and figured it was probably suicidal to try to climb down through the fire. "Girls, let us go up on the roof! Get on the roof!" he bellowed. The other owner, Max Blanck, was paralyzed by fear. He stood frozen with a look of terror on his face, holding his youngest daughter in one arm and his elder daughter's hand with the other.[6] A clerk, who was evacuating with the firm's order book, decided to throw it down and save his boss's life instead.

Most of the workers on the eighth floor were able to get out, but the workers on the ninth floor had little warning until the fire was already upon them. They ran like terrified schools of fish from one potential exit to another. There were two elevators, but they were slow and overloaded. There was no sprinkler system. There was a fire escape, but it was rickety and blocked. On normal days the workers were searched as they headed home, to prevent theft. The factory had been designed to force them through a single choke point in order to get out. Some of the doors were locked. As the fire surrounded them, the workers were left to make desperate life-and-death decisions with limited information in a rising atmosphere of fire, smoke, and terror.

Three friends, Ida Nelson, Katie Weiner, and Fanny Lansner, were in the changing room when the screams of "Fire!" reached them. Nelson decided to sprint for one of the stairwells. Weiner went to the elevators and saw an elevator car descending the shaft. She hurled herself into space, diving onto the roof. Lansner took neither course and didn't make it out.[7]

Mary Bucelli later described her own part in the vicious scramble to get out first: "I can't tell you because I gave so many pushes and kicks. I gave and received. I was throwing them down wherever I met them," she said of her co-workers. "I was only looking for my own life. . . . At a moment like that, there is big confusion and you must understand that you cannot see anything. . . . You see a multitude of things, but you can't distinguish anything. With the confusion and the fight that you take, you can't distinguish anything."[8]

Joseph Brenman was one of the relatively few men in the factory. A crowd of women were pushing between him and the elevators. But they were small, and many of them were faint. He shoved them aside and barreled his way onto the elevator and to safety.

The fire department arrived quickly but its ladders could not reach the eighth floor. The water from its hoses could barely reach that high, just enough to give the building exterior a light dousing.

Shame

THE HORROR OF THE TRIANGLE SHIRTWAIST FIRE TRAUMATIZED THE CITY. People were not only furious at the factory owners, but felt some deep responsibility themselves. In 1909 a young Russian immigrant named Rose Schneiderman had led the women who worked at Triangle and other factories on a strike to address the very issues that led to the fire disaster. The picketers were harassed by company guards. The city looked on indifferently, as it did upon the lives of the poor generally. After the fire there was a collective outpouring of rage, fed by collective guilt at the way people had self-centeredly gone about their lives, callously indifferent to the conditions and suffering of the people close around them. "I can't begin to tell you how disturbed the people were everywhere," Frances Perkins remembered. "It was as though we had all done something wrong. It shouldn't have been. We were sorry. Mea culpa! Mea culpa!"[9]

A large memorial march was held, and then a large meeting, with all the leading citizens of the city. Perkins was on stage as a representative of the Consumers' League when Rose Schneiderman electrified the crowd: "I would be a traitor to those poor burned bodies if I were to come here to talk good fellowship. We have tried you, good people of the public—and we have found you wanting!

"The old Inquisition had its rack and its thumbscrews and its instruments of torture with iron teeth. We know what these things are today: the iron teeth are our necessities, the thumbscrews are the high-powered and swift machinery close to which we must work, and the rack is here in the firetrap structures that will destroy us the minute they catch fire. . . .

"We have tried you, citizens! We are trying you now and you have a couple of dollars for the sorrowing mothers and brothers and sisters by way of a charity gift. But every time the workers come out in the only way they know to protest against conditions which are unbearable, the strong hand of the law is allowed to press down heavily upon us. . . . I can't talk fellowship to you who are gathered here. Too much blood has been spilled!"[10]

The fire and its aftershocks left a deep mark on Frances Perkins. Up until that point she had lobbied for worker rights and on behalf of the poor, but she had been on a conventional trajectory, toward a conventional marriage, perhaps, and a life of genteel good works. After the fire, what had been a career turned into a vocation. Moral indignation set her on a different course. Her own desires and her own ego became less central and the cause itself became more central to the structure of her life. The niceties of her class fell away. She became impatient with the way genteel progressives went about serving the poor. She became impatient with their prissiness, their desire to stay pure and above the fray. Perkins hardened. She threw herself into the rough and tumble of politics. She was willing to take morally hazardous action if it would prevent another catastrophe like the one that befell the women at the Triangle factory. She was willing to compromise and work with corrupt officials if it would produce results. She pinioned herself to this cause for the rest of her life.

Summoned

TODAY, COMMENCEMENT SPEAKERS TELL GRADUATES TO FOLLOW THEIR passion, to trust their feelings, to reflect and find their purpose in life. The assumption behind these clichés is that when you are figuring out how to lead your life, the most important answers are found deep inside yourself. When you are young and just setting out into adulthood, you should, by this way of thinking, sit down and take some time to discover yourself, to define what is really important to you, what your priorities are, what arouses your deepest passions. You should ask certain questions: What is the purpose of my life? What do I want from life? What are the things that I truly value, that are not done just to please or impress the people around me?

By this way of thinking, life can be organized like a business plan. First you take an inventory of your gifts and passions. Then you set goals and come up with some metrics to organize your progress toward those goals. Then you map out a strategy to achieve your purpose, which will help you distinguish those things that move you toward your goals from those things that seem urgent but are really just distractions. If you define a realistic purpose early on and execute your strategy flexibly, you will wind up leading a purposeful life. You will have achieved self-determination, of the sort captured in the oft-quoted lines from William Ernest Henley's poem "Invictus": "I am the master of my fate / I am the captain of my soul."

This is the way people tend to organize their lives in our age of individual autonomy. It's a method that begins with the self and ends with the self, that begins with self-investigation and ends in self-fulfillment. This is a life determined by a series of individual choices. But Frances Perkins found her purpose in life using a different method, one that was more common in past eras. In this method, you don't ask, What do I want from life? You ask a different set of questions: What does life want from me? What are my circumstances calling me to do?

In this scheme of things we don't create our lives; we are summoned by life. The important answers are not found inside, they are found outside. This perspective begins not within the autonomous self, but with the concrete circumstances in which you happen to be embedded. This perspective begins with an awareness that the world existed long before you and will last long after you, and that in the brief span of your life you have been thrown by fate, by history, by chance, by evolution, or by God into a specific place with specific problems and needs. Your job is to figure certain things out: What does this environment need in order to be made whole? What is it that needs repair? What tasks are lying around waiting to be performed? As the novelist Frederick Buechner put it, "At what points do my talents and deep gladness meet the world's deep need?"

Viktor Frankl described this sort of call in his famous 1946 book *Man's Search for Meaning*. Frankl was a Jewish psychiatrist in Vienna who was rounded up in 1942 by the Nazis and sent to a ghetto and then to a series of concentration camps. His wife, mother, and brother died in the camps. Frankl spent most of his time in camp laying tracks for railway lines. This was not the life he had planned for himself. This was not his passion, or his dream. This is not what he would be doing if he were marching to the beat of his own drummer. But this was the life events had assigned to him. And it became clear to him that what sort of person he would wind up being depended upon what sort of inner decision he would make in response to his circumstances.

"It did not really matter what we expected from life," he wrote, "but rather what life expected from us. We needed to stop asking the meaning of life, and instead think of ourselves as those who were being questioned by life—daily and hourly."[11] Frankl concluded that fate had put a moral task and an intellectual task before him. It had given him an assignment.

His moral task was to suffer well, to be worthy of his sufferings. He could not control how much he suffered, or whether or when he would end up in the gas chamber or as a corpse by the side of the road, but he could control his inner response to his sufferings. The Nazis tried to dehumanize and insult their victims, and some prisoners went along with this degradation or retreated into their memories of a happier past. But some prisoners struggled against the insults and fortified their own integrity. "One could make a victory of those experiences, turning life into an inner triumph," Frankl realized. One could struggle against the insults by asserting small acts of dignity, not necessarily to change your outer life or even your ultimate fate, but to strengthen the beams and pillars of your inner structure. He could exercise what he called an "inner hold," a rigorous control of his own inner state, a disciplined defense of his own integrity.

"Suffering had become a task on which we did not want to turn our backs," Frankl wrote.[12] Once he became aware of the task events had assigned to him, he understood the meaning and ultimate purpose of his life and the opportunity the war had given him to realize that purpose. And once he understood the meaning of these events, survival itself became easier. As Nietzsche observed, "He who has a why to live for can bear almost any how."

Frankl's other assignment was to take the circumstances into which he had been put and turn them into wisdom he could take to the world. Frankl had been given a great intellectual opportunity, the opportunity to study human beings under the most horrific conditions. He had the chance to share his observations with his fellow prisoners, and, if he survived, he figured he could spend the rest of his life sharing this knowledge with the world beyond.

When he had the mental energy, he spoke with groups of prisoners, telling them to take their lives seriously and struggle to preserve their inner hold. He told them to focus their minds upward on the image of a loved one, to preserve, share, and strengthen love for their absent wife or child or parent or friend, even in the midst of circumstances that conspire to destroy love, even though the loved one, having been sent to a different camp, might already be dead. Amid the grit and grime and the corpses one could still rise upward: "I called to the Lord from my narrow prison and he answered me in the freedom of space." One could, Frankl wrote, still participate in a rapturous passion for one's beloved and thus understand the full meaning of the words "The angels are lost in perpetual contemplation of an infinite glory."

He told potential suicides that life had not stopped expecting things from them, and that something in the future was still expected of them. In the darkness after lights out, he told his fellow prisoners that someone was watching them—a friend, a wife, somebody alive or dead, or God—who did not want to be disappointed.[13] Life, he concluded, "ultimately means taking the responsibility to find the right answer to its problems and to fulfill the tasks which it constantly sets before the individual."[14]

Few people are put in circumstances that horrific and extreme, but all of us are given gifts, aptitudes, capacities, talents, and traits that we did not strictly earn. And all of us are put in circumstances that call out for action, whether they involve poverty, suffering, the needs of a family, or the opportunity to communicate some message. These circumstances give us the great chance to justify our gifts.

Your ability to discern your vocation depends on the condition of your eyes and ears, whether they are sensitive enough to understand the assignment your context is giving you. As the Jewish Mishnah puts it, "It's not your obligation to complete the work, but neither are you free to desist from beginning it."

Vocation

FRANKL, LIKE PERKINS, HAD A VOCATION. A VOCATION IS NOT A CAREER. A person choosing a career looks for job opportunities and room for advancement. A person choosing a career is looking for something that will provide financial and psychological benefits. If your job or career isn't working for you, you choose a different one.

A person does not choose a vocation. A vocation is a calling. People generally feel they have no choice in the matter. Their life would be unrecognizable unless they pursued this line of activity.

Sometimes they are called by indignation. Frances Perkins witnessed the Triangle fire and was indignant that this tear in the moral fabric of the world could be permitted to last. Other people are called by an act. A woman picks up a guitar and from that moment knows that she is a guitarist. Playing is not something she does; a guitarist is who she is. Still other people are called by a Bible verse or a literary passage. One summer morning in 1896, Albert Schweitzer came upon the biblical passage "Whosoever would save his life shall lose it and whosoever shall lose his life for my sake shall save it." He knew at the moment he was called to give up his very successful career as a musical scholar and organist to go into medicine and become a jungle doctor.

A person with a vocation is not devoted to civil rights, or curing a disease, or writing a great novel, or running a humane company because it meets some cost-benefit analysis. Such people submit to their vocations for reasons deeper and higher than utility and they cling to them all the more fiercely the more difficulties arise. Schweitzer would write, "Anybody who proposes to do good must not expect people to roll any stones out of his way, and must calmly accept his lot even if they roll a few more onto it. Only force that in the face of obstacles becomes stronger can win."[15]

It is important to point out how much the sense of vocation is at odds with the prevailing contemporary logic. A vocation is not about fulfilling your desires or wants, the way modern economists expect us to do. A vocation is not about the pursuit of happiness, if by "happiness" you mean being in a good mood, having pleasant experiences, or avoiding struggle and pain. Such a person becomes an instrument for the performance of the job that has been put before her. She molds herself to the task at hand. While serving as an instrument in the fight against Soviet tyranny, Aleksandr Solzhenitsyn put it this way: "It makes me happier, more secure, to think that I do not have to plan and manage everything for myself, that I am only a sword made sharp to smite the unclean forces, an enchanted sword to cleave and disperse them. Grant, O Lord, that I may not break as I strike! Let me not fall from Thy hand!"

And yet people with vocations are generally not morose. In the first place, there is the joy they typically take in their own activities. Dorothy L. Sayers, best known today as a mystery writer but also a respected scholar and theologian in her time, used to make a distinction between serving the community and serving the work. People who seek to serve the community end up falsifying their work, she wrote, whether the work is writing a novel or baking bread, because they are not single-mindedly focused on the task at hand. But if you serve the work—if you perform each task to its utmost perfection—then you will experience the deep satisfaction of craftsmanship and you will end up serving the community more richly than you could have consciously planned. And one sees this in people with a vocation—a certain rapt expression, a hungry desire to perform a dance or run an organization to its utmost perfection. They feel the joy of having their values in deep harmony with their behavior. They experience a wonderful certainty of action that banishes weariness from even the hardest days.

The Triangle Shirtwaist Factory fire wasn't the only event that defined Frances Perkins's purpose in life, but it was a major one. This horror had been put in front of her. And like many people, she found a fiercer resolve amid a flood of righteous rage. It wasn't just that so many people had died—after all, they could not be brought back to life; it was also the "ongoing assault on the common order that the fire came to symbolize." There is a universal way people should be treated, a way that respects their dignity as living creatures, and this way was being violated by their mistreatment. The person who experiences this kind of indignation has found her vocation.

The Rigorous Childhood

PERKINS WAS BORN ON BEACON HILL IN BOSTON ON APRIL 10, 1880. HER ancestors had come over in the great Protestant migration in the middle of the seventeenth century, settling first in Massachusetts and then in Maine. One ancestor, James Otis, was an incendiary Revolutionary War hero. Another, Oliver Otis Howard, served as a general in the Civil War before founding Howard University, the historically black college in Washington, D.C. Howard visited the Perkins home when Frances was fifteen. Because he had lost his arm in the war, Frances served as his scribe.[16]

The Perkinses had been farmers and brickmakers through the centuries, mostly near the Damariscotta River east of Portland, Maine. Frances's mother was a member of the large Bean family. They gave their daughter a traditional Yankee upbringing: parsimonious, earnest, and brutally honest. In the evenings, Fred Perkins read Greek poetry and recited Greek plays with friends. He began to teach Frances Greek grammar when she was seven or eight. Frances's mother was heavy, artistic, and assertive. When Frances was ten, her mother took her to a hat shop. The fashionable hats of the day were narrow and tall, with feathers and ribbons. But Susan Bean Perkins plopped a low-crowned, simple, three-cornered hat onto Frances's head. What she said next reflects a very different sort of child rearing than is common today. While today we tend to tell children how wonderful they are, in those days parents were more likely to confront children with their own limitations and weaknesses. They were more likely to confront them with an honesty that can seem brutal to us today:

"There, my dear, that is your hat," her mother said. "You should always wear a hat something like this. You have a very broad face. It's broader between the two cheekbones than it is up at the top. Your head is narrower above the temples than it is at the cheekbones. Also, it lops off very suddenly into your chin. The result is you always need to have as much width in your hat as you have width in your cheekbones. Never let yourself get a hat that is narrower than your cheekbones, because it makes you look ridiculous."[17]

These days, New England Yankee culture has been diluted by the softening influence of the global culture, but then it was still hard and distinct. Yankees were reticent, self-reliant, egalitarian, and emotionally tough. Sometimes that toughness devolved into frigidity. But sometimes it was motivated by and intermixed with a fierce love and tenderness. New Englanders tended to have an acute awareness of their own sinfulness, and they worshipped a God who demonstrated his love through restraint and correction. They worked hard. They did not complain.

One evening, Perkins, then a young woman, came downstairs wearing a new party dress. Her father told her that it made her look ladylike. Perkins reflected later, "Even if I had ever succeeded in making myself look pretty—which, mind you, I'm not saying I ever succeeded in doing—my father would never have told me. That would have been a sin."[18]

The Yankees also combined what you might call social conservatism with political liberalism. Traditional and stern in their private lives, they believed in communal compassion and government action. They believed that individuals have a collective responsibility to preserve the "good order." Even in the mid-eighteenth century, the New England colonies had levels of taxation for state and local governments that were twice as high as the levels in colonies such as Pennsylvania and Virginia. They also put tremendous faith in education. For the past 350 years, New England schools have been among the best in the United States. New Englanders have, to this day, some of the highest levels of educational attainment in the nation.[19]

Perkins's parents saw to it that she was educated, but she never earned good grades. She had a natural facility with words, and in high school she used her glibness to slide by. She then went off to Mount Holyoke College, a member of the class of 1902. The rules at the college, and at colleges generally, were, again, very different from the rules today. Today, students live more or less unsupervised in their dorms. They are given the freedom to conduct their private lives as they see fit. Then, they were placed under restrictions, many of which seem absurd now, that were designed to inculcate deference, modesty, and respect. Here are some of the rules that formed part of the deference code when Perkins entered Holyoke: "Freshmen should keep a respectful silence in the presence of sophomores. Freshmen meeting a sophomore on the campus should bow respectfully. No Freshman shall wear a long skirt or hair high on head before the mid-year examinations."[20] Perkins survived the restraint, and the hazing that went along with this class structure, and became one of the social stars of her class, elected class president her senior year.

Today, teachers tend to look for their students' intellectual strengths, so they can cultivate them. But a century ago, professors tended to look for their students' moral weaknesses, so they could correct them. A Latin teacher, Esther Van Dieman, diagnosed Perkins's laziness, her tendency to be too easy on herself. Van Dieman used Latin grammar the way a drill instructor might use forced marches, as an ordeal to cultivate industriousness. She forced Perkins to work, hour upon hour, on precise recitations of the Latin verb tenses. Perkins would burst into tears in frustration and boredom, but later expressed appreciation for the enforced discipline: "For the first time I became conscious of character."[21]

Perkins was interested in history and literature, and she floundered badly in chemistry. Nonetheless, her chemistry teacher, Nellie Goldthwaite, hounded her into majoring in chemistry. The idea was that if she was tough enough to major in her weakest subject, she'd be tough enough to handle whatever life threw at her. Goldthwaite urged Perkins to take the hardest courses even if it meant earning mediocre grades. Perkins took the challenge. Goldthwaite became her faculty adviser. Years later, Perkins told a student with the school's alumnae quarterly, "The undergraduate mind should concentrate on the scientific courses, which temper the human spirit, harden and refine it, and make of it a tool with which one may tackle any kind of material."[22]

Mount Holyoke was the sort of school that leaves a permanent mark on its students. It did not see its role, as modern universities tend to, in purely Adam I cognitive terms. It was not there merely to teach people how to think. It was not there merely to help students question their assumptions. Instead, it successfully performed the broader role of college: helping teenagers become adults. It inculcated self-control. It helped its students discover new things to love. It took young women and ignited their moral passions by giving them a sense that humans are caught in a web of good and evil and that life is an epic struggle between these large forces. A dozen voices from across the institution told students that while those who lead flat and unre-markable lives may avoid struggle, a well-lived life involves throwing oneself into struggle, that large parts of the most worthy lives are spent upon the rack, testing moral courage and facing opposition and ridicule, and that those who pursue struggle end up being happier than those who pursue pleasure.

Then it told them that the heroes in this struggle are not the self-aggrandizing souls who chase after glory; they are rather the heroes of renunciation, those who accept some arduous calling. Then it tried to cut down their idealism and make it permanent by criticizing mere flights of compassion and self-congratulatory sacrifice. It emphasized that performing service is not something you do out of the goodness of your heart but as a debt you are repaying for the gift of life.

Then it gave them concrete ways to live this life of steady, heroic service. Over the decades, Mount Holyoke sent hundreds of women to missionary and service jobs in northwest Iran, Natal in southern Africa, and Maharashtra in western India. "Do what nobody else wants to do; go where nobody else wants to go," the school's founder, Mary Lyon, implored her students.

In 1901 a new president arrived, Mary Woolley, one of the first women to graduate from Brown and a biblical studies scholar. She wrote an essay titled "Values of College Training for Women" for *Harper's Bazaar* that captures the tone of high moral ambition that characterized life at the school. "Character is the main object for edu-cation," she declared, continuing, "A true perspective implies poise." Today, the word "poise" suggests social grace. But in that day it re-ferred to the deeper qualities of steadiness and balance. "The lack of these qualities is often the weak place in the armor, and good im-pulses, high purposes, real ability, fail of their end."[23]

The Mount Holyoke education was dominated by theology and the classics—Jerusalem and Athens. The students were to take from religion an ethic of care and compassion, and from the ancient Greeks

and Romans a certain style of heroism—to be courageous and un-
flinching in the face of the worst the world could throw at you. In her
Harper's Bazaar essay, Woolley quoted the Stoic philosopher Epicte-
tus: "To live in the presence of great truths and eternal laws, to be led
by permanent ideals, that is what keeps a man patient when the world
ignores him and calm and unspoiled when the world praises him."
Perkins and Woolley would remain friends until Woolley's death.

Perkins also went to college at a time when the social gospel movement was at its most influential. In response to urbanization and
industrialization, the leaders of the movement, including Walter
Rauschenbusch, rejected the individualistic and privatized religion
that was prevalent in many genteel churches. It is not enough, Rauschenbusch argued, to heal the sinfulness in each individual human heart.
There is also suprapersonal sin—evil institutions and social structures
that breed oppression and suffering. The leaders of the social gospel
movement challenged their listeners to test and purify themselves by
working for social reform. The real Christian life, they said, is not a
solitary life of prayer and repentance. It is a life of sacrificial service,
which involves practical solidarity with the poor and membership in a
larger movement working to repair God's kingdom on earth.

As class president, Perkins helped select her class motto, "Be ye
steadfast." The full verse, which Perkins read to her classmates in their
final prayer meeting, is from 1 Corinthians. "Therefore my beloved
brethren, be ye steadfast, unmovable, always abounding in the work
of the Lord, forasmuch as ye know that your labor is not in vain in the
Lord."

Holyoke took Perkins, who had been taught, because of her sex
and because of her stature, to think lowly of herself, and it persuaded
her and the other women that she could do something heroic. But it
achieved this task in an ironic way. It didn't tell her that she was awesome and qualified for heroism. It forced her to confront her natural
weaknesses. It pushed her down. It pushed her down and then taught
her to push herself upward and outward. Perkins came to Holyoke
sweet and glib, diminutive and charming. She left stronger, fortified,
ardent for service and clearly unsuited to the narrow bourgeois world
in which she'd grown up. When Frances Perkins's mother came to see
her daughter graduate from Mount Holyoke, she remarked in a tone

of dismay, "I don't recognize my daughter Fanny anymore. I can't understand it. She's a stranger to me."[24]

Tender Toughness

PERKINS KNEW SHE WANTED SOME SORT OF HEROIC LIFE, BUT SHE STRUG-gled after graduation to find a specific role. She was too inexperienced to be a social worker; the agencies would not hire her. She tried teaching at an upscale school for girls in Lake Forest, Illinois, but it was uninspiring. Eventually she also commuted in to Chicago and became involved with Hull House.

Hull House was a settlement house cofounded by Jane Addams, the leading American social reformer of her day. The idea was to give women a new range of service careers, to link the affluent with the poor, and to re-create the sense of community that had been destroyed by the disruptions of industrialization. It was modeled after Toynbee Hall in London, in which affluent university men organized social gatherings with the poor in the same manner in which they would organize them with one another.

At Hull House, affluent women lived among the poor and working classes, serving as counselors, assistants, and advisers and taking on projects to make their lives better. They offered job training, child care, a savings bank, English lessons, even art classes.

Today, community service is sometimes used as a patch to cover over inarticulateness about the inner life. Not long ago, I asked the head of a prestigious prep school how her institution teaches its students about character. She answered by telling me how many hours of community service the students do. That is to say, when I asked her about something internal, she answered by talking about something external. Her assumption seemed to be that if you go off and tutor poor children, that makes you a good person yourself.

And so it goes. Many people today have deep moral and altruistic yearnings, but, lacking a moral vocabulary, they tend to convert moral questions into resource allocation questions. How can I serve the greatest number? How can I have impact? Or, worst of all: How can I use my beautiful self to help out those less fortunate than I?

The atmosphere at Hull House was quite different. The people who organized the place had a specific theory about how to build character, equally for those serving the poor and for the poor themselves. Addams, like many of her contemporaries, dedicated her life to serving the needy, while being deeply suspicious of compassion. She was suspicious of its shapelessness, the way compassionate people tended to ooze out sentiment on the poor to no practical effect. She also rejected the self-regarding taint of the emotion, which allowed the rich to feel good about themselves because they were doing community service. "Benevolence is the twin of pride," Nathaniel Hawthorne had written. Addams had no tolerance for any pose that might put the server above those being served.

As with all successful aid organizations, she wanted her workers to enjoy their work, to love their service. At the same time, she wanted them to hold their sentiments in check and to struggle relentlessly against any feelings of superiority. At Hull House, social workers were commanded to make themselves small. They were commanded to check their sympathies and exercise scientific patience as they investigated the true needs of each individual. The social worker was to be a practical adviser, almost in the manner of today's management consultant—to investigate options, offer friendship and counsel, but never let her own opinions prevail over the decisions of the beneficiaries. The idea was to let the poor determine their own lives rather than becoming dependent upon others.

Addams observed a phenomenon one still sees frequently today: Many people graduate from college energetic, lively, and impressive, but by age thirty they have become duller and more cynical versions of themselves. Their ambitions have shrunk. At school, Addams wrote in her memoir, *Twenty Years at Hull House,* students are taught to be self-sacrificial and self-forgetting, to put the good of society above the good of their ego. But when they graduate they are told to look out for themselves, to settle down into marriage and, perhaps, career. The young women are effectively asked to repress their desire to right wrongs and alleviate suffering. "The girl loses something vital out of her life to which she is entitled," Addams wrote. "She is restricted and unhappy; her elders, meanwhile, are unconscious of the situation and we have all the elements of tragedy."[25] Addams saw Hull House not only as a place to help the poor; it was a place where the affluent could surrender to an ennobling vocation. "The final return of the deed is upon the head of the doer," Addams wrote.[26]

Perkins spent as much time at Hull House as possible, first staying over for weekends, then longer stretches. When she left, she had more of a scientific mentality—data must be gathered. She knew how to navigate the landscape of poverty. She also had more courage. Her next job was with an organization in Philadelphia founded by a Hull House alumna. Bogus employment agencies were luring immigrant women into boardinghouses, sometimes drugging them and forcing them into prostitution. Perkins exposed 111 of these places by applying for such jobs herself, confronting the pimps face-to-face. Then, in 1909, with some experience under her belt, she joined Florence Kelley in New York at the National Consumers League. Kelley was a hero and inspiration to Perkins. "Explosive, hot-tempered, determined, she was no gentle saint," Perkins would later write. "She lived and worked like a missionary, no sacrifice too great, no effort too much. She was a deeply emotional and profoundly religious woman, although the expression was often unconventional."[27] While at the Consumers' League, Perkins lobbied against child labor and other atrocities.

In New York, she also fell in with the bohemian Greenwich Village crowd: Jack Reed, who later became involved in the Russian Revolution; Sinclair Lewis, who once proposed marriage to her, at least semiseriously; and Robert Moses, who was part of the counterculture then but who would go on to become the domineering uber-engineer of New York City.

Reticence

PERKINS WAS GETTING A BIT TOUGHER AT EVERY STEP ALONG THE WAY—AT Mount Holyoke, at Hull House—and yet she was also getting more idealistic, more fervent about her cause. The Triangle Factory fire was the moment when those two processes took a definitive leap.

The United States ambassador to the United Nations, Samantha Power, perceptively observes that some people put themselves "at stake" when they get involved in a cause. That is to say, they feel that their own reputation and their own identity are at stake when decisions are made. They are active in the cause in part because of what it says about them, and they want their emotions and their identity and their pride to be validated along the way. Perkins was not "at stake" after the fire. She went to work in Albany, lobbying the state legislature for worker safety legislation. She left behind the prejudices of her upscale New York social set. She left behind the gentility of progressive politics. She would compromise ruthlessly if it meant making progress. Her mentor, Al Smith, a rising figure in New York politics, told Perkins that before long, the genteel progressives would lose interest in any cause. If you want to usher real change, he told her, you have to work with the sleazy legislators and the rough party pols. You have to be practical, subordinate your personal purity to the cause. Perkins learned that in a fallen world it is often the "tainted" people who help you do the most good. In Albany she began to work closely with the denizens of the Tammany Hall political machine, who were regarded with horror in the polite circles in which she had previously traveled.

In Albany, Perkins also learned how to deal with older men. One day she was standing by the elevators of the state capitol when a crude little senator named Hugh Frawley came out and started describing the confidential details of the backroom negotiations and moaning about the shameful work he was compelled to perform. Swept up in self-pity, he cried, "Every man's got a mother, you know."

Perkins kept a folder titled "Notes on the Male Mind" and recorded this episode in it. It played a major role in her political education: "I learned from this that the way men take women in political life is to associate them with motherhood. They know and respect their mothers—99 percent of them do. It's a primitive and primary attitude. I said to myself, 'That's the way to get things done. So behave, dress, and so comport yourself that you remind them subconsciously of their mothers.' "[28]

Perkins was then thirty-three, and perky, though certainly not beautiful. Up until then, she had dressed in the conventional fashion of the day. But from that point on she began dressing like a mother. She wore somber black dresses with white bow ties at the neck. She wore pearls and a black tricorn hat and adopted a matronly demeanor. The press picked up on the change and started calling her "Mother Perkins" for the way she led sixty-something state legislators. She despised the nickname, but she found that the method worked. She suppressed her sexuality, her femininity, and even part of her identity in order to win the confidence of the old men around her. It's a questionable tactic today, when women should not have to suppress themselves to succeed, but in the 1920s, it was necessary.

Among other projects, Perkins lobbied furiously for a bill to limit the workweek to 54 hours. She tried to befriend the machine bosses to get them to support the bill. They did their best to deceive and outmaneuver her, but she won support from some of the rank and file. "Me sister was a poor girl and she went to work when she was young," one machine pol, Big Tim Sullivan, confided to her. "I feel kind sorry for them poor girls that work the way you say they work. I'd like to do them a good turn. I'd like to do you a good turn."[29]

When the 54-hour workweek bill finally came to a vote, the legislators exempted one of the most egregious but politically influential industries, the canners. The activists for the bill had spent the previous months insisting that there could be no exemptions. All industries, especially the canners, had to be covered by the legislation. At the crucial moment, Perkins stood at the edge of the legislative chamber. On the spot, she had to decide whether to accept this deeply flawed bill or reject it as a matter of principle. Her colleagues argued vociferously for rejecting it. Instead, she took half a loaf. She told legislators her organization would support the bill. "This is my responsibility. I'll do it and hang for it if necessary."[30] Many Progressives were indeed outraged. But her tough-minded mentor, Florence Kelley, completely endorsed her decision. Forever after Perkins was known as a "half-a-loaf girl," in public or private life, as someone who would take as much as circumstances allowed.[31]

Around this time she met Paul Wilson, a handsome, wellborn progressive, who became a close aide to New York's reformist mayor, John Purroy Mitchel. Wilson fell in love with Perkins and slowly won her over. "Before you came into my life," she wrote to him, "it was a lonesome place—cold and raw and trembling except on the outside. . . . You stormed into my heart somehow and I could never let you go."[32]

The courtship was odd. Perkins's letters to Wilson are romantic, earnest, and passionate. But with her friends and co-workers she was extremely reticent, and decades later she would deny that she had ever felt strong emotions. They were married on September 26, 1913, at Grace Church in Lower Manhattan. They did not invite their friends or tell them of the wedding in advance. Perkins and Wilson informed their families, but too late for them to attend. Perkins dressed for the wedding alone in her apartment on Waverly Place and probably walked over. The two witnesses were just people who happened to be in the building at the time. There was no luncheon or tea afterward.

When she described her decision to marry in later years, she adopted the matter-of-fact tone that you might use for making a dental appointment. "There was a New England pride in me," Perkins said decades later. "I wasn't anxious to get married. To tell the truth, I was reluctant. I was no longer a child but a grown woman. I hadn't wanted to marry. I liked life better in a single harness."[33] But people were constantly asking her when she would find a husband, so she decided to get it out of the way, thinking, "I know Paul Wilson well. I like him. . . . I enjoy his friends and company and I might as well marry and get it off my mind."

Their first years were relatively happy. They lived in a gracious townhouse on Washington Square, not far from where Perkins had been drinking tea when the Triangle fire erupted. Wilson served in the mayor's office. Perkins continued with her social work. Their home became a center for political activists of the day.

Soon things began to deteriorate. John Mitchel was voted out of office. Wilson had an affair with a society lady, which caused a furor and then was never mentioned again. Perkins began to feel stifled in the marriage and asked for a separation. "I've made some wretched blunders," Perkins wrote to Wilson. "I've become a different kind of person with a lesser degree of working efficiency and paler kind of spiritual efficiency."[34]

Then she got pregnant. The boy died shortly after birth. Perkins was consumed by grief, but that, too, was never mentioned again. Afterward, Perkins became executive secretary of the Maternity Center Association, a voluntary organization that sought to lower maternal and infant death rates. She also had a daughter, Susanna, named after the wife of the second governor of the Plymouth Colony.

Perkins wanted to have another child, but by 1918 Wilson was showing signs of mental illness. He seems to have been manic-depressive. He couldn't withstand any pressure. "It was always up and down. He was sometimes depressed, sometimes excited," Perkins said later. From 1918 on there were never anything but very short periods of reasonably comfortable accommodations to life. In one of these manic phases, Wilson invested his life's savings in a gold scheme and was wiped out. Perkins was sometimes afraid to be alone with him, because he was prone to violent rages and was much stronger than she was. He would spend significant parts of the next several decades in asylums and institutional care, where Perkins would visit him on weekends. When he was home he was unable to handle any responsibility. He had a nurse—euphemistically known as a secretary—to look after him. "He was becoming a kind of nonperson," Perkins's biographer, George Martin, wrote, "someone to be talked at rather than with."[35]

Her New England reticence kicked in. She called the loss of their family fortune "this accident," and she realized she would have to work to support the family. She pushed such "accidents" "into the background. I haven't brooded over them and had a Freudian collapse."[36] For the next several decades she tried to rope off her private life, conceal it from public view. This attitude was partly a product of her Yankee upbringing. But she was also reticent as a matter of philosophy and conviction. She believed that private emotions were too intricate to be exposed to public glare; she would have been horrified by the culture of exposure that is so prevalent today.

There is a general struggle between two philosophic dispositions, what the social critic Rochelle Gurstein calls the party of reticence and the party of exposure. The party of reticence believes that the tender emotions of the inner world are brutalized and polluted when they are exposed to the glare of public exhibition. The party of exposure believes that anything secret is suspect and that life works better when everything is brought out into the open and discussed. Perkins was definitely a member of the party of reticence. She stood with those who believe that everything that is complex, nuanced, contradictory, paradoxical, and mysterious about private sensations is reduced to banality when it is paraded about and summarized in pat phrases. Damage is done when people bring intimate things before mere acquaintances or total strangers. Precious emotions are lifted out of the context of trust and intimacy and trampled. Therefore people should keep what is private, private. Though she was a believer in government when it came to serving the poor and protecting the weak, she had a strong aversion to government when it trampled the right to privacy.

There was a cost to this philosophy. She was not superbly introspective. She did not excel at intimacy. She did not have a particularly happy private life. It is hard to know what would have happened if her husband had not spent so much time in mental institutions, but it is likely that her public vocation would have crowded out her energy and capacity for private intimacy nonetheless. She was built for the public campaign. She did not receive love well, or give it, or display vulnerability. Even her care for her daughter often took the form of a moral improvement crusade, which backfired. Frances exerted iron control over herself and expected it in her daughter.

But that daughter, Susanna, inherited her father's manic temperament. Starting when she was sixteen, when Perkins moved to Washington to serve in the Roosevelt administration, they seldom shared a home. Throughout her life, Susanna suffered severe bouts of depression. Susanna married a man who conducted a flagrant affair. By the 1940s, she was something of a hippie, twenty years before the term existed. She became involved with various countercultural groups. She developed a fixation on the Romanian sculptor Constantin Brancusi. She went out of her way to shock polite society and embarrass her mother. Perkins once invited Susanna to a society event and begged her to dress appropriately. Susanna chose a flamboyant green dress and wore her hair piled wildly atop her head, with garish flowers adorning her hair and neck.

"I have given way to morbid superstition that I am the cause of others' nervous collapse, my husband, my daughter," Perkins confessed. "[It] frightens and oppresses me."[37] Susanna was never really able to work and was supported by Frances. Even at age seventy-seven, Frances turned over her rent-controlled apartment in New York so that Susanna would have a place to live. She had to take a job to pay her daughter's bills.

Every virtue can come with its own accompanying vice. The virtue of reticence can yield the vice of aloofness. Perkins was not emotionally vulnerable to those close to her. Her public vocation never completely compensated for her private solitude.

Duty

NEW YORK'S GOVERNOR AL SMITH WAS PERKINS'S FIRST AND GREATEST political love. He was loyal, approachable, voluble and a man with the common touch. Smith also gave Perkins her first big break in government. He appointed her to the Industrial Commission, the body that regulated workplace conditions across the Empire State. The job brought a generous $8,000 a year salary and put Perkins in the middle of the major strikes and industrial disputes. She was not only a rare woman in a man's world, she was in the manliest precincts of the man's world. She'd travel to factory towns and throw herself in the middle of bitter disputes between energized labor organizers and determined corporate executives. There is no boasting in any of her reminiscences that this was a brave and even reckless thing to do. To her, this was simply a job that needed doing. The word "one" plays a crucial role in her descriptions of her own life. Sometimes she would use the formulation "I did this," but more often her diction was formal and archaic: "One did this . . ."

Nowadays we think of the use of "one" as pompous and starched. But for Perkins it was simply a way to avoid the first person pronoun. It was a way to suggest that any proper person would of course be duty-bound to do what she had done under the circumstances.

During the 1910s and 1920s in Albany, Perkins also had occasion to work with Franklin Delano Roosevelt. He did not impress her. She found him shallow and a bit arrogant. He had a habit of throwing his head back as he spoke. Later, when he was president, that gesture suggested confidence and buoyant optimism. But when he was young, Perkins just thought it made him look supercilious.

Roosevelt disappeared from Perkins's life when he suffered his polio attack. When he returned, she felt he had changed. He almost never spoke of his illness, but Perkins felt it "purged the slightly arrogant attitude he had displayed."[38]

One day, as Roosevelt was reentering politics, Perkins sat on a stage and watched him drag himself up to the podium to deliver a speech. His hands, supporting his weight on the podium, never stopped trembling. Perkins realized that after the speech, someone would have to cover his awkward movements as he lurched down from the stand.

She gestured to a woman behind her, and as he concluded, they hurried up to Roosevelt, nominally to congratulate him, but actually to shield his movements with their skirts. Over the years, this became a routine.

Perkins admired the way Roosevelt gratefully and humbly accepted help. "I began to see what the great teachers of religion meant when they said that humility is the greatest of virtues," she later wrote, "and if you can't learn it, God will teach it to you by humiliation. Only so can a man be really great, and it was in those accommodations to necessity that Franklin Roosevelt began to approach the stature of humility and inner integrity which made him truly great."[39]

When Roosevelt was elected governor of New York, he offered Perkins the job of Industrial Commissioner. She wasn't sure she should take it, because she wasn't sure she could successfully manage an agency. "I believe that such talent as I may have for public service lies much more in the judicial and legislative work of the Department than in the administrative," she wrote in a note to Roosevelt. On the day he offered her the job, she told him that she would give him a day to reconsider, to consult with others. "If anyone says it's unwise to appoint me or will make trouble with the leaders, just disregard today. . . . I'm not going to tell anyone so you're not sewed up."[40]

Roosevelt responded, "That's very decent, I must say, but I'm not going to change my mind." He was pleased to appoint a woman to such a senior job, and Perkins's reputation as a public servant was exemplary. As one biographer, George Martin, put it, "As an administrator she was good, perhaps even more than good; as a judge or legislator she was quite extraordinary. She had a judicial temperament and a strong sense in all situations of what was fair. She was always open to new ideas and yet the moral purpose of the law, the welfare of mankind, was never overlooked."[41]

When he was elected president, Roosevelt asked Perkins to become his secretary of labor. Again, she resisted. When rumors of her potential nomination circulated during the transition, Perkins wrote FDR a letter saying that she hoped they were untrue. "You are quoted as saying that the newspaper predictions on cabinet posts are 80 percent wrong. I write to say that I honestly hope that what they've been printing about me is among the 80 percent of incorrect items. I've had my 'kick' out of the gratifying letters etc., but for your own sake and that of the U.S.A. I think that someone straight from the ranks of some group of organized workers should be appointed—to establish firmly the principle that labor is in the President's councils."[42] She also touched lightly on her family problems, which she feared might become a distraction. Roosevelt wrote a little squib on a piece of scratch paper and sent it back: "Have considered your advice and don't agree."[43]

Perkins's grandmother had told her that when somebody opens a door, you should always walk through. So Perkins confronted FDR with terms if she was to become his labor secretary. If she were to join the cabinet, FDR would have to commit to a broad array of social insurance policies: massive unemployment relief, a giant public works program, minimum wage laws, a Social Security program for old age insurance, and the abolition of child labor. "I suppose you are going to nag me about this forever," Roosevelt told her. She confirmed she would.

Perkins was one of only two top aides to stay with Roosevelt for his entire term as president. She became one of the tireless champions of the New Deal. She was central to the creation of the Social Security system. She was a major force behind many of the New Deal jobs programs such as the Civilian Conservation Corps, the Federal Works Agency, and the Public Works Administration. Through the Fair Labor Standards Act she established the nation's first minimum wage law and its first overtime law. She sponsored federal legislation on child labor and unemployment insurance. During World War II she resisted calls to draft women, sensing that women would benefit more over the long run if they could take the jobs that were being abandoned by drafted men.

Perkins excelled at reading Franklin Roosevelt. After he died, Perkins wrote a biographical work, *The Roosevelt I Knew,* which remains one of the most astute character sketches ever written about the man. Overshadowing all Roosevelt's decisions, Perkins wrote, "was his feeling that nothing in human judgment is final. One may courageously take the step that seems right today because it can be modified tomorrow if it does not work well." He was an improviser, not a planner. He took a step and adjusted, a step and adjusted. Gradually a big change would emerge.

This mentality develops, she continued, in "a man who is more an instrument than an engineer. The prophets of Israel would have called him an instrument of the Lord. The prophets of today could only explain his type of mind in terms of psychology, about which they know so pitiably little."[44]

Perkins devised a strategy to deal with this man who was prone to changing his mind and shifting direction depending upon who was the last adviser he encountered. Before her meeting with the president she would prepare a one-page memo outlining the concrete options before him. They would go over her outline and Roosevelt would state his preference. Then Perkins would force him to repeat himself: "Do you authorize me to go ahead with this? Are you sure?"

They would have a little more discussion, and then Perkins would underline his decision a second time: "Are you sure you want item number one? Do you want items number two and three? You understand that this is what we do and this is who is opposed?" The purpose of this exercise was to sear a photograph of the decision into Roosevelt's memory. Then she would ask him a third time, asking him whether he explicitly remembered his decision and understood the opposition he would face. "Is that all right? Is it still okay?"

FDR did not always stand up for Perkins when she needed it. He was too slippery a politician to extend loyalty downward all of the time. She was not popular with many of the men in the cabinet. For one thing, she had a tendency to go on at meetings. She was certainly not popular with the press. Her sense of privacy and her fierce desire to protect her husband prevented her from hanging around with reporters or ever letting down her guard. The reporters, in turn, were unsympathetic.

As the years went by, she became exhausted by the job. Her reputation waned. Twice she sent Roosevelt a letter of resignation and twice he rejected it. "Frances, you can't go now. You mustn't put this on me now," Roosevelt pleaded. "I can't think of anybody else. I can't get used to anyone else. Not now! Do stay there and don't say anything. You are all right."

In 1939 she became the target of impeachment proceedings. The case revolved around an Australian longshoreman named Harry Bridges who led a general strike in San Francisco. Bridges's critics called him a Communist and demanded that he be deported for subversive activities. When the Soviet Union fell and the files were opened, it turned out they were right. Bridges was a Communist agent, known by the code name Rossi.[45]

But at the time, that wasn't so clear. Deportation hearings, operated by the Labor Department, dragged on. In 1937, more evidence against Bridges surfaced, and in 1938, the department began proceedings to deport him. These proceedings were blocked by a court decision, which was then appealed to the Supreme Court. The delay inflamed Bridges's critics, which included business groups and the leaders of rival unions.

Perkins bore the brunt of their criticism. Why was the labor secretary shielding a subversive? One congressman accused her of being a Russian Jew and a Communist herself. In January 1939, J. Parnell Thomas of New Jersey introduced impeachment charges against her. The press coverage was brutal. Franklin Roosevelt was given a chance to rise to her defense, but, wary of soiling his own reputation by association, he just let her hang out there. Most of her allies in Congress remained silent, too. The Federation of Women's Clubs also refused to defend her. *The New York Times* wrote an ambiguous editorial. The common sentiment was that she was in fact a Communist, and nobody wanted to get in the line of fire of those who were persecuting her. It was left to the Tammany Hall pols to remain reliably steadfast beside her.

Perkins's grandmother had always told her that when social disaster strikes, "all are to act as though nothing had happened." Perkins soldiered on. Her description of that period is awkwardly phrased but revealing. "Of course if I had wept at all, or if I'd let myself down at all, I would have disintegrated," Perkins said later. "That's the kind of person which we New Englanders are. We disintegrate if we do these things. All the qualities in us of integrity and the ability to keep our heads clear and make decisions and take actions that are influenced by our personal suffering or personal effect on ourselves, that integrity would have been scattered, and I would not have had that inner core within myself which makes it possible for me to rely upon myself under the guidance of God to do the right thing."[46]

Put in plain language, Perkins was aware that there was a fragility within herself. If she relaxed the hold she had on herself, then all might fall apart. Over the years, Perkins had made frequent visits to the All Saints Convent in Catonsville, Maryland. She would go to the convent for two or three days at a time, gathering for prayers five times a day, eating simple meals, and tending the gardens. She spent most of those days in silence, and when the nuns came to mop her floor, they sometimes had to mop around her, for she was on her knees in prayer. During the impeachment crisis, Perkins visited the convent whenever she could. "I have discovered the rule of silence is one of the most beautiful things in the world," she wrote to a friend. "It preserves one from the temptation of the idle world, the fresh remark, the wisecrack, the angry challenge. . . . It is really quite remarkable what it does for one."[47]

She also reflected on a distinction that had once seemed unimportant to her. When a person gives a poor man shoes, does he do it for the poor man or for God? He should do it for God, she decided. The poor will often be ungrateful, and you will lose heart if you rely on immediate emotional rewards for your work. But if you do it for God, you will never grow discouraged. A person with a deep vocation is not dependent on constant positive reinforcement. The job doesn't have to pay off every month, or every year. The person thus called is performing a task because it is intrinsically good, not for what it produces.

Finally, on February 8, 1939, Perkins was able to meet her accusers. She appeared before the House Judiciary Committee as it considered articles of impeachment against her. She delivered a long and detailed recitation of the administrative procedures initiated against Bridges, the reasons for them, and the legal constraints preventing further action. The questions ranged from the skeptical to the brutal. When opponents made vicious charges against her, she asked them to repeat their question, believing that no person can be scurrilous twice. The photographs of the hearing make her look haggard and exhausted, but she impressed the committee with her detailed knowledge of the case.

Eventually, in March, the committee ruled that there were insufficient facts to support impeachment. She was cleared, but the report was vague and elliptical. It generated little press coverage and her reputation was permanently marred. Unable to resign, she soldiered on in the administration for another six years, helping out mostly behind the scenes. She was stoic about it all, never showing any public weakness or any self-pity. After her government service ended, when she could have written a memoir to give her side of the story, she declined.

During the Second World War, she served as an administrative troubleshooter. She urged Roosevelt to do something to help European Jewry. She became alarmed by the way federal action was beginning to infringe on privacy and civil liberties.

When FDR died in 1945, she was finally released from the cabinet, though President Truman asked her to serve on the Civil Service Commission. Instead of writing that memoir, she wrote a book about Roosevelt instead. It was a tremendous success, but it contains very little autobiography.

Perkins did not really experience private joy until the end of her life. In 1957, a young labor economist asked her to teach a course at Cornell. The job paid about $10,000 a year, scarcely more than she had earned decades before as New York Industrial Commissioner, but she needed the money to pay for her daughter's mental health care.

At first, she lived in residential hotels during her time in Ithaca, but she was then invited to live in a small bedroom at Telluride House, a sort of fraternity house for some of Cornell's most gifted students. She was delighted by the invitation. "I feel like a bride on her wedding night!" she told friends.[48] While there, she drank bourbon with the boys and tolerated their music at all hours.[49] She attended the Monday house meetings, though she rarely spoke. She gave them copies of Baltasar Gracian's *The Art of Worldly Wisdom,* a seventeenth-century guidebook by a Spanish Jesuit priest on how to retain one's integrity while navigating the halls of power. She became close friends with Allan Bloom, a young professor who would go on to achieve fame as the author of *The Closing of the American Mind*. Some of the boys had trouble understanding how this small, charming, and unassuming old lady could have played such an important historical role.

She did not like airplanes and traveled alone by bus, sometimes having to make four or five connections to get to a funeral or a lecture. She tried to destroy some of her papers, to foil future biographers. She traveled with a copy of her will in her handbag, so that if she died she "wouldn't cause any trouble."[50] She died alone, in a hospital, on May 14, 1965, at age eighty-five. A few of the Telluride House boys served as pallbearers, including Paul Wolfowitz, who would go on to serve in the Reagan and Bush administrations. The minister read the "be ye steadfast" passage from 1 Corinthians that Perkins herself had read upon her graduation from Mount Holyoke College more than six decades before.

If you look back at her college yearbook photo, you see a small, cute, almost mousy young lady. It would be hard to foresee from that vulnerable expression that she would be able to endure so much hardship—the mental illnesses of her husband and daughter, the ordeal of being the solitary woman in a hypermasculine world, the decades of political battles and negative press.

But it would also be hard to foresee how much she would accomplish throughout the hardship. She faced her own weaknesses—laziness, glibness—early in life and steeled herself for a life of total commitment. She suppressed her own identity so she could lobby for her cause. She took on every new challenge and remained as steadfast as her motto. She was, as Kirstin Downey would put it in the title of her fine biography, "The Woman Behind the New Deal."

On the one hand she was a fervent liberal activist, of the sort we are familiar with today. But she combined this activism with reticent traditionalism, hesitancy, and a puritanical sensibility. Daring in politics and economics, she was conservative in morality. She practiced a thousand little acts of self-discipline to guard against self-indulgence, self-glorification, or, until the impeachment and the end of her life, self-reflection. Her rectitude and reticence pinched her private life and made her bad at public relations. But it helped her lead a summoned life, a life in service to a vocation.

Perkins didn't so much choose her life. She responded to the call of a felt necessity. A person who embraces a calling doesn't take a direct route to self-fulfillment. She is willing to surrender the things that are most dear, and by seeking to forget herself and submerge herself she finds a purpose that defines and fulfills herself. Such vocations almost always involve tasks that transcend a lifetime. They almost always involve throwing yourself into a historical process. They involve compensating for the brevity of life by finding membership in a historic commitment. As Reinhold Niebuhr put it in 1952:

> Nothing that is worth doing can be achieved in our lifetime; therefore we must be saved by hope. Nothing which is true or beautiful or good makes complete sense in any immediate con-

text of history; therefore we must be saved by faith. Nothing we do, however virtuous, can be accomplished alone; therefore we are saved by love. No virtuous act is quite as virtuous from the standpoint of our friend or foe as it is from our standpoint. Therefore we must be saved by the final form of love, which is forgiveness.[51]

CHAPTER 3

SELF-CONQUEST

IDA STOVER EISENHOWER WAS BORN IN 1862 IN THE SHENANDOAH VAL-
ley of Virginia, one of eleven children. Her childhood was more or
less a series of catastrophes. When she was a young girl, Union soldiers invaded her home, hunting for her two teenage brothers. They
threatened to burn down the barn and ransacked the town and surrounding country. Her mother died when Ida was nearly five, and her
father died when she was eleven.

The children were scattered among distant relations. Ida became
the assistant cook for the large household that was putting her up. She
baked pies, pastries, and meats, darned socks, and patched clothing.
She was not, however, sad and pitiable. From the start, she had spark
and drive and pushed daringly against her hardships. She was an overworked orphan, but folks in town remembered her as something of a
tomboy, wiry and unafraid, galloping bareback through town on any
borrowed horse, and one time falling and breaking her nose.

Girls were generally not educated beyond eighth grade at the time,
but Ida, who in early adolescence had memorized 1,365 Bible verses in
six months on her own, possessed a tremendous drive to improve herself, in both Adam I and Adam II terms. One day, when she was fifteen, her host family went off on a family outing, leaving her alone.
She packed her belongings and sneaked away, walking to Staunton,
Virginia. She got a room and a job and enrolled herself in the local
high school.

She graduated, taught for two years, and at twenty-one came into a $1,000 inheritance. She used $600 of that (more than $10,000 today) to buy an ebony piano, which was to remain the most treasured possession of her life. The rest she devoted to her education. She hitched on with a Mennonite caravan heading west, though she was not a Mennonite, and settled with her brother at the grandly named Lane University in Lecompton, Kansas. There were fourteen freshmen the year Ida matriculated, and classes were held in the parlor of a residential house.

Ida studied music. She was, according to faculty reports, not the brightest student, but she was diligent, and she earned good grades through hard digging. Her classmates found a joyful, gregarious personality and an extremely optimistic nature, and they elected her valedictorian.[1] She also met her temperamental opposite while at Lane, a dour and stubborn fellow named David Eisenhower. Inexplicably, they fell in love, and they remained together for life. Their children could not remember a serious argument between them, though David gave Ida ample cause.

They were married within the River Brethren church, a small orthodox sect that believed in plain dress, temperance, and pacifism. After a daring girlhood, Ida devoted herself to a strict, but not too strict, life. The women of the River Brethren sect wore bonnets as part of their religious garb. One day Ida and a friend decided they no longer wanted to wear the bonnets. They were ostracized at church, forced to sit alone in the back. But eventually they won the day and were readmitted, bonnetless, into the community. Ida was strict in her faith but fun-loving and humane in practice.

David opened a store with a partner named Milton Good near Abilene, Kansas. Later, after the store failed, David told his family that Good had disappeared and stolen all the store's money. That was a face-saving lie, which his sons appeared to believe. The fact is that David Eisenhower was solitary and difficult. He seems to have abandoned the business or had a falling-out with his partner. After the business collapsed, David left for Texas, leaving Ida with an infant son at home and another on the way. "David's decision to quit the store and abandon his pregnant wife is incomprehensible," the historian Jean Smith writes. "He had no job lined up or a profession on which to fall back."[2]

David eventually found a job doing manual labor in a railroad yard. Ida followed him to Texas and set up home in a shack along the tracks, where Dwight was born. By the time Ida was twenty-eight, they'd hit bottom. They had $24.15 in cash and few possessions except the piano back in Kansas, and David had no marketable skills.[3]

The extended Eisenhower family came to the rescue. David was offered a job at a creamery in Abilene, and they moved back to Kansas and back to the middle class. Ida raised five boys, all of whom would go on to remarkable success and all of whom would spend their lives revering her. Dwight would later call her "the finest person I've ever known."[4] In *At Ease,* the memoir composed late in life, Ike revealed how much he idolized her, though his prose, characteristically, was restrained: "Her serenity, her open smile, her gentleness with all and her tolerance of their ways, despite an inflexible religious conviction and her own strict pattern of personal conduct, made even a brief visit with Ida Eisenhower memorable for a stranger. And for her sons, privileged to spend a boyhood in her company, the memories are indelible."[5]

There was no drinking, card playing, or dancing in the house. There was not much demonstrated love. Dwight's father was quiet, somber, and inflexible, while Ida was warm and down to earth. But there were Ida's books, her tutelage, and her commitment to education. Dwight became an avid reader of classical history, reading about the battles of Marathon and Salamis and heroes like Pericles and Themistocles. There was also Ida's vibrant, funny personality, and her maxims, which came in a steady, tough-minded flow: "God deals the cards and we play them," "Sink or swim," "Survive or perish." The family prayed and read the Bible every day, the five brothers taking turns and forfeiting the right to be the reader when they stumbled over a line. Though Dwight was not religious later in life, he was steeped in the biblical metaphysic and could cite verses with ease. Ida, though devout herself, strongly believed that religious views were a matter of personal conscience and not to be imposed on others.

During Eisenhower's presidential campaigns, Abilene was portrayed as an idyllic, Norman Rockwell piece of rural America. In reality, it was a harsh environment covered by a thick code of respectability and propriety. Abilene had gone from boomtown to Bible Belt, from whorehouses to schoolmarms, without any of the intervening phases.

Victorian morality was reinforced by puritan rigor, what one historian has called Augustinianism come to America.

Ida began raising her boys in a house Ike would later calculate to be about 833 square feet. Thrift was essential, self-discipline a daily lesson. Before modern medicine, with sharp tools and hard physical labor to be done, there was a greater chance of accidents and more catastrophic consequences when they came. One year an invasion of grasshoppers ruined the crops.[6] Dwight suffered a leg infection as a teenager and refused to let the doctors amputate because it would have ended his football career. He slipped in and out of consciousness and had one of his brothers sleep on the threshold of his room to prevent the doctor from cutting off the leg while Ike was asleep. Once, when Dwight was babysitting his three-year-old brother, Earl, he left a pocketknife open on a windowsill. Earl got up on a chair, tried to grasp the knife, but it slipped from his hands and plunged into his eye, damaging the eye and producing a lifelong sense of guilt in Dwight.

Somebody should write a history of how the common death of children shaped culture and beliefs. It must have created a general sense that profound suffering was not far off, that life was fragile and contained unbearable hardships. After Ida lost one son, Paul, she converted to the sect that would later become the Jehovah's Witnesses, in search of a more personal and compassionate expression of faith. Eisenhower himself would later lose his own firstborn son, Doud Dwight, known in the family as "Icky," an experience that darkened his world ever after. "This was the greatest disappointment and disaster in my life," he would write decades later, "the one I have never been able to forget completely. Today, when I think of it, even now as I write about it, the keenness of our loss comes back to me as fresh and terrible as it was in that long dark day soon after Christmas, 1920."[7]

The fragility and remorselessness of this life demanded a certain level of discipline. If a single slip could produce disaster, with little in the way of a social safety net to cushion the fall; if death, or drought, or disease, or betrayal could come crushingly at any moment; then character and discipline were paramount requirements. This was the shape of life: an underlying condition of peril, covered by an ethos of self-restraint, reticence, temperance, and self-wariness, all designed to minimize the risks. People in that culture developed a moral abhorrence of anything that might make life even more perilous, like debt or childbirth out of wedlock. They developed a stern interest in those activities that might harden resilience.

Any child raised by Ida Eisenhower was going to value education, but the general culture placed much less emphasis on it than ours does now. Of the two hundred children who entered first grade with Dwight in 1897, only thirty-one graduated with him from high school. Academics were less important because you could get a decent job without a degree. What mattered more to long-term stability and success was having steady habits, the ability to work, the ability to sense and ward off sloth and self-indulgence. In that environment, a disciplined work ethic really was more important than a brilliant mind.

One Halloween evening, when he was about ten, Eisenhower's older brothers received permission to go out trick-or-treating, a more adventurous activity in those days than it is now. Ike wanted to go with them, but his parents told him he was too young. He pleaded with them, watched his brothers go, and then became engulfed by uncontrolled rage. He turned red. His hair bristled. Weeping and screaming, he rushed out into the front yard and began pounding his fists against the trunk of an apple tree, scraping the skin off and leaving his hands bloody and torn.

His father shook him, lashed him with a hickory switch, and sent him up to bed. About an hour later, with Ike sobbing into his pillow, his mother came up and sat silently rocking in the chair next to his bed. Eventually she quoted a verse from the Bible: "He that conquereth his own soul is greater than he who taketh a city."

As she began to salve and bandage his wounds, she told her son to beware the anger and hatred burning inside. Hatred is a futile thing, she told him, which only injures the person who harbors it. Of all her boys, she told him, he had the most to learn about controlling his passions.

When he was seventy-six, Eisenhower wrote, "I have always looked back on that conversation as one of the most valuable moments of my life. To my youthful mind, it seemed to me that she talked for hours, but I suppose the affair was ended in fifteen or twenty minutes. At least she got me to acknowledge that I was wrong and I felt enough ease in my mind to fall off to sleep."[8]

That concept—conquering your own soul—was a significant one in the moral ecology in which Eisenhower grew up. It was based on the idea that deep inside we are dual in our nature. We are fallen, but also splendidly endowed. We have a side to our nature that is sinful—selfish, deceiving, and self-deceiving—but we have another side to our nature that is in God's image, that seeks transcendence and virtue. The essential drama of life is the drama to construct character, which is an engraved set of disciplined habits, a settled disposition to do good. The cultivation of Adam II was seen as a necessary foundation for Adam I to flourish.

Sin

TODAY, THE WORD "SIN" HAS LOST ITS POWER AND AWESOME INTENSITY. It's used most frequently in the context of fattening desserts. Most people in daily conversation don't talk much about individual sin. If they talk about human evil at all, that evil is most often located in the structures of society—in inequality, oppression, racism, and so on—not in the human breast.

We've abandoned the concept of sin, first, because we've left behind the depraved view of human nature. In the eighteenth and even the nineteenth century, many people really did embrace the dark self-estimation expressed in the old Puritan prayer "Yet I Sin": "Eternal Father, Thou art good beyond all thought, but I am vile, wretched, miserable, blind . . ." That's simply too much darkness for the modern mentality.

Second, in many times and many places, the word "sin" was used to declare war on pleasure, even on the healthy pleasures of sex and entertainment. Sin was used as a pretext to live joylessly and censoriously. "Sin" was a word invoked to suppress the pleasures of the body, to terrify teenagers about the perils of masturbation.

Furthermore, the word "sin" was abused by the self-righteous, by dry-hearted scolds who seem alarmed, as H. L. Mencken put it, by the possibility that someone somewhere might be enjoying himself, who always seem ready to rap somebody's knuckles with a ruler on the supposition that that person is doing wrong. The word "sin" was abused by people who embraced a harsh and authoritarian style of parenting, who felt they had to beat the depravity out of their children. It was abused by those who, for whatever reason, fetishize suffering, who believe that only through dour self-mortification can you really become superior and good.

But in truth, "sin," like "vocation" and "soul," is one of those words that it is impossible to do without. It is one of those words—and there will be many in this book—that have to be reclaimed and modernized.

Sin is a necessary piece of our mental furniture because it reminds us that life is a moral affair. No matter how hard we try to reduce everything to deterministic brain chemistry, no matter how hard we try to reduce behavior to the sort of herd instinct that is captured in big data, no matter how hard we strive to replace sin with nonmoral words, like "mistake" or "error" or "weakness," the most essential parts of life are matters of individual responsibility and moral choice: whether to be brave or cowardly, honest or deceitful, compassionate or callous, faithful or disloyal. When modern culture tries to replace sin with ideas like error or insensitivity, or tries to banish words like "virtue," "character," "evil," and "vice" altogether, that doesn't make life any less moral; it just means we have obscured the inescapable moral core of life with shallow language. It just means we think and talk about these choices less clearly, and thus become increasingly blind to the moral stakes of everyday life.

Sin is also a necessary piece of our mental furniture because sin is communal, while error is individual. You make a mistake, but we are all plagued by sins like selfishness and thoughtlessness. Sin is baked into our nature and is handed down through the generations. We are all sinners together. To be aware of sin is to feel intense sympathy toward others who sin. It is to be reminded that as the plight of sin is communal, so the solutions are communal. We fight sin together, as communities and families, fighting our own individual sins by helping others fight theirs.

Furthermore, the concept of sin is necessary because it is radically true. To say you are a sinner is not to say that you have some black depraved stain on your heart. It is to say that, like the rest of us, you have some perversity in your nature. We want to do one thing, but we end up doing another. We want what we should not want. None of us wants to be hard-hearted, but sometimes we are. No one wants to self-deceive, but we rationalize all the time. No one wants to be cruel, but we all blurt things out and regret them later. No one wants to be a bystander, to commit sins of omission, but, in the words of the poet Marguerite Wilkinson, we all commit the sin of "unattempted loveliness."

We really do have dappled souls. The same ambition that drives us to build a new company also drives us to be materialistic and to exploit. The same lust that leads to children leads to adultery. The same confidence that can lead to daring and creativity can lead to self-worship and arrogance.

Sin is not some demonic thing. It's just our perverse tendency to fuck things up, to favor the short term over the long term, the lower over the higher. Sin, when it is committed over and over again, hardens into loyalty to a lower love.

The danger of sin, in other words, is that it feeds on itself. Small moral compromises on Monday make you more likely to commit other, bigger moral compromises on Tuesday. A person lies to himself and soon can no longer distinguish when he is lying to himself and when he isn't. Another person is consumed by the sin of self-pity, a passion to be a righteous victim that devours everything around it as surely as anger or greed.

People rarely commit the big sins out of the blue. They walk through a series of doors. They have an unchecked problem with anger. They have an unchecked problem with drinking or drugs. They have an unchecked problem of sympathy. Corruption breeds corruption. Sin is the punishment of sin.

The final reason sin is a necessary part of our mental furniture is that without it, the whole method of character building dissolves. From time immemorial, people have achieved glory by achieving great external things, but they have built character by struggling against their internal sins. People become solid, stable, and worthy of self-respect because they have defeated or at least struggled with their own demons. If you take away the concept of sin, then you take away the thing the good person struggles against.

The person involved in the struggle against sin understands that each day is filled with moral occasions. I once met an employer who asks each job applicant, "Describe a time when you told the truth and it hurt you." He is essentially asking those people if they have their loves in the right order, if they would put love of truth above love of career.

In places like Abilene, Kansas, the big sins, left unchallenged, would have had very practical and disastrous effects. Sloth could lead to a failure of a farm; gluttony and inebriation to the destruction of a family; lust to the ruination of a young woman; vanity to excessive spending, debt, and bankruptcy.

In places like that, people had an awareness not only of sin but of the different kinds of sins and the different remedies for each. Some sins, such as anger and lust, are like wild beasts. They have to be fought through habits of restraint. Other sins, such as mockery and disrespect, are like stains. They can be expunged only by absolution, by apology, remorse, restitution, and cleansing. Still others, such as stealing, are like a debt. They can be rectified only by repaying what you owe to society. Sins such as adultery, bribery, and betrayal are more like treason than like crime; they damage the social order. Social harmony can be rewoven only by slowly recommitting to relationships and rebuilding trust. The sins of arrogance and pride arise from a perverse desire for status and superiority. The only remedy for them is to humble oneself before others.

In other words, people in earlier times inherited a vast moral vocabulary and set of moral tools, developed over centuries and handed down from generation to generation. This was a practical inheritance, like learning how to speak a certain language, which people could use to engage their own moral struggles.

Character

IDA EISENHOWER WAS FUNNY AND WARM-HEARTED, BUT STOOD SENTRY against backsliding. She forbade dancing and card games and drinking in her home precisely because her estimation of the power of sin was so high. Since self-control is a muscle that tires easily, it is much better to avoid temptation in the first place rather than try to resist it once it arises.

In raising her boys she showed them bottomless love and warmth. She allowed them more freedom to get into scrapes than parents generally do today. But she did demand that they cultivate the habit of small, constant self-repression.

Today, when we say that somebody is repressed, we tend to mean it as a criticism. It means they are uptight, stiff, or unaware of their true emotional selves. That's because we live in a self-expressive culture. We tend to trust the impulses inside the self and distrust the forces outside the self that seek to push down those impulses. But in this earlier moral ecology, people tended to distrust the impulses inside the self. These impulses could be restrained, they argued, through habit.

In 1877, the psychologist William James wrote a short treatise called "Habit." When you are trying to lead a decent life, he wrote, you want to make your nervous system your ally and not your enemy. You want to engrave certain habits so deep that they will become natural and instinctual. James wrote that when you set out to engrave a habit—say, going on a diet or always telling the truth—you want to launch yourself with as "strong and decided an initiative as possible." Make the beginning of a new habit a major event in your life. Then, "never suffer an exception" until the habit is firmly rooted in your life. A single slip undoes many fine acts of self-control. Then take advantage of every occasion to practice your habit. Practice a gratuitous exercise of self-discipline every day. Follow arbitrary rules. "Asceticism of this sort is like the insurance which a man pays on his house of goods. The tax does him no good at the time, and may possibly never bring him a return. But if the fire does come, his having paid it will be his salvation from ruin."

What William James and Ida Eisenhower were trying to inculcate, in their different ways, was steadiness over time. Character, as the Yale law professor Anthony T. Kronman has put it, is "an ensemble of settled dispositions—of habitual feelings and desires."[9] The idea is largely Aristotelian. If you act well, eventually you will be good. Change your behavior and eventually you rewire your brain.

Ida emphasized the importance of practicing small acts of self-control: following the rules of etiquette when sitting at the table, dressing in one's Sunday best when going to church, keeping the Sabbath afterward, using formal diction in letter writing as a display of deference and respect, eating plain food, avoiding luxury. If you are in the army, keep your uniform neat and your shoes polished. If you are at home, keep everything tidy. Practice the small outward disciplines.

In the culture of that time, people also believed that manual labor was a school for character. In Abilene, everybody, from business owners to farmers, did physical labor every day, greasing the buggy axles, shoveling coal, sifting the unburned lumps from the stove ash. Eisenhower grew up in a home with no running water, and the boys' chores began at dawn—waking up at five to build the morning fire, hauling water from the well—and continued through the day—carrying a hot lunch to their father at the creamery, feeding the chickens, canning up to five hundred quarts of fruit annually, boiling the clothing on washday, raising corn to be sold for spending money, digging trenches when plumbing became available, and wiring the house when electricity came to town. Ike grew up in an atmosphere that is almost the inverse of the way many children are raised today. Today's children are spared most of the manual labor Dwight had to perform, but they are not given nearly as much leeway to roam over forests and town when the chores were done. Dwight had a great deal of assigned work, but also a great deal of freedom to roam around town.

David Eisenhower, Dwight's father, practiced this sort of disciplined life in a harsh and joyless way. He was defined by his punctilious sense of rectitude. He was rigid, cool, and strictly proper. After his bankruptcy he had a horror of taking on any debt, of slipping even a bit. When he was a manager at his company he forced his employees to save 10 percent of their salary every month. They had to report to him what they had done with their 10 percent, either putting it in the bank or investing it in stocks. He wrote down each answer each month, and if he was not satisfied with their report, they lost their job.

He seemed never to relax, never taking his boys out hunting or fishing or playing with them much at all. "He was an inflexible man with a stern code," one of the boys, Edgar, was to recall. "Life to him was a very serious proposition, and that's the way he lived it, soberly and with due reflection."[10]

Ida, on the other hand, always had a smile on her lips. She was always willing to be a little naughty, to violate her sense of rectitude, even taking a shot of alcohol if the situation warranted. Ida seemed to understand, as her husband did not, that you can't rely just on self-control, habit, work, and self-denial to build character. Your reason and your will are simply too weak to defeat your desires all the time. Individuals are strong, but they are not self-sufficient. To defeat sin you need help from outside.

Her character-building method had a tender side as well. Fortunately, love is the law of our nature. People like Ida understand that love, too, is a tool to build character. The tender character-building strategy is based on the idea that we can't always resist our desires, but we can change and reorder our desires by focusing on our higher loves. Focus on your love for your children. Focus on your love of country. Focus on your love for the poor and downtrodden. Focus on your love of your hometown or alma mater. To sacrifice for such things is sweet. It feels good to serve your beloved. Giving becomes cheerful giving because you are so eager to see the things you love prosper and thrive.

Pretty soon you are behaving better. The parent focusing on the love of his or her children will drive them to events day after day, will get up in the middle of the night when they are sick, will drop everything when they are in crisis. The lover wants to sacrifice, to live life as an offering. A person motivated by such feelings will be a bit less likely to sin.

Ida demonstrated that it is possible to be strict and kind, disciplined and loving, to be aware of sin and also aware of the possibility of forgiveness, charity, and mercy. Decades later, when Dwight Eisenhower took the presidential oath of office, Ida asked him to have the Bible open to 2 Chronicles 7:14: "If my people, which are called by my name, shall humble themselves, and pray, and seek my face, and turn from their wicked ways; then I will hear from heaven, and will forgive their sin, and will heal their land." The most powerful way to fight sin is by living in a sweet, loving way. It's how you do the jobs you do, whether it's a prestigious job or not. As others have noted, God loves adverbs.

Self-Control

DWIGHT SEEMS TO HAVE BELONGED TO THE CATEGORY OF THOSE WHO BE-
lieve that religion is good for society but who are not religious themselves. There's no evidence that he had an explicit sense of God's grace
or any theological thoughts about redemption. But he inherited both
his mother's garrulous nature and her sense that that nature had to be
continually repressed and conquered. He just held these beliefs in secular form.

He was rambunctious from birth. His childhood was remembered
in Abilene for a series of epic brawls. At West Point, he was defiant, rebellious, and misbehaving. He ran up a string of demerits, for
gambling, smoking, and general disrespectfulness. At graduation, he
ranked 125th out of 164 men for discipline. Once he was demoted
from sergeant to private for dancing too exuberantly at a ball. He
was also bedeviled, throughout his military career and his presidency,
with the barely suppressed temper that his parents had seen on that
Halloween evening. Throughout his military career, his subordinates
came to look for the telltale signs of his looming fury, such as certain set expressions that signaled an imminent profanity-laced explo-
sion. Dubbed "the terrible-tempered Mr. Bang" by a World War II
journalist, Eisenhower's capacity for rage was always there, just under
the surface.[11] "It was like looking into a Bessemer furnace," one of
his aides, Bryce Harlow, recalled. His wartime doctor, Howard
Snyder, noticed the "twisted cord-like temple arteries standing out
on the side of his head" just before one of Eisenhower's explosions.
"Ike's subordinates were awed by his capacity for rage," his biographer
Evan Thomas wrote.[12] Eisenhower's appointments secretary, Tom
Stephens, noticed that the president tended to wear brown whenever
he was in a foul temper. Stephens would see Eisenhower from the
office window. "Brown suit today!" he would call out to the staff as
forewarning.[13]

Ike was even more divided than most of us. He was a master of
army expletives, but he almost never cursed in front of women. He
would turn away if someone told a dirty joke.[14] He was reprimanded
at West Point for habitually smoking cigarettes in the halls, and by the
end of the war he was a four-pack-a-day smoker. But one day he quit

cold turkey: "I simply gave myself an order." "Freedom," he would later say in his 1957 State of the Union address, "has been defined as the opportunity for self-discipline."[15]

His internal torment could be convulsive. By the end of World War II, his body was a collection of aches and pains. He spent the nights staring at the ceiling, racked by insomnia and anxiety, drinking and smoking, tortured by throat infections, cramps, spiking blood pressure. But his capacity for self-repression—what might be called noble hypocrisy—was also immense. He was not naturally good at hiding his emotions. He had a remarkably expressive face. But day by day he put on a false front of confident ease and farm-boy garrulousness. He became known for his sunny, boyish temperament. Evan Thomas writes that Ike told his grandson, David, that that smile "came not from some sunny feel-good philosophy but from getting knocked down by a boxing coach at West Point. 'If you can't smile when you get up from a knockdown,' the coach said, 'you're never going to lick an opponent.'"[16] He thought it was necessary to project easy confidence in order to lead the army and win the war:

> I firmly determined that my mannerisms and speech in public would always reflect the cheerful certainty of victory—that any pessimism and discouragement I might ever feel would be reserved for my pillow. To translate this conviction into tangible results, I adopted a policy of circulating through the whole force to the full limit imposed by physical considerations. I did my best to meet everyone from general to private with a smile, a pat on the back and a definite interest in his problems.[17]

He devised stratagems for dismissing his true passions. For example, in his diaries he made lists of people who offended him as a way of sealing off his anger toward them. When he felt a surge of hatred, he refused to let it rule him. "Anger cannot win. It cannot even think clearly," he noted in his diary.[18] Other times he would write an offender's name on a piece of paper and then drop it into the wastebasket, another symbolic purging of emotion. Eisenhower was not an authentic man. He was a passionate man who lived, as much as his mother did, under a system of artificial restraints.

Organization Man

IDA SENT IKE OFF FROM ABILENE TO WEST POINT ON JUNE 8, 1911. SHE RE-
mained an ardent pacifist, determinedly opposed to the soldier's vocation, but she told her son, "It is your choice." She saw the train off,
went home, and shut herself in her room. The remaining boys could
hear her sobbing through the door. His brother Milton later told Ike
it was the first time he had ever heard their mother cry.[19]

Ike graduated from West Point in the class of 1915. He thus spent
his early career in the shadow of World War I. Trained for combat, he
never saw action in the war that was supposed to end all wars. He
never even left the United States. He spent those years training troops,
coaching football, and doing logistics. He lobbied furiously to be sent
to war, and in October 1918, when he was twenty-eight, he received
orders. He was to ship out to France on November 18. The war, of
course, ended on November 11. It was a bitter blow. "I suppose we'll
spend the rest of our lives explaining why we didn't get into this war,"
he lamented in a letter to a fellow officer. Then he made an uncharacteristically unrestrained vow: "By God, from now on I am cutting
myself a swath that will make up for this."[20]

That vow didn't immediately come true. Eisenhower was promoted to lieutenant colonel in 1918, in advance of his coming deploy-
ment. He would not be promoted again for twenty years, until 1938.
The army had a glut of officers who'd been elevated during the war,
and there were not many openings for advancement in an army that
by the 1920s was shrinking and assuming a marginal role in American
life. His career stagnated, while the careers of his civilian brothers
zoomed ahead. By the time he was in his forties, he was easily the least
accomplished of the boys in the Eisenhower family. He was in middle
age. He did not receive his first star until he was fifty-one. Nobody
expected great things of him.

During these interwar years Ike served as an infantry officer, football coach, and staff officer, intermittently attending school at the Infantry Tank School, the Command and General Staff School, and
eventually the War College. Ike would occasionally unleash his frustration at the bureaucratic bungling of his institution, at the way it

smothered his opportunities and wasted his talents. But on the whole, his response was amazingly restrained. He became the classic Organization Man. From Ida's rules of conduct, Ike slid easily into the military code of conduct. He subsumed his own desires for the sake of the group.

He wrote in one of his memoirs that by the time he was in his thirties he had learned "the basic lesson of the military—that the proper place for a soldier is where he is ordered by his superiors."[21] He was given a run-of-the-mill assignment. "I found no better cure than to blow off steam in private and then settle down to the job at hand."[22]

As a staff officer—never a coveted or glamorous role—Eisenhower learned to master procedure, process, teamwork, and organization. He learned the secrets of thriving within the organization. "When I go to a new station I look to see who is the strongest and ablest man on the post. I forget my own ideas and do everything in my power to promote what he says is right."[23] Later, in *At Ease,* he wrote, "Always try to associate yourself closely and learn as much as you can from those who know more than you, who do better than you, who see more clearly than you." He was a fanatic about both preparation and then adaptation: "The plans are nothing, but the planning is everything," he would say. Or, "Rely on planning, but never trust plans."

He also gained a perspective on himself. He began carrying around an anonymous little poem:

> Take a bucket, fill it with water,
> Put your hand in—clear up to the wrist.
> Now pull it out; the hole that remains
> Is a measure of how much you'll be missed. . . .
>
> The moral of this quaint example:
> To do just the best that you can,
> Be proud of yourself, but remember,
> There is no Indispensible Man![24]

Mentors

IN 1922, EISENHOWER WAS ORDERED TO PANAMA, WHERE HE JOINED THE
20th Infantry Brigade. Two years in Panama did two things for Ike.
First, it allowed him a change of scene after the death of his firstborn
son, Icky. Second, it introduced him to General Fox Connor. As the
historian Jean Edward Smith put it, "Fox Connor was understatement personified: self-possessed, soft-spoken, eminently formal, and
polite—a general who loved reading, a profound student of history,
and a keen judge of military talent."[25] Connor was completely devoid
of theatricality. From Connor Ike learned the maxim "Always take
your job seriously, never yourself."

Fox Connor served as the beau ideal of the humble leader. "A sense
of humility is a quality I have observed in every leader whom I have
deeply admired," Eisenhower later wrote. "My own conviction is that
every leader should have enough humility to accept, publicly, the responsibility for the mistakes of the subordinates he has himself selected and, likewise, to give them credit, publicly, for their triumphs."
Connor, Ike continued, "was a practical officer, down to earth, equally
at home in the company of the most important people in the region
and with any of the men in the regiment. He never put on airs of any
kind, and he was as open and honest as any man I have ever known. . . .
He has held a place in my affections for many years that no other, not
even a relative, could obtain."[26]

Connor also revived Ike's love of the classics, military strategy, and
world affairs. Eisenhower called his service under Connor "a sort of
graduate school in military affairs and the humanities, leavened by the
comments and discourses of a man who was experienced in his knowledge of men and their conduct. . . . It was the most interesting and
constructive [period] of my life." On a visit to Panama, Ike's boyhood
friend Edward "Swede" Hazlett noted that Eisenhower had "fitted up
the 2nd story screened porch of their quarters as a rough study, and
here, with drawing board and texts, he put in his spare time re-fighting
the campaigns of the old masters."[27]

At the same time, Ike was particularly affected by the training of a
horse, "Blackie." In his memoirs, he wrote:

In my experience with Blackie—and earlier with allegedly incompetent recruits at Camp Colt—is rooted my enduring conviction that far too often we write off a backward child as hopeless,
a clumsy animal as worthless, a worn-out field as beyond restora-
tion. This we do largely out of our own lack of willingness to
take the time and spend the effort to prove ourselves wrong: to
prove that a difficult boy can become a fine man, that an animal
can respond to training, that the field can regain its fertility.[28]

General Connor arranged for Eisenhower to attend the Command
and General Staff School at Fort Leavenworth, Kansas. He would
graduate first in his class of 245 officers. Like Blackie, he was not to be
written off.

In 1933, after graduating from the War College as one of the youngest officers ever to attend, Eisenhower was appointed General Douglas
MacArthur's personal assistant. For the next several years, Eisenhower
worked with MacArthur, primarily in the Philippines, helping that
nation prepare for its independence. Douglas MacArthur was the the-
atrical one. Ike respected MacArthur but was put off by his grandios-
ity. He described MacArthur as "an aristocrat, but as for me, I'm just
folks."[29]

Under MacArthur, Eisenhower met the ultimate test of his temper.
Their small office rooms adjoined, separated by only a slatted door.
"He called me to his office by raising his voice,"[30] Eisenhower remembered. "He was decisive, personable, and he had one habit that never
ceased to startle me. In reminiscing or in telling stories, he talked of
himself in the third person."[31]

Several times, Ike asked to leave his staff assignment. MacArthur
denied the request, insisting Eisenhower's work in the Philippines was
far more important than anything he could do as a mere lieutenant
colonel in the American army.

Ike was disappointed, but he remained with MacArthur for six more
years, working behind the scenes with more and more planning work
falling on his shoulders.[32] Ike remained respectful in his boss's presence
but eventually came to detest MacArthur for the way he put himself
above the institution. After one of MacArthur's more memorable acts
of egomania, Eisenhower erupted in the privacy of his diary:

But I must say it is almost incomprehensible that after 8 years of working for him, writing every word he publishes, keeping his secrets, preventing him from making too much of an ass of himself, trying to advance his interests while keeping myself in the background, he should suddenly turn on me. He'd like to occupy a throne room surrounded by experts in flattery; while in a dungeon beneath, unknown to the world, would be a bunch of slaves doing his work and producing the things that, to the public, would represent the brilliant accomplishment of his mind. He's a fool, but worse he is a puking baby.[33]

Eisenhower served loyally and humbly, putting himself inside the mind of his superior, adopting his perspectives as his own, getting his work done efficiently and on time. In the end, the officers he served—MacArthur included—ended up promoting him. And when the great challenge of his life came during World War II, Ike's ability to repress his own passions served him well. He never greeted war with a sense of romantic excitement, the way his lifelong colleague George S. Patton did. He saw it as another hard duty to be endured. He had learned to focus less on the glamor and excitement of wartime heroics and more on the dull, mundane things that would prove to be the keys to victory. Preserving alliances with people you might find insufferable. Building enough landing craft to make amphibious invasions possible. Logistics.

Eisenhower was a masterful wartime commander. He suppressed his own frustrations in order to keep the international alliance together. He ferociously restrained national prejudices, which he felt as acutely as anyone, in order to keep the disparate armies on the same team. He passed credit for victories on to his subordinates and, in one of the most famous unsent messages in world history, was willing to put the blame for failures upon himself. This was the memo he was going to release if the D-Day invasion failed. "Our landings . . . have failed . . . and I have withdrawn the troops," he wrote. "My decision to attack at this time and place was based upon the best information available. The troops, the air and the Navy did all that bravery and devotion could do. If any blame or fault attaches to the attempt it is mine alone."

Eisenhower's disciplined and self-regulating life had its downsides.

He was not a visionary. He was not a creative thinker. In war, he was not a great strategist. As president, he was often oblivious to the most consequential emerging historical currents of his time—from the civil rights movement to the menace of McCarthyism. He was never good with abstract ideas. He behaved disgracefully in failing to defend General George C. Marshall from attacks upon his patriotism, to his great regret and shame later on. And all that artificial self-restraint could make him cold when he should have been warm, ruthlessly practical when he should have been chivalrous and romantic. His behavior toward his mistress, Kay Summersby, at the end of the war is repellent. Summersby had served, and presumably, loved Eisenhower through the hardest years of his life. He did not give her even the benefit of a good-bye. One day, she found that her name had been dropped from his travel roster. She received an icy typewritten note from Ike on official Army stationery: "I am sure you understand that I am personally much distressed that an association that has been so valuable to me has to be terminated in this particular fashion but it is by reasons over which I have no control. . . . I hope that you will drop me a note from time to time—I will always be interested in how you are getting along."[34] He had become so practiced at suppressing his own emotions that in this moment he was even able to suppress any hint of compassion, any ember of gratitude.

Eisenhower was occasionally aware of his shortcomings. Thinking of his hero George Washington, he said, "I've often felt the deep wish that the Good Lord had endowed me with his clarity of vision in big things, his strength of purpose and his genuine greatness of mind and spirit."[35]

But for some, life is the perfect school; it teaches them exactly those lessons they will need later on. Eisenhower was never a flashy man, but two outstanding traits defined the mature Eisenhower, traits that flowed from his upbringing and that he cultivated over time. The first was his creation of a second self. Today, we tend to live within an ethos of authenticity. We tend to believe that the "true self" is whatever is most natural and untutored. That is, each of us has a certain sincere way of being in the world, and we should live our life being truthful to that authentic inner self, not succumbing to the pressures outside ourself. To live artificially, with a gap between your inner nature and your outer conduct, is to be deceptive, cunning, and false.

Eisenhower hewed to a different philosophy. This code held that artifice is man's nature. We start out with raw material, some good, some bad, and this nature has to be pruned, girdled, formed, repressed, molded, and often restrained, rather than paraded in public. A personality is a product of cultivation. The true self is what you have built from your nature, not just what your nature started out with.

Eisenhower was not a sincere person. He hid his private thoughts. He recorded them in his diary, and they could be scathing. Of Senator William Knowland, he wrote, "In his case, there seems to be no final answer to the question, 'How stupid can you get?' "[36] But in public he wore a costume of affability, optimism, and farm-boy charm. As president, he was perfectly willing to appear stupider than he really was if it would help him perform his assigned role. He was willing to appear tongue-tied if it would help him conceal his true designs. Just as he learned to suppress his anger as a boy, he learned to suppress his ambitions and abilities as an adult. He was reasonably learned in ancient history, admiring especially the crafty Athenian leader Themistocles, but he never let that on. He did not want to appear smarter than other people, or somehow superior to the average American. Instead he cultivated the image of simple, unlearned charm. As president he would supervise a detailed meeting about an arcane topic, issuing clear and specific instructions about what was to be done. Then he would go out to a press conference and massacre the English language in an effort to disguise his designs. Or he would just pretend the whole subject was over his head: "That's just too complicated for a dumb bunny like me."[37] He was willing to appear more stupid than he really was. (This is how we know he was not a New Yorker.)

Ike's simplicity was strategic. After his death, his vice president, Richard Nixon, recollected, "[Ike] was a far more complex and devious man than most people realized, and in the best sense of these words. Not shackled to a one-track mind, he always applied two, three, or four lines of reasoning to a single problem. . . . His mind was quick and facile."[38] He was a famously good poker player. "Ike's wide smile, open as the Kansas sky," Evan Thomas writes, "concealed a deep secretiveness. He was honorable but occasionally opaque, outwardly amiable but inwardly seething."[39]

Once, before a press conference, his press secretary, Jim Hagerty, informed him of an increasingly delicate situation in the Formosa

Strait. Ike smiled and said, "Don't worry, Jim, if that question comes up, I'll just confuse them." Predictably, the question was raised by journalist Joseph Harsch. Good-naturedly, Eisenhower responded:

The only thing I know about war is two things: the most changeable factor in war is human nature in its day-by-day manifestation; but the only unchanging factor about war is human nature. And the next thing is that every war is going to astonish you in the way it occurred and the way it is carried out. . . . So I think you just have to wait, and that is the kind of prayerful decision that may some day face a president.[40]

After the conference, Thomas writes, "Eisenhower himself joked that he must have given fits to Russian and Chinese translators trying to explain to their bosses what he meant."[41]

Ike's double nature could make it hard for people to really know him. "I don't envy you trying to figure Dad out," John Eisenhower told the biographer Evan Thomas. "I can't figure him out." After his death, his widow, Mamie, was asked whether she had really known her husband. "I'm not sure anyone did," she replied.[42] But self-repression helped Eisenhower to control his natural desires and to fulfill the tasks assigned to him, both by his military superiors and by history. He looked simple and straightforward, but his simplicity was a work of art.

Moderation

HIS FINAL TRAIT WHICH RIPENED WITH HIS FULL MATURITY WAS MODERATION.

Moderation is a generally misunderstood virtue. It is important to start by saying what it is not. Moderation is not just finding the midpoint between two opposing poles and opportunistically planting yourself there. Neither is moderation bland equanimity. It's not just having a temperate disposition that doesn't contain rival passions or competing ideas.

On the contrary, moderation is based on an awareness of the inevitability of conflict. If you think that the world can fit neatly together, then you don't need to be moderate. If you think all your personal qualities can be brought together into simple harmony, you don't need to hold back, you can just go whole hog for self-actualization and growth. If you think all moral values point in the same direction, or all political goals can be realized all at once by a straightforward march along one course, you don't need to be moderate, either. You can just head in the direction of truth as quickly as possible.

Moderation is based on the idea that things do not fit neatly together. Politics is likely to be a competition between legitimate opposing interests. Philosophy is likely to be a tension between competing half-truths. A personality is likely to be a battleground of valuable but incompatible traits. As Harry Clor put it in his brilliant book *On Moderation,* "The fundamental division in the soul or psyche is at the root of our need for moderation." Eisenhower, for example, was fueled by passion and policed by self-control. Neither impulse was entirely useless and neither was entirely benign. Eisenhower's righteous rage could occasionally propel him toward justice, but it could occasionally blind him. His self-control enabled him to serve and do his duty, but it could make him callous.

The moderate person contains opposing capacities to the *n*th degree. A moderate person can start out hot on both ends, both fervent in a capacity for rage and fervent in a desire for order, both Apollonian at work and Dionysian at play, both strong in faith and deeply doubtful, both Adam I and Adam II.

A moderate person can start out with these divisions and rival tendencies, but to live a coherent life, the moderate must find a series of balances and proportions. The moderate is forever seeking a series of temporary arrangements, embedded in the specific situation of the moment, that will help him or her balance the desire for security with the desire for risk, the call of liberty with the need for restraint. The moderate knows there is no ultimate resolution to these tensions. Great matters cannot be settled by taking into account just one principle or one viewpoint. Governing is more like sailing in a storm: shift your weight one way when the boat tilts to starboard, shift your weight the other way when it tilts to port—adjust and adjust and adjust to circumstances to keep the semblance and equanimity of an even keel.

Eisenhower understood this intuitively. Writing to Swede, his boyhood friend, in his second term as president, he mused "Possibly I am something like a ship which, buffeted and pounded by wind and wave, is still afloat and manages in spite of frequent tacks and turnings to stay generally along its plotted course and continues to make some, even if slow and painful, headway."[43]

As Clor observes, the moderate knows she cannot have it all. There are tensions between rival goods, and you just have to accept that you will never get to live a pure and perfect life, devoted to one truth or one value. The moderate has limited aspirations about what can be achieved in public life. The paradoxes embedded into any situation do not allow for a clean and ultimate resolution. You expand liberty at the cost of encouraging license. You crack down on license at the cost of limiting liberty. There is no escaping this sort of trade-off.

The moderate can only hope to have a regulated character, stepping back to understand opposing perspectives and appreciating the merits of each. The moderate understands that political cultures are traditions of conflict. There are never-ending tensions that pit equality against achievement, centralization against decentralization, order and community against liberty and individualism. The moderate doesn't try to solve those arguments. There are no ultimate solutions. The moderate can only hope to achieve a balance that is consistent with the needs of the moment. The moderate does not believe there are some policy solutions that are right for all times (this seems obvious, but the rule is regularly flouted by ideologues in nation after nation). The moderate does not admire abstract schemes but understands that it is necessary to legislate along the grain of human nature, and within the medium in which she happens to be placed.

The moderate can only hope to be disciplined enough to combine in one soul, as Max Weber put it, both warm passion and a cool sense of proportion. He aims to be passionate about his ends but deliberate about the proper means to realize them. The best moderate is blessed with a spirited soul and also the proper character to tame it. The best moderate is skeptical of zealotry because he is skeptical of himself. He distrusts passionate intensity and bold simplicity because he know that in politics the lows are lower than the highs are high—the damage leaders do when they get things wrong is greater than the benefits they create when they get things right. Therefore caution is the proper attitude, an awareness of the limits the foundation of wisdom.

For many people at the time and for many years after, Eisenhower seemed like an emotionally flat simpleton with a passion for Western novels. His star has risen among historians as his inner turmoil has become better appreciated. And at the end of his presidency, he delivered a speech that still stands today as a perfect example of moderation in practice.

Ike's speech came at a crucial pivot point in American politics and even public morality. On January 20, 1961, John F. Kennedy gave an inaugural address that signaled a cultural shift. Kennedy's speech was meant to indicate a new direction in the march of history. One generation and one era was ending and another generation would, as he put it, "begin anew." There would be a "new endeavor" and "a new world of law." The possibilities, he argued, were limitless. "Man holds in his mortal hands the power to abolish all forms of human poverty," he declared. Kennedy issued a call to uninhibited action. "We shall pay any price, bear any burden, meet any hardship. . . ." He called on his listeners not just to tolerate problems, but to end them: "Together let us explore the stars, conquer the deserts, eradicate disease." It was the speech of a man supremely confident in himself. It inspired millions of people around the world and set the tone and standard for political rhetoric ever since.

Three days earlier, however, Eisenhower had given a speech that epitomized the worldview that was fading away. Whereas Kennedy emphasized limitless possibilities, Eisenhower warned against hubris. Whereas Kennedy celebrated courage, Eisenhower celebrated prudence. Whereas Kennedy exhorted the nation to venture boldly forth, Eisenhower called for balance.

The word "balance" recurs throughout his text—a need to balance competing priorities, "balance between the private economy and the public economy, balance between the cost and hoped-for advantages, balance between the clearly necessary and the comfortably desirable, balance between our essential requirements as a nation and the duties imposed by the nation upon the individual; balance between the actions of the moment and the national welfare of the future. Good judgment seeks balance and progress; lack of it eventually finds imbalance and frustration."

Eisenhower warned the country against belief in quick fixes. Americans, he said, should never believe that "some spectacular and costly action could become the miraculous solution to all current difficulties." He warned against human frailty, particularly the temptation to be shortsighted and selfish. He asked his countrymen to "avoid the impulse to live only for today, plundering, for our own ease and convenience, the precious resources of tomorrow." Echoing the thrifty ethos of his childhood, he reminded the nation that we cannot "mortgage the material assets of our grandchildren without risking the loss also of their political and spiritual heritage."

He warned, most famously, about the undue concentration of power, and the way unchecked power could lead to national ruin. He warned first about the military-industrial complex—"a permanent armaments industry of vast proportions." He also warned against "a scientific-technological elite," a powerful network of government-funded experts who might be tempted to take power away from the citizenry. Like the nation's founders, he built his politics on distrust of what people might do if they have unchecked power. He communicated the sense that in most times, leaders have more to gain from being stewards of what they have inherited than by being destroyers of what is there and creators of something new.

This was the speech of a man who had been raised to check his impulses and had then been chastened by life. It was the speech of a man who had seen what human beings are capable of, who had felt in his bones that man is a problem to himself. It was the speech of a man who used to tell his advisers "Let's make our mistakes slowly," because it was better to proceed to a decision gradually than to rush into anything before its time. This is the lesson that his mother and his upbringing had imparted to him decades before. This was a life organized not around self-expression, but self-restraint.

CHAPTER 4

STRUGGLE

O N THE NIGHT OF APRIL 18, 1906, WHEN SHE WAS EIGHT YEARS OLD, Dorothy Day was living in Oakland, California.

She had, as usual, said her prayers at bedtime. She was the only religiously observant member of her household and had become, as she wrote later, "disgustingly, proudly pious."[1] She had always had a sense, she wrote in her diary decades later, of an immanent spiritual world.

The earth began shaking. When the rumbling began, her father rushed into the children's bedroom, snatched her two brothers, and rushed for the front door. Her mother grabbed her baby sister from Dorothy's arms. Her parents apparently figured Dorothy could take care of herself. She was left alone in her brass bed as it rolled back and forth across the polished floor. The night of the San Francisco earthquake, she felt that God was visiting her. "The earth became a sea which rocked our house in a most tumultuous manner," she recalled.[2] She could hear the water in the rooftop tank splashing above her head. These sensations "were linked up with my idea of God as a tremendous Force, a frightening impersonal God, a Hand stretched out to seize me, His child, and not in love."[3]

When the earth settled, the house was a mess. There were broken dishes all over the floor, along with books, chandeliers, and pieces of the ceiling and chimney. The city was in ruins, too, temporarily reduced to poverty and need. But in the days after, Bay Area residents pulled together. "While the crisis lasted, people loved each other," she wrote in her memoir decades later. "It was as though they were united in Christian solidarity. It makes one think of how people could, if they would, care for each other in times of stress, unjudgingly in pity and love."

As the writer Paul Elie has put it, "A whole life is prefigured in that episode"—the crisis, the sense of God's nearness, the awareness of poverty, the feeling of loneliness and abandonment, but also the sense that that loneliness can be filled by love and community, especially through solidarity with those in deepest need.[4]

Day was born with a passionate, ideal nature. Like Dorothea, the main character in George Eliot's novel *Middlemarch,* her nature demanded that she live an ideal life. She was unable to be satisfied with mere happiness, being in a good mood, enjoying the normal pleasures that friendships and accomplishments bring. As Eliot put it, "Her flame quickly burned up that light fuel; and, fed from within, soared after some illimitable satisfaction, some object which would never justify weariness, which would reconcile self-despair with the rapturous consciousness of life beyond self." Day needed spiritual heroism, some transcendent purpose for which she could sacrifice.

Children's Crusade

DOROTHY'S FATHER HAD BEEN A JOURNALIST, BUT THE NEWSPAPER PRINTING plant burned down in the quake and his job was gone. The family possessions lay in ruins. Day experienced the family's humiliating descent into poverty. Her father moved them to Chicago, where he set out to write a novel that was never published. A distant, distrustful man, he forbade his children to leave the house without permission or to invite friends in. Day remembered Sunday dinners marked by gloomy silence but for the sound of everybody chewing. Her mother did her best, but she suffered four miscarriages, and one night she fell into hysterics, smashing every dish in the home. The next day she was back to normal. "I lost my nerve," she explained to her children.

In Chicago, Day noticed that her own family was much less affectionate than the families around her. "We were never hand holders. We were always withdrawn and alone, unlike Italians, Poles, Jews and other friends who I had who were fresh and spontaneous in their affections." She went to church and sang hymns with neighboring families. In the evenings she got on her knees and inflicted her piety on her sister: "I used to plague my sister with my long prayers. I would kneel until my knees ached and I was cold and stiff. She would beg me to come to bed and tell her a story." One day she had a conversation with her best friend, Mary Harrington, about a certain saint. Later in life, writing her memoirs, Day couldn't remember exactly which saint they were talking about, but she remembered "my feeling of lofty enthusiasm, and how my heart almost burst with desire to take part in such high endeavor. One verse of the Psalms often comes to mind, 'Enlarge Thou my heart, O Lord, that Thou mayst enter in.' . . . I was filled with a natural striving, a thrilling recognition of the possibilities of spiritual adventure."[5]

Parents in those days did not feel it necessary to entertain their children. Day remembered spending happy hours on the beach with her friends, fishing in creeks for eels, running away to an abandoned shack at the edge of a swamp, setting up a fantasy world and pretending that they would live there alone forever. Day also remembered long days of intolerable boredom, especially over the summer break. She tried to ease the tedium by doing household chores and reading. She read Charles Dickens, Edgar Allan Poe, and *The Imitation of Christ* by Thomas à Kempis, among other books.

With adolescence came a fascination with sex. She knew right away that she was thrilled by it, but she also had been taught that it was dangerous and evil. One afternoon, when she was fifteen, Day was out in a park with her baby brother. The weather was perfect. The world was full of life, and there must have been boys around. In a letter she wrote at the time to her best friend, she describes a "wicked thrilling feeling at my heart." In the next passage, she remonstrates herself priggishly, "It is wrong to think so much about human love. All those feelings and cravings that come to us are sexual desires. We are prone to have them at this age, I suppose, but I think they are impure. It is sensual and God is spiritual."

In her superb memoir *The Long Loneliness,* she reprints long passages from this letter. Her fifteen-year-old self continued, "How weak I am. My pride forbids me to write this and to put it down on paper makes me blush, but all the old love comes back to me. It is a lust of the flesh and I know that unless I forsake all sin, I will not gain the kingdom of heaven."

The letter has all the self-involvement and paint-by-numbers self-righteousness that you'd expect in a precocious teenager. She's got the basic concept of her religion down, but not the humanity and the grace. But there's also an arduous spiritual ambition at work. "Maybe if I stayed away from books more this restlessness would pass. I am reading Dostoyevsky." She resolves to fight her desires: "Only after a hard bitter struggle with sin and only after we have overcome it, do we experience blessed joy and peace. . . . I have so much work to do to overcome my sins. I am working always, always on guard, praying without ceasing to overcome all physical sensations to be purely spiritual."

Reflecting on that letter in *The Long Loneliness,* which was published when she was in her fifties, Day confessed that it "was filled with pomp and vanity and piety. I was writing of what interested me most, the conflict of flesh and spirit, but I was writing self-consciously and trying to pretend to myself I was being literary."[6] But that letter displays some of the features that would eventually make Day one of the most inspiring religious figures and social workers of the twentieth century: her hunger to be pure, her capacity for intense self-criticism, her desire to dedicate herself to something lofty, her tendency to focus on hardship and not fully enjoy the simple pleasures available to her, her conviction that fail as she might, and struggle as she would, God would ultimately redeem her from her failings.

Bohemia

DAY WAS ONE OF THREE STUDENTS IN HER HIGH SCHOOL TO WIN A COL-lege scholarship, thanks to her excellence in Latin and Greek. She went to the University of Illinois, where she cleaned and ironed to pay for room and board and was an indifferent student. She threw herself, willy-nilly, into activities that she hoped would lead to an epic life. She joined the writers' club, accepted for an essay in which she described what it was like to go without food for three days. She also joined the Socialist Party, broke from religion, and began doing what she could to offend the churchgoers. She decided the sweetness of girlhood was gone. It was time to be at war with society.

At age eighteen, after a couple of years at Illinois, she decided that college life was unsatisfying. She moved to New York to become a writer. She wandered the city for months, desperately lonely: "In all that great city of seven millions, I found no friends; I had no work, I was separated from my fellows. Silence in the midst of city noises oppressed me. My own silence, the feeling that I had no one to talk to overwhelmed me so that my very throat was constricted; my heart was heavy with unuttered thoughts; I wanted to weep my loneliness away."[7]

During this lonely period she became indignant at the poverty she saw in New York, its different smell from the poverty she had seen in Chicago. "Everyone must go through something analogous to a conversion," she would later write, "conversion to an idea, a thought, a desire, a dream, a vision—without vision the people perish. In my teens I read Upton Sinclair's *The Jungle* and Jack London's *The Road* and became converted to the poor, to a love for and desire to be always with the poor and suffering—the workers of the world. I was converted to the idea of the Messianic mission of the proletariat." Russia was very much on people's minds then. Russian writers defined the spiritual imagination. The Russian Revolution inflamed young radicals' visions for the future. Dorothy's closest college friend, Rayna Simons, moved to Moscow to be part of that future, and died of illness after a few months there. In 1917, Day attended a rally celebrating the Russian Revolution. She felt a sense of exaltation; the victory of the masses was at hand.

Dorothy finally found work at a radical paper, *The Call*, for five dollars a week. There she covered labor unrest and the lives of factory workers. She interviewed Leon Trotsky one day and a millionaire's butler the next. Newspaper life was intense. She was carried along by events, not reflecting on them, just letting them sweep over her.

Although more an activist than an aesthete, she fell in with a bohemian crowd, with the critic Malcolm Cowley, the poet Allen Tate, and the novelist John Dos Passos. She formed a deep friendship with the radical writer Michael Gold. They would walk along the East River for hours, happily talking about their reading and their dreams. Occasionally, Gold would break into joyful song, in Hebrew or Yiddish. She had a close though apparently platonic relationship with the playwright Eugene O'Neill, who shared her obsessions with loneliness, religion, and death. Day's biographer Jim Forest writes that Dorothy would sometimes put O'Neill to bed, drunk and shaking with the terrors, and hold him until he fell asleep. He asked her to have sex with him, but she refused.

She protested on behalf of the working classes. But the most vital dramas of her life were going on inside. She had become an even more avid reader, especially of Tolstoy and Dostoyevsky.

It's hard now to recapture how seriously people took novel reading then, or at least how seriously Day and others took it—reading important works as wisdom literature, believing that supreme artists possessed insights that could be handed down as revelation, trying to mold one's life around the heroic and deep souls one found in books. Day read as if her whole life depended upon it.

Fewer people today see artists as oracles and novels as a form of revelation. The cognitive sciences have replaced literature as the way many people attempt to understand their own minds. But Day was "moved to the depths of my being" by Dostoyevsky. "The scene in *Crime and Punishment* where the young prostitute reads from the New Testament to Raskolnikov, sensing sin more profound than her own; that story, 'The Honest Thief'; those passages in *The Brothers Karamazov*; Mitya's conversion in jail, the very legend of the Grand Inquisitor, all this helped to lead me on." She was especially drawn to the scene in which "Father Zossima spoke glowingly of that love for God which resulted in a love for one's brother. The story of his conversion to love is moving, and that book, with its picture of religion, had a lot to do with my later life."[8]

She didn't just read Russian novels, she seemed to live them out. She was a heavy drinker and barfly. Malcolm Cowley wrote that gangsters loved her because she could drink them under the table, though that is hard to believe, given her rail-thin frame. The tragedies of her raucous life were there, too. A friend named Louis Holladay took an overdose of heroin and died in her arms.[9] In her memoir, she describes her moves from one rancid and airless apartment to another, but even she, self-critical as she was, leaves out some of the messiness. She leaves out her promiscuity, calling it "a time of searching" and referring vaguely to "the sadness of sin, the unspeakable dreariness of sin."[10]

In the spring of 1918, she volunteered as a nurse at King's County Hospital as a deadly flu epidemic swept through the city and the world. (More than 50 million people died of it between March 1918 and June 1920.)[11] She began work at six each morning and worked twelve-hour days, changing linens, emptying bedpans, administering shots, enemas, and douches. The hospital was run like a military unit. When the head nurse entered the ward, the junior nurses stood at attention. "I liked the order of life and the discipline. By contrast the life that I had been leading seemed disorderly and futile," she recalled. "One of the things that this year in the hospital made me realize is that one of the hardest things in the world is to organize ourselves and discipline ourselves."[12]

She met a newspaperman named Lionel Moise at the hospital. They had a tumultuous physical relationship. "You are hard," she wrote to him lustfully. "I fell in love with you because you are hard." She got pregnant. He told her to get an abortion, which she did (also neglecting to mention it in her memoirs). One night, after he dumped her, she unhooked the gas pipe from the heater in her apartment and attempted suicide. A neighbor found her in time.

In her memoirs she writes that she left the hospital job because it eventually made her numb to suffering, and it left her no time to write. She neglected to mention that she had also agreed to marry a man twice her age named Berkeley Tobey, a rich man from the Northwest. They traveled to Europe together, and after the trip was over, she left him. In her memoirs she describes it as a solo trip, embarrassed that she had used Tobey for a chance to go to Europe. "I didn't want to write what I was ashamed of," she would later tell the journalist Dwight MacDonald. "I felt I had used him and was ashamed."[13]

She also, crucially, was arrested twice, first in 1917 at age twenty and then in 1922 at age twenty-five. The first time, it was in the name of political activism. She had become active in advocating for the rights of women; she was arrested for taking part in a suffragist protest in front of the White House and sentenced, with the rest of the protesters, to thirty days in jail. The prisoners began a hunger strike, but Day, sitting there gnawed by hunger, soon slipped into a deep depression. She flipped from feeling solidarity with the hunger strikers to feeling that it was all somehow wrong and meaningless. "I lost all consciousness of any cause. I had no sense of being a radical. I could only feel darkness and desolation all around me. . . . I had an ugly sense of the futility of human effort, man's helpless misery, the triumph of might. . . . Evil triumphed. I was a petty creature, filled with self-deception, self-importance, unreal, false, and rightly scorned and punished."[14]

In jail she asked for a Bible and read it intensely. Other prisoners told her stories of the solitary confinement cells where prisoners would be locked up for six months at a time. "Never would I recover from this wound, this ugly knowledge I had gained of what men were capable of in their treatment of each other."[15]

Day was taking a stand against injustice, but she was doing it without an organizing transcendent framework. She seems to have felt, unconsciously and even then, that for her, activism without faith would fail.

Her second imprisonment was even more emotionally devastating. She had gone to stay with a friend, a drug addict, in her apartment on Skid Row, in a building that served as both a whorehouse and a residence for members of the IWW, the radical union. The police raided the place, looking for subversives. The cops assumed that Day and her friend were prostitutes. They were forced to stand out on the street, semiclad, before they were hauled off to jail.

She was a victim of the Red hysteria of the time. But she also felt she was a victim of her own imprudence and lack of integrity. She took the arrest as an indictment of her scattered life. "I do not think that ever again, no matter of what I am accused, can I suffer more than I did then of shame and regret, and self-contempt. Not only because I had been caught, found out, branded, publicly humiliated, but because of my own consciousness that I deserved it."[16]

These are episodes of extraordinary self-scrutiny and self-criticism. Looking back years later, Day took a dim view of her own rowdy life. She saw it as a form of pride, as an attempt to define what was good and bad for herself, without reference to anything larger. "The life of the flesh called to me as a good and wholesome life, regardless of man's laws, which I felt rebelliously were made for the repression of others. The strong could make their own law, live their own lives; in fact they were beyond good and evil. What was good and what was evil? It is easy enough to stifle conscience for a time. The satisfied flesh has its own law."

But Day was not just lost in a world of shallow infatuations, tumultuous affairs, fleshly satisfaction, and selfishness. Her extreme self-criticism flowed from a deep spiritual hunger. She used the word "loneliness" to describe this hunger. For many of us, that word brings to mind solitude. And Day was indeed solitary, and she did suffer from it. But Day also used the word "loneliness" to describe spiritual isolation. She had a sense that there was some transcendent cause or entity or activity out there and that she would be restless until she found it. She was incapable of living life on the surface only—for pleasures, success, even for service—but needed a deep and total commitment to something holy.

Childbirth

DAY HAD SPENT HER TWENTIES THROWING HERSELF DOWN DIFFERENT AVenues, looking for a vocation. She tried politics. She took part in protests and marches. But they didn't satisfy. Unlike Frances Perkins, she was unfit for the life of politics, with its compromises, self-seeking, shades of gray, and dirty hands. She needed a venue that would involve internal surrender, renunciation of self, commitment to something pure. She looked back on her early activism with disquiet and self-criticism. "I do not know how sincere I was in my love of the poor and my desire to serve them. . . . I wanted to go on picket lines, to go to jail, to write, to influence others and so make my mark on the world. How much ambition and how much self-seeking there was in all of this."[17]

Then Day went the literary route. She wrote a novel about her disordered early life called *The Eleventh Virgin,* which was accepted by a New York publisher and optioned for $5,000 by a Hollywood studio.[18] But this sort of literature did not cure the longing, either, and the book would eventually make her feel ashamed—she later thought of buying up every existing copy.

She thought that romantic love might satisfy her longing. She fell in love with a man named Forster Batterham, and they lived together, unmarried, in a house on Staten Island that Day bought with the proceeds of her novel. She describes Forster romantically in *The Long Loneliness* as an anarchist, an Englishman by descent, and a biologist. In fact, the truth is more prosaic. He made gauges in a factory; he had grown up in North Carolina and gone to Georgia Tech. He had an interest in radical politics.[19] But Day's love for him was real. She loved him for his convictions, for his stubborn attachment to them, for his love of nature. She would, after their disagreements about fundamental things had become clear, still beg him to marry her. Day was still a passionate, sexual woman, and her lust for him was real, too. "My desire for you is a painful rather than pleasurable emotion," she wrote in a letter that was released after her death. "It is a ravishing hunger which makes me want you more than anything in the world. And makes me feel as though I could barely exist until I saw you again." On September 21, 1925, during one of their separations, she wrote to him, "I made myself a beautiful new nightie, all lacie and exotic, also several new pairs of panties which you will be interested in I am sure. I think of you much and dream of you every night and if my dreams could affect you over long distance, I am sure they would keep you awake."

When you read of Day and Batterham living their secluded life in Staten Island, reading, talking, making love, you get the impression that they, like many young couples newly in love, were trying to build what Sheldon Vanauken would call a "Shining Barrier," a walled garden, cut off from the world, in which their love would be pure. Ultimately, Day's longing could not be contained within the Shining Barrier. Living with Batterham, taking long walks with him on the beach, she still felt a desire for something more. Among other things, she wanted a child. She felt her house was empty without one. In 1925, at age twenty-eight, she was thrilled when she learned she was pregnant. Batterham did not share her feelings. A self-styled radical, a modern man, he did not believe in bringing more human beings into the world. He certainly did not believe in the bourgeois institution of marriage, and he would never consent to marry her.

While she was pregnant, it occurred to Day that most of the descriptions of childbirth had been written by men. She set out to rectify this. Shortly after giving birth, she wrote an essay on the experience, which eventually appeared in the *New Masses*. Day vividly described the physical struggle of the birth itself:

> Earthquake and fire swept my body. My spirit was a battle-
> ground on which thousands were butchered in a most horrible

manner. Through the rush and roar of the cataclysm which was all about me I heard the murmur of the doctor and answered the murmur of the nurse in my head. In a white blaze of thankfulness I knew that ether was forthcoming.

When her daughter Tamar arrived, she was overwhelmed by gratitude: "If I had written the greatest book, composed the greatest symphony, painted the most beautiful painting or carved the most exquisite figure, I could not have felt the more exalted creator than I did when they placed my child in my arms." She felt the need for someone to thank. "No human creature could receive or contain so vast a flood of love and joy as I often felt after the birth of my child. With this came the need to worship, to adore."[20]

But whom to thank? Whom to worship? A sense of God's reality and immanence came upon her, particularly on her long walks, when she found herself praying. She had trouble praying on her knees, but while she was walking, words of gratitude, praise, and obedience seemed to leap from her. A walk that began in misery could end in exultation.

Day was not answering the question of whether God exists. She was simply made aware of a presence beyond herself. She was surrendering to the belief that independent of one's own will, there is something significant that gives shape to life. If the life of a radical was a life of assertion and agency, a desire to steer history, she was turning to a life of obedience. God was in charge. As she later put it, she came to see that "worship, adoration, thanksgiving, supplication—these were the noblest acts of which men were capable of in this life."[21] The birth of her child began her transformation from a scattered person to a centered one, from an unhappy bohemian to a woman who had found her calling.

DAY HAD NO OBVIOUS outlet for her faith. She was a member of no church. She was not comfortable with theology or traditional religious doctrines. But she felt hunted by God. "How can there be no God," she asked Forster, "when there are all these beautiful things?"

Her attention turned to the Catholic Church. It was not church history that drew her, or papal authority, or even the political and social positions taken by the church. She knew nothing about Catholic theology and only knew the Church itself as a backward and politically reactionary force. It was the people, not theology. It was the Catholic immigrants she had covered and served—their poverty, their dignity, their communal spirit, and their generosity toward those who were down and out. Day's friends told her that she didn't need a religious institution to worship God, certainly not one as retrograde as the Catholic Church, but Day's experience as a radical taught her to associate herself as closely as possible with those who were suffering, to join in their walk, which meant joining their church.

She observed that Catholicism already organized the lives of many poor urban families. It had won their allegiance. They poured into its churches on Sundays and holy days and in moments of joy and mourning. In the same way, the Catholic faith would provide structure for her life, and she hoped it would provide structure for her daughter. "We all crave order, and in the book of Job, hell is described as a place where no order is. I felt that 'belonging' to a church would bring order into [Tamar's] life, which I felt was lacking in my own."[22]

Day's adult faith was warmer and more joyful than the faith she'd experienced as a teenager. Day was particularly attracted to Saint Teresa of Avila, the sixteenth-century Spanish mystic and nun whose experiences closely paralleled Day's own: the deeply spiritual childhood, the terror in the face of her own sinfulness, the occasional moments of what could be described as sexual ecstasy in His presence, the intense ambition to reform human institutions and serve the poor.

Teresa lived a life of renunciation. She slept under a single woolen blanket. There was no heat in her convent except for a stove in one room. Her days were filled with prayer and penance. But she also possessed a lightness of spirit. Day said she loved the fact that Saint Teresa wore a bright red dress the day she entered the convent. She loved the fact that one day Teresa shocked her fellow nuns by taking out castanets and dancing. When she was the Mother Superior and the nuns under her became melancholy, she had the kitchen serve them steak. Teresa said that life is like a "night spent in an uncomfortable inn," so you might as well do what you can to make it more pleasant.

Day was becoming a Catholic, but she wasn't close to any practicing Catholics. But she encountered a nun walking down a street and asked her for instruction. The nun was shocked by Day's ignorance of

Catholic teaching and berated her for it, but she welcomed her in. Day began attending services weekly, even when she didn't feel like it. She asked herself, "Do I prefer the Church or my own will?" She decided that even though she would have found it more pleasant to spend Sunday mornings reading the papers, she preferred the church to her own will.

The path to God eventually meant breaking with Forster. He was scientific, skeptical, and empirical. He bet his life on a material universe, clinging to his conviction as fiercely as Day ultimately would to her view of a divinely created one.

Their separation took some time and required much tearing. One day, over a meal, Forster asked the questions many of Day's radical friends were asking: Had she lost her mind? Who was pushing her to an archaic and backward institution like the Church? Who was the secret person in her life corrupting her in this way?

Day was surprised by the passion and power behind his questions. Finally she quietly said, "It is Jesus. I guess it is Jesus Christ who is the one who is pushing me to the Catholics."[23]

Forster turned white and went silent. He didn't move. He just sat there glaring at her. She asked if they could talk some more about religion. He didn't answer her at all, or nod, or shake his head. Then he clasped his hands together on the table in a gesture that reminded Day of the way schoolboys act when they want their teachers to think they are good. He sat for several seconds in this posture, then raised his clasped hands and brought them smashing down on the table, rattling the cups and dishes. Day was terrified that he would lose control and start striking her with his clasped hands. But he didn't. He got up and told Day that she was mentally disturbed. Then he walked around the table once and went out of the house.[24]

These scenes did not end their love, or their lust, for each other. Day still pleaded with Forster to marry her and to give Tamar a real father. Even after she had effectively renounced him for the Church, she wrote to him, "I dream of you every night—that I am lying in your arms and can feel your kisses and it is torture to me, but so sweet too. I do love you more than anything else in the world, but I cannot help my religious sense, which tortures me unless I do as I believe right."[25]

Dorothy's love for Forster paradoxically opened her up to faith.

Her love for him broke through her shell and exposed the soft and more vulnerable regions of the heart to other loves. It provided her with a model. As Day put it, "It was through a whole love, both physical and spiritual, I came to know God."[26] This is a more mature understanding than her tendency, as a teenager, to divide the world between flesh on one side and spirit on the other.

Conversion

THE CONVERSION PROCESS WAS A DREARY, JOYLESS AFFAIR. DAY, BEING Day, made it hard on herself. She criticized herself at each moment, doubting her own motives and practices. She was divided between the radicalism of her former self and the devotion to the Church that her new life required. One day, walking to the post office, she was enveloped with scorn for her own faith. "Here you are in a stupor of content. You are biological. Like a cow. Prayer for you is like the opiate of the people." She kept repeating that phrase in her head: "The opiate of the people." But, she reasoned as she continued her walk, she wasn't praying to escape pain. She was praying because she was happy, because she wanted to thank God for her happiness.[27]

She had Tamar baptized in July 1927. There was a party afterward, and Forster brought some lobsters he had caught. But then he quarreled with Day, telling her again that it was all just so much mumbo-jumbo, and then he left.

She officially joined the church on December 28, 1927. The moment brought her no consolation. "I had no sense of peace, no joy, no conviction that what I was doing was right. It was just something that I had to do, a task to be gotten through."[28] As she performed the sacraments, the Baptism, Penance, Holy Eucharist, she felt herself a hypocrite. She went through the motions, getting down on her knees, coldly. She was afraid somebody might see her. She was afraid she was betraying the poor and going over to the losing side of history, to an institution lined up on the side of property, of the powerful and the elites. "Are you sure of yourself?" she asked herself. "What kind of affectation is this? What act is this you are going through?"

Self-critical as always, Day questioned herself over the following months and years, wondering whether her faith was deep or practical enough: "How little, how puny my work had been since becoming a Catholic, I thought. How self-centered, how ingrown, how lacking in a sense of community! My summer of quiet reading and prayer, my self-absorption seemed sinful as I watched my brothers in their struggle, not for themselves but for others."[29]

In choosing religion, she chose an arduous path. It is often said that religion makes life easier for people, provides them with the comforting presence of a loving and all-knowing father. That is certainly not how Day experienced it. She experienced it as difficult self-conflict, the sort of self-conflict that Joseph Soloveitchik described in a famous footnote in his book *Halakhic Man*. Here is an abridged version of that footnote:

> This popular ideology contends that the religious experience is tranquil and neatly ordered, tender and delicate; it is an enchanted stream for embittered souls and still waters for troubled spirits. The person "who comes in from the field, weary" (Gen. 25:29), from the battlefield and campaigns of life, from the secular domain which is filled with doubts and fears, contradictions and refutations, clings to religion as does a baby to its mother and finds in her lap "a shelter for his head, the nest of his forsaken prayers" and there is comforted for his disappointments and tribulations. This Rousseauian ideology left its stamp on the entire Romantic movement from the beginning of its growth until its final (tragic!) manifestations in the consciousness of contemporary man. Therefore, the representatives of religious communities are inclined to portray religion, in a wealth of colors that dazzle the eye, as a poetic Arcadia, a realm of simplicity, wholeness, and tranquillity. This ideology is intrinsically false and deceptive. That religious consciousness in man's experience, which is most profound and most elevated, which penetrates to the very depths and ascends to the very heights, is not that simple and comfortable.
>
> On the contrary, it is exceptionally complex, rigorous, and tortuous. Where you find its complexity, there you find its greatness. The consciousness of *homo religiosis* flings bitter accusations against itself and immediately is filled with regret, judges its desires and yearnings with excessive severity, and at

the same time steeps itself in them, casts derogatory aspersions on its own attributes, flails away at them, but also subjugates itself to them. It is in a condition of spiritual crisis, of psychic ascent and descent, of contradiction arising from affirmation and negation, self-abnegation and self-appreciation. Religion is not, at the outset, a refuge of grace and mercy for the despondent and desperate, an enchanted stream for crushed spirits, but a raging clamorous torrent of man's consciousness with all its crises, pangs, and torments.

Early in her religious journey, Day met three women who were in love but weren't sleeping with the men they intended to marry, even though it was obvious how much they wanted to. Day looked at their self-denial and began to feel "that Catholicism was something rich and real and fascinating. . . . I saw them wrestling with moral problems, with the principles by which they lived, and this made them noble in my eyes."[30]

Day attended mass daily, which meant rising at dawn. She prayed according to the monastic rhythms through the day. She dedicated time each day to the religious disciplines, reading the scripture, saying the rosary. She fasted and went to confession.

These rituals could become routine, like playing the scales for a musician, but Day found the routine, even when it was dull, necessary: "Without the sacraments of the church, primarily the Eucharist, the Lord's Supper, as it is called, I certainly do not think that I could go on. . . . I do not always approach it from need, or with joy and thanksgiving. After 38 years of almost daily communion, one can confess to a routine, but it is like the routine of taking daily food."[31]

These routines created a spiritual center for her life. From the fragmentation of her early life she moved toward integration.

Living Out the Gospel

DAY WAS NOW IN HER EARLY THIRTIES. THE GREAT DEPRESSION WAS BITING with full force. In 1933 she started a newspaper called *The Catholic Worker* to mobilize the proletariat and apply Catholic social teaching toward the goal of creating a society in which it is easier for people to be good. It wasn't only a newspaper; it was a movement, located in ramshackle offices in Lower Manhattan, with everybody working for free. Within three years it had a circulation of 150,000, with distribution in five hundred parishes across the country.[32]

The newspaper hosted a soup kitchen, feeding as many as fifteen hundred each morning. It sponsored a series of hospitality houses for the indigent, providing nearly fifty thousand nights of lodging between 1935 and 1938. Day and her colleagues also organized and inspired more than thirty other hospitality houses across the United States and in England. They eventually opened and inspired agrarian communes from California to Michigan to New Jersey. They organized marches and events. These were, in part, efforts to build community, to heal the loneliness that marks human existence.

To Day, separation was sin: separation from God, separation from one another. Unity was holiness: the fusion between people and spirits. *The Catholic Worker* fused a lot of things together. It was a newspaper but also an activist aid organization. It was a religious publication, but it also advocated for economic change. It was about inner life, but also political radicalism. It brought the rich and poor into contact. It joined theology and economics, material concerns and spiritual ones, body and soul.

Day insisted on being radical, to get down to the roots of social problems. The paper was Catholic, but she embraced a philosophy of personalism, which is an affirmation of the dignity of each person, created in the image of God. Being a personalist, Day had a suspicion of bigness, whether it was big government or big corporations. Day even had a suspicion of big philanthropy. She was constantly urging her co-workers to "stay small": Start your work from where you live, with the small concrete needs right around you. Help ease tension in your workplace. Help feed the person right in front of you. Personalism holds that we each have a deep personal obligation to live simply, to look after the needs of our brothers and sisters, and to share in the happiness and misery they are suffering. The personalist brings his whole person to serve another whole person. This can only be done by means of intimate contact within small communities.

Day spent the rest of her life, until her death on November 29, 1980, as a Catholic worker, working on the newspaper and serving bread and soup to the poor and mentally disabled. She wrote eleven books and more than a thousand articles. The service work was pro-saic. This was before computers and copiers. Each month the staff had to type out tens of thousands of address labels in order to send the paper out to subscribers. The reporters sold the paper themselves on the street. Day felt that it was not enough to just care for the poor, "one must live with them, share with them their suffering too. Give up one's privacy, and mental and spiritual comforts as well as physical."[33] She didn't just visit the shelters and hospitality houses from the comfort of her own home. She lived in the hospitality houses herself, with those she was serving.

The work was relentless—endlessly serving coffee and soup, rais-ing money, writing articles for the paper. "Breakfast a thick slice of dry bread," Day wrote in her diary one day, "and some very bad cof-fee. I dictate a dozen letters. My brain is a fog. I am too weak to climb stairs. I have prescribed for myself this day in bed but I keep thinking it is my spirit that is all wrong. I am surrounded by repellent disorder, noise, people, and have no spirit of inner solitude or poverty."[34]

We sometimes think of saints, or of people who are living like saints, as being ethereal, living in a higher spiritual realm. But often enough they live in an even less ethereal way than the rest of us. They are more fully of this earth, more fully engaged in the dirty, practical problems of the people around them. Day and her colleagues slept in cold rooms. They wore donated clothes. They did not receive salaries. Day's mind was not engaged by theology most of the time, but by how to avoid this or that financial crisis, or arrange for this person to get that treatment. In a 1934 journal entry she described the activities of a single day, a mixture of the sacred and the profane: she woke up, got to mass, made breakfast for the staff, answered mail, did the book-keeping, read some literature, wrote an inspirational message to be mimeographed and handed out. Then a relief worker came in looking for a confirmation outfit for a twelve-year-old girl, then a convert came in to share his religious writings, then a Fascist came by to whip up hatred among the residents, then an art student arrived with some drawings of Saint Catherine of Siena, and so on and so on.

The atmosphere was similar to the one Albert Schweitzer, the Ger-man medical missionary, described at his hospital in the African jun-gle. He did not hire idealists for that hospital, nor did he hire people who had a righteous sense of how much they were giving to the world. He certainly did not hire people who set out "to do something special." He only wanted people who would perform constant acts of service with the no-nonsense attitude that they will simply do what needs doing. "Only a person who feels his preference to be a matter of course, not something out of the ordinary, and who has no thought of heroism but only of a duty undertaken with sober enthusiasm, is capable of being the sort of spiritual pioneer the world needs."[35]

Day was not a naturally social creature. She had a writer's personality, somewhat aloof and often craving solitude. But she forced herself to be with people, almost all day, every day. Many of those she served had mental disabilities, or suffered from alcoholism. Bickering was constant. The guests could be rude, nasty, and foul-mouthed. Yet she forced herself to sit at the table and focus on the specific person in front of her. That person might be drunk and incoherent, but Day would sit, showing respect and listening.

She would carry notebooks with her and use spare moments to write, journal entries for herself and a constant string of columns, essays, and reports for others. Other people's sins became an occasion to reflect on her own greater ones. As she wrote one day in her journal: "Drunkenness and all the sins which follow in its wake are so obviously ugly and monstrous, and mean such unhappiness for the poor sinner that it is all the more important that we do not judge or condemn. In the eyes of God the hidden subtle sins must be far worse. We must make every effort of will to love more and more—to hang on to each other with love. They should serve to show us the hideousness of our own sins so that we truly repent and abhor them."[36]

She guarded against spiritual pride, against the feeling of self-righteousness that might come over her because she was doing good works. "I have to stop myself sometimes," she wrote. "I have found myself rushing from one person to another—soup bowls and more soup bowls, plates of bread and more plates of bread, with the gratitude of the hungry becoming a loud din in my ears. The hunger of my ears can be as severe as someone else's stomach hunger; the joy of hearing those expressions of gratitude."[37] The sin of pride is around every corner, Day believed, and there are many corners even in a charity house. To serve others is to live under a great temptation.

Suffering

————

AS A YOUNG WOMAN, DAY FOLLOWED THE MODE OF DOSTOYEVSKY—HER life was filled with drinking and disorder even while she was God-haunted. But, as Paul Elie notes, internally she was not a Dostoyevskyan; she was a Tolstoyan. She was not a trapped animal compelled to suffer by circumstance; she ardently chose suffering. At each step along the way, when most people would have sought out comfort and ease—what economists call self-interest or what psychologists call happiness—she chose a different route, seeking discomfort and difficulty in order to satisfy her longing for holiness. She wasn't just choosing to work at a nonprofit institution in order to have a big impact; she was seeking to live in accord with the Gospels, even if it meant sacrifice and suffering.

When most people think about the future, they dream up ways they might live happier lives. But notice this phenomenon. When people remember the crucial events that formed them, they don't usually talk about happiness. It is usually the ordeals that seem most significant. Most people shoot for happiness but feel formed through suffering.

Day was unusual, maybe even perverse, in that she sometimes seemed to seek out suffering as a road to depth. She probably observed, as we all do, that people we call deep have almost always endured a season of suffering, or several such seasons. But she seemed to seek out those seasons, and to avoid some of the normal pleasures of life that would have brought simple earthly happiness. She often sought out occasions for moral heroism, occasions to serve others in acts of enduring hardship.

For most of us, there is nothing intrinsically noble about suffering. Just as failure is sometimes just failure (and not your path to becoming the next Steve Jobs), suffering is sometimes just destructive, to be exited or medicated as quickly as possible. When it is not connected to some larger purpose beyond itself, suffering shrinks or annihilates people. When it is not understood as a piece of a larger process, it leads to doubt, nihilism, and despair.

But some people can connect their suffering to some greater design. They place their suffering in solidarity with all the others who have suffered. These people are clearly ennobled by it. It is not the suffering itself that makes all the difference, but the way it is experienced. Think of the way Franklin Roosevelt came back deeper and more empathetic after being struck by polio. Often, physical or social suffering can give people an outsider's perspective, an attuned awareness of what others are enduring.

The first big thing suffering does is it drags you deeper into yourself. The theologian Paul Tillich wrote that people who endure suffering are taken beneath the routine busyness of life and find they are not who they believed themselves to be. The pain involved in, say, composing a great piece of music or the grief of having lost a loved one smashes through a floor they thought was the bottom floor of their soul, revealing a cavity below, and then it smashes through that floor, revealing another cavity, and so on and so on. The person in pain descends to unknown ground.

Suffering opens up ancient places of pain that had been hidden. It exposes frightening experiences that had been repressed, shameful wrongs that had been committed. It spurs some people to painfully and carefully examine the basement of their own soul. But it also presents the pleasurable sensation that one is getting closer to the truth. The pleasure in suffering is that you feel you are getting beneath the superficial and approaching the fundamental. It creates what modern psychologists call "depressive realism," an ability to see things exactly the way they are. It shatters the comforting rationalizations and pat narratives we tell about ourselves as part of our way of simplifying ourselves for the world.

Then, too, suffering gives people a more accurate sense of their own limitations, of what they can control and not control. When people are thrust down into these deeper zones, thrust into lonely self-scrutiny, they are forced to confront the fact that they can't determine what goes on there.

Suffering, like love, shatters the illusion of self-mastery. Those who suffer can't tell themselves to stop feeling pain, or to stop missing the one who has died or gone. And even when tranquillity begins to come back, or in those moments when grief eases, it is not clear where that relief comes from. The healing process, too, feels as though it's part of some natural or divine process beyond individual control. For people in this striving culture, in this Adam I world where everything is won by effort, exertion, and control, suffering teaches dependence. It teaches that life is unpredictable and that the meritocrat's efforts at total control are an illusion.

Suffering, oddly, also teaches gratitude. In normal times we treat the love we receive as a reason for self-satisfaction (I deserve to be loved), but in seasons of suffering we realize how undeserved this love is and how it should in fact be a cause for thanks. In proud moments we refuse to feel indebted, but in humble moments, people know they don't deserve the affection and concern they receive.

People in this circumstance also have a sense that they are swept up in some larger providence. Abraham Lincoln suffered through depression through his life and then suffered through the pain of conducting a civil war, and emerged with the sense that Providence had taken control of his life, that he was a small instrument in a transcendent task.

It's at this point that people in the midst of difficulty begin to feel a call. They are not masters of the situation, but neither are they helpless. They can't determine the course of their pain, but they can participate in responding to it. They often feel an overwhelming moral responsibility to respond well to it. They may start their suffering asking "Why me?" or "Why evil?" But they soon realize the proper question is "What am I supposed to do if I am confronted with suffering, if I am the victim of evil?"

People who seek this proper response to their ordeal sense that they are at a deeper level than the level of personal happiness. They don't say, "Well, I'm fighting a lot of pain over the loss of my child. I should try to balance my hedonic account by going to a lot of parties and whooping it up."

The right response to this sort of pain is not pleasure. It's holiness. I don't mean that in a purely religious sense. I mean seeing the pain as part of a moral narrative and trying to redeem something bad by turning it into something sacred, some act of sacrificial service that will put oneself in fraternity with the wider community and with eternal moral demands. Parents who have lost a child start foundations; their dead child touches the lives of people they never met. Suffering simultaneously reminds us of our finitude and pushes us to see life in the widest possible connections, which is where holiness dwells.

Recovering from suffering is not like recovering from a disease.

Many people don't come out healed; they come out different. They crash through the logic of individual utility and behave paradoxically. Instead of recoiling from the sorts of loving commitments that often lead to suffering, they throw themselves more deeply into them. Even while experiencing the worst and most lacerating consequences, some people double down on vulnerability and become available to healing love. They hurl themselves deeper and more gratefully into their art, loved ones, and commitments.

This way, suffering becomes a fearful gift, very different from that other gift, happiness, conventionally defined. The latter brings pleasure, but the former cultivates character.

Service

AS THE DECADES WORE ON, NEWS OF DOROTHY DAY'S EXAMPLE SPREAD. She has inspired generations of young Catholics because she wasn't merely a champion of Catholic social teaching, but a concrete living example. Catholic social teaching is based, in part, on the idea that each life has equal dignity, that the soul of a drug-addled homeless person is just as invaluable as the most laudable high achiever. It is based on the conviction that God has a special love for the poor. As it says in Isaiah, "True worship is to work for justice and care for the poor and oppressed." This teaching emphasizes that we are one human family. God's servants are therefore called upon to live in solidarity with one another, in community. Day formed her organization around these principles.

The Long Loneliness was published in 1952. It sold well and has been in print ever since. As her work became famous, her houses attracted flocks of admirers, and that, too, presented its own spiritual challenges. "I get tired of hearing people say how wonderful it is, what we do. Lots of times it's not as wonderful as they think. We are overworked, or feel tired and irritable, and we have heard some rude remark from someone in the line and our patience is exhausted and we're ready to explode."[38] Still, she was afraid she and her flock would be corrupted by this admiration. It also made her feel lonely.

Surrounded by people almost all the time, Day was often isolated from those she loved. Her family was estranged from her, mystified by her Catholicism. After Forster, she never loved another man and remained celibate the rest of her life. "It was years before I awakened without that longing for a face pressed against my breast, an arm about my shoulder. The sense of loss was there. It was a price I had paid."[39] It's not clear why she felt she had to pay this price, to bear this loneliness and this chastity, but she did.

Living in the hospitality houses, going on long lecture tours, even meant being away from her daughter, Tamar. "It took me hours to get to sleep," she wrote in her diary in 1940. "I miss Tamar terribly, unhappily at night, but in the day not sadly. My nights are always sadness and desolation and it seems as soon as I lie down, I am on a rack of bitterness and pain. Then in the day I am again strong enough to make an act of faith and love and go on in peace and joy."[40]

She was a single mother leading a diverse and demanding social movement. She traveled often, while a parade of others looked after Tamar. She often felt she was failing as a mother. Tamar grew up within the Catholic Worker family when she was young, and then went to boarding school when she got older. While she was sixteen, Tamar fell in love with a volunteer at *The Catholic Worker* named David Hennessy. Dorothy told Tamar she was too young to marry. She ordered her not to write to David for a year and to return his letters unopened. She wrote to David urging him to leave her daughter alone, but David returned those letters without reading them.

The couple persevered, finally marrying, with Dorothy's blessing, when Tamar was eighteen, on April 19, 1944. They moved to a farm in Easton, Pennsylvania, where Tamar gave birth to the first of the nine grandchildren she was to present to her mother. The marriage between Tamar and David lasted until the end of 1961, when they divorced. David was unemployed for long periods and struggled with mental illness. Tamar eventually moved back near a Catholic Worker farm on Staten Island. People described her as a gentle, hospitable person, without the propulsive spiritual longing her mother wrestled with. She accepted people as they were and loved them unconditionally. She died in 2008, at the age of eighty-two, in New Hampshire. Tamar remained wedded to the Social Worker movement, but she had precious little time to spend with her mother.

Impact

TORN BETWEEN COMPETING DEMANDS AND VOCATIONS, DAY WAS REST-
less through much of her adult life. At times she even thought of leaving the newspaper. "The world is too much with me in the Catholic
Worker. The world is suffering and dying. I am not suffering and
dying in the CW. I am writing and talking about it."[41] She also thought
about becoming invisible, about getting a job in a hospital as a maid,
about finding a room to live in somewhere, preferably next door to a
church: "There in the solitude of the city, living and working with
the poor, to learn to pray, to work, to suffer, to be silent."

In the end, she decided not to leave. She built a series of communities, around the newspaper, the hospitality houses, the rural communes. The communities provided her with families and joy.

"Writing," she wrote in one column in 1950, "is an act of community. It is a letter, it is comforting, consoling, helping, advising on our
part as well as asking for it on yours. It is part of our human association with each other. It is an expression of our love and concern for
each other."[42]

She returned to this theme again and again, wrestling with her divided self: her solitary nature and also her craving for others. "The
only answer in this life, to the loneliness we are all bound to feel, is
community," she wrote. "The living together, working together,
sharing together, loving God and loving our brother, and living close
to him in community so we can show our love for Him."[43] At the end
of *The Long Loneliness* she cries out, in one of her great bursts of gratitude,

> I found myself, a barren woman, the joyful mother of chil-
> dren. It is not easy always to be joyful, to keep in mind the duty
> to delight. The most significant thing about The Catholic
> Worker is poverty, some say. The most significant thing about
> The Catholic Worker is community, others say. We are not
> alone anymore. But the final word is love. At times it has been,
> in the words of Father Zossima, a harsh and dreadful thing, and
> our very faith in love has been tried through fire.
>
> We cannot love God unless we love each other, and to love

we must know each other. We know Him in the breaking of bread, and we know each other in the breaking of bread, and we are not alone anymore. Heaven is a banquet and life is a banquet, too, even with a crust, where there is companionship.[44]

It may seem from the outside as if Day was doing the sort of community service that young people are called upon to do these days— serving soup, providing shelter. But in fact, her life rested on very different foundations and pointed in very different directions than the lives of many do-gooders today.

The Catholic Worker movement was meant to ease the suffering of the poor, but that was not its main purpose or organizing principle. The main idea was to provide a model of what the world would look like if Christians really did lead the lives that the Gospels command and love. It was not only to help the poor, but to address their own brokenness, that people served. "Going to bed at night with the foul smell of unwashed bodies. Lack of privacy," Day wrote in her diary. "But Christ was born in a [manger] and a stable is apt to be unclean and odorous. If the Blessed Mother could endure it, why not I."[45]

As the journalist Yishai Schwartz has written, for Day, "every significant action only attains its significance because of its relation to the Divine." Every time she found somebody a piece of clothing, that was an act of prayer. Day was revolted by "the idea of doled-out charity," which denigrates and disrespects the poor. For her, each act of service was a gesture upward to the poor and toward God, and the fulfillment of an internal need. Day felt it was necessary, Schwartz writes, to "internalize poverty as a private virtue," to embrace poverty as a way to achieve communion with others and come closer to God. To separate community service from prayer would have been to separate it from its life-altering purpose.

The loneliness, suffering, and pain Dorothy Day endured have a sobering effect on anybody who reads her diaries. Does God really call for this much hardship? Did she not renounce too many of the simple pleasures that the world provides? In some sense she did. But in some sense this is a false impression left by overreliance on her diaries and her own writing. Like many people, Day's mood was darker in her journals than it was in her daily life. She didn't write when happy; she was engaged in the activities that made her happy. She wrote when she was brooding about something and used her diaries to contemplate the sources of her pain.

The diaries give the impression of someone in torment, but the oral histories give the impression of someone who was constantly surrounded by children, by dear friends, by admiration and a close community. As one admirer, Mary Lathrop, put it, "She had an enormous capacity for close friendships. Really quite extraordinary. Each friendship was unique, and she had many, many of them—people who loved her, and people that she loved."[46]

Others remembered her intense love of music and the sensual things of the world. As Kathleen Jordan put it, "there was Dorothy's deep sense of beauty. . . . I'd interrupt her during the opera time [while she was listening to the Metropolitan Opera on the radio]. I'd walk in and see her almost in ecstasy. That taught me a great deal about what proper prayer meant to her. . . . She used to say, 'Remember what Dostoyevsky said: "Beauty will save the world." ' We would see that in her. She didn't separate the natural and supernatural."[47]

Nanette

BY 1960, MORE THAN THREE DECADES HAD PASSED SINCE SHE HAD LEFT Forster Batterham. He had spent almost all of those years living with an innocent and charming woman named Nanette. When cancer struck Nanette, Forster called on Dorothy once again, to minister to her as she died. Of course Day responded without a second thought. For several months she spent much of each day with Nanette on Staten Island. "Nanette has been having a very hard time," Day recounted in the diary, "not only pressure but pain all through her. She lay there and cried pitifully today. There is so little one can do, except just be there and say nothing. I told her how hard it was to comfort her, one could only keep the silence in the face of suffering, and she said bitterly, 'Yes, the silence of death.' I told her I would say a rosary."[48]

Day did what sensitive people do when other people are in trauma. We are all called at certain moments to comfort people who are enduring some trauma. Many of us don't know how to react in such situations, but others do. In the first place, they just show up. They provide a ministry of presence. Next, they don't compare. The sensitive person understands that each person's ordeal is unique and should not be compared to anyone else's. Next, they do the practical things—making lunch, dusting the room, washing the towels. Finally, they don't try to minimize what is going on. They don't attempt to reassure with false, saccharine sentiments. They don't say that the pain is all for the best. They don't search for silver linings. They do what wise souls do in the presence of tragedy and trauma. They practice a passive activism. They don't bustle about trying to solve something that cannot be solved. The sensitive person grants the sufferer the dignity of her own process. She lets the sufferer define the meaning of what is going on. She just sits simply through the nights of pain and darkness, being practical, human, simple, and direct.

Forster, on the other hand, behaved terribly through the ordeal. He kept running away, leaving Nanette with Dorothy and the other caregivers. "Forster in a sad state," Day wrote in her diary, "resolutely refusing to spend time with Nanette. Nanette in a sad state all day, legs swelling badly, also stomach. Later in the evening she cried out she was losing her mind and screamed continually."[49]

Day found herself suffering with Nanette and fighting off anger toward Forster. "I get so impatient at him and his constant fleeing from her, his self-pity and his weeping that I feel hard and must fight to overcome it. Such fear of sickness and death."

On January 7, 1960, Nanette asked to be baptized. The next day she died. Day remembered her final hours: "This morning at 8:45 Nanette died after an agony of two days. The Cross was not as hard as this, she said. People in concentration camps suffered like this, she said, showing her arms. She died peacefully after a slight hemorrhage. She had a slight smile, calm and peaceful."

Apotheosis

WHEN THE RADICALISM OF THE LATE 1960S CAME ALONG, DAY BECAME ACtive in the peace movement, and in many of the other political activities of the era, but she couldn't have been more different from those radicals in her fundamental approach to life. They preached liberation, freedom, and autonomy. She preached obedience, servitude, and self-surrender. She had no patience for the celebration of open sexuality and the lax morality. She was repelled when some young people wanted to use a Dixie cup to serve the sacramental wine. She was out of step with the spirit of the counterculture and complained about all the rebellious young people: "All this rebellion makes me long for obedience—hunger and thirst for it."

In 1969 she wrote a journal entry disagreeing with those who sought to build community outside the permanent disciplines of the Church. Day had always understood the flaws in the Catholic Church, but she also understood the necessity of the structure. The radicals around her saw only the flaws and wanted to throw everything away. "It is as though the adolescents had just discovered their parents were fallible and they are so shocked they want to throw out the institutions of the home and go in for 'community.' . . . They call them 'young adults' but it seems to me they are belated adolescents with all the romanticism that goes with it."

The years confronting genuine dysfunction in the shelters had made Day realistic. "I can't bear romantics," she told one interviewer. "I want a religious realist." Much of the activism she saw around her was far too easy and self-forgiving. She had paid a terrible price to perform community service and to practice her faith—the breakup of her relationship with Forster, the estrangement from her family. "For me, Christ was not bought for thirty pieces of silver, but with my heart's blood. We buy not cheap on this market."

All around her people were celebrating nature and natural man, but Day believed that natural man is corrupt and is only saved by repressing natural urges. "We must be pruned to grow," she wrote, "and cutting hurts the natural man. But if this corruption is to put on incorruption, if one is to *put on Christ,* the new man, pain of one kind or another is inevitable. And how joyful a thought that in spite of one's dullness and lethargy one is indeed growing in the spiritual life."

The word "counterculture" was used a lot in the late 1960s, but Day was living according to a true counterculture, a culture that stood athwart not only the values of the mainstream culture of the day— the commercialism, the worship of success—but also against the values of the Woodstock counterculture the media was prone to celebrate—the antinomianism, the intense focus on the liberated individual and "doing your own thing." The Woodstock counterculture seemed, superficially, to rebel against mainstream values, but as the ensuing decades have demonstrated, it was just a flipside version of the culture of the Big Me. Both capitalism and Woodstock were about the liberation of self, the expression of self. In commercial society you expressed self by shopping and building a "lifestyle." In Woodstock culture you expressed self by casting off restraint and celebrating yourself. The bourgeois culture of commerce could merge with the bohemian culture of the 1960s precisely because both favored individual liberation, both encouraged people to measure their lives by how they were able to achieve self-gratification.

Day's life, by contrast, was about the surrender of self and ultimately the transcendence of self. Toward the end of her life she would occasionally appear on television talk shows. There is a simplicity and directness to her presence on these shows, and great self-possession. Through *The Long Loneliness* and her other writings she practiced a sort of public confession, which has attracted people ever since. She was open about her interior life, as Frances Perkins and Dwight Eisenhower never were. She was the opposite of reticent. The premise behind her confession was not mere self-revelation, though. It was the idea that in the long run our problems are all the same. As Yishai Schwartz writes, "Confessions are meant to reveal universal truths through specific examples. Through introspection and engagement with the priest, the penitent uses her experiences to transcend her own life. Confession is thus a private moral act with a public moral purpose. For in reflecting on private decisions, we better understand the problems and struggles of humanity—itself composed of billions of individuals struggling with their own decisions." Day's confessions were theological, too. Her attempts to understand herself and humanity were really efforts to understand God.

She certainly never achieved complete spiritual tranquillity and self-satisfaction. On the day she died, there was a card inserted into the final page of her journal, inscribed with a prayer of penance from Saint Ephraim the Syrian that begins, "O Lord and master of my life, take from me the spirit of sloth, faintheartedness, lust of power and idle talk. But give to thy servant rather the spirit of chastity, humility, patience and love."

But over the course of her life, she built a steady inner structure. Her work for others yielded a certain steadiness in herself, which was so absent in the early years. And at the end there was gratitude. For her tombstone inscription she simply chose the words DEO GRATIAS. Toward the close of her life she met with Robert Coles, a Harvard child psychiatrist, who had become a friend and confidant. "It will soon be over," she told him. And then she described a moment when she tried to make a literary summation of her life. She had been writing all those years and it would have been natural to write a memoir. She sat down one day to compose something like that. She told Coles what happened:

I try to think back; I try to remember this life that the Lord gave me; the other day I wrote down the words "a life remembered," and I was going to try to make a summary for myself, write what mattered most—but I couldn't do it. I just sat there and thought of our Lord, and His visit to us all those centuries ago, and I said to myself that my great luck was to have had Him on my mind for so long in my life!

Coles wrote, "I heard the catch in her voice as she spoke, and soon her eyes were a little moist, but she quickly started talking of her great love for Tolstoy, as if, thereby, she had changed the subject."[50] That moment represents a calm apotheosis, a moment when after all the work and all the sacrifice and all the efforts to write and change the world, the storm finally abates and a great calm comes over. Adam I lies down before Adam II. The loneliness ends. At the culmination of that lifetime of self-criticism and struggle there was thankfulness.

CHAPTER 5

SELF-MASTERY

GEORGE CATLETT MARSHALL WAS BORN IN 1880 AND GREW UP IN Uniontown, Pennsylvania. Uniontown was a small coal city, with a population of about thirty-five hundred, just then being transformed by industrialization. His father was a successful businessman—thirty-five years old when George was born—who had established himself as a figure of some consequence in town. He was proud of his old southern family. Supreme Court Justice John Marshall was a distant relative. His father was also somewhat stiff and reserved, especially at home, where he played the role of lord of the manor.

In midlife, though, Marshall's father sold his coal business and invested in a real estate scheme around the Luray Caverns in Virginia, which quickly went bankrupt. He lost all the wealth it had taken him twenty years to acquire. He retreated from the world, spending his time on family genealogy. The family began its descent. Later in life, George Marshall would remember trips to a hotel kitchen, where they would ask for leftover scraps to serve as dog food and the occasional stew. It was "painful and humiliating," he would later remember, "a black spot on my boyhood."[1]

Marshall was not a bright, sparkling boy. When he was nine, his father enrolled him in the local public school. His placement was determined by an interview with the school superintendent, Professor Lee Smith. The man asked him a series of simple questions to gauge Marshall's intelligence and preparation, but Marshall could not answer them. As his father looked on, he hemmed and hawed, stuttered and squirmed. Later, after he had led the U.S. Army through World War II, served as secretary of state, and won the Nobel Peace Prize, Marshall still remembered that excruciating episode, when he had so publicly failed his father. His father, Marshall recalled, "suffered very severely"[2] from the embarrassment.

Marshall lagged academically. He developed a terror of any sort of public presentation, an intense fear of being laughed at by other students, and a painful self-consciousness that inevitably fueled more failure and humiliation. "I did not like school," he would recall later in life. "The truth is I was not even a poor student. I was simply not a student, and my academic record was a sad affair."[3] He grew mischievous and troublesome. After his sister Marie called him the "dunce of the class," she found a frog in her bed that night. When visitors he did not approve of came to the house, he dropped water bombs off the roof onto unsuspecting heads. But he was also ingenious. He started a small business transporting groups of girls across a creek on a raft he built himself.[4]

After elementary school, he wanted to follow his older and favored brother Stuart to the Virginia Military Institute. He would later recall in an interview with his great biographer, Forrest Pogue, his brother's cruel response:

> When I was begging to go to VMI, I overheard Stuart talking to my mother; he was trying to persuade her not to let me go because he thought I would disgrace the family name. Well, that made more of an impression on me than all the instructors, parental pressure or anything else. I decided right then that I was going to wipe his eye. I did finally get ahead of what my brother had done. That was the first time I had ever done that, and it was where I really learned my lesson. The urgency to succeed came from hearing that conversation; it had a psychological effect on my career.[5]

This is a common trait among modest people who achieve extraordinary success. It's not that they were particularly brilliant or talented. The average collegiate GPA for a self-made millionaire is somewhere in the low B range. But at some crucial point in their lives, somebody told them they were too stupid to do something and they set out to prove the bastards wrong.

Marshall was not totally without family warmth and support. While his father was perpetually disappointed in his son, his mother rejoiced in him, offering unconditional love and support. She sold the last of her family's property so he could go away to college, including the lot in Uniontown upon which she had been hoping to build a house of her own.[6] Marshall also had learned from his humiliations in school and at home that his rise in the ranks of life would not come from his natural talent. It would come from grinding, the dogged plod, and self-discipline. When Marshall got to VMI (he seems to have been admitted without having to take the entrance exam), he found a way of living and a pattern of discipline exactly to his liking.

He arrived at VMI in 1897 and was instantly drawn to its southern traditions. VMI had a moral culture that brought together several ancient traditions: a chivalric devotion to service and courtesy, a stoic commitment to emotional self-control, and a classical devotion to honor. The school was haunted by the memories of southern chivalry: of the Civil War general Stonewall Jackson, a former professor there; of the 241 cadets, some as young as fifteen, who marched out on May 15, 1864, to turn back a Union force at the Battle of New Market; and by the ghost of the Confederate hero Robert E. Lee, who served as a beau ideal of what a man was supposed to be.

VMI taught Marshall a sense of reverence, the imaginative ability to hold up a hero in his mind to copy in all appropriate ways, to let him serve as a standard by which to judge himself. Not long ago, there was a great move to debunk heroes. Even today, the word "irreverent" is often used as a high compliment. But in the world of Marshall's youth, there was a greater intent to cultivate a capacity for veneration. The work of the Roman biographer Plutarch is based on the premise that the tales of the excellent can lift the ambitions of the living. Thomas Aquinas argued that in order to lead a good life, it is necessary to focus more on our exemplars than on ourselves, imitating their actions as much as possible. The philosopher Alfred North Whitehead argued, "Moral education is impossible without the habitual vision of greatness." In 1943, Richard Winn Livingstone wrote, "One is apt to think of moral failure as due to weakness of character: more often it is due to an inadequate ideal. We detect in others, and occasionally in ourselves, the want of courage, of industry, of persistence, which leads to defeat. But we do not notice the more subtle and disastrous weakness, that our standards are wrong, that we have never learned what is good."[7]

By cultivating the habit of reverence—for ancient heroes, for the elderly, for leaders in one's own life—teachers were not only offering knowledge of what greatness looks like, they were trying to nurture a talent for admiration. Proper behavior is not just knowing what is right; it is having the motivation to do what is right, an emotion that propels you to do good things.

School days were filled with tales—sometimes false or romanticized tales—of the great paragons of history, Pericles, Augustus, Judah Maccabee, George Washington, Joan of Arc, Dolley Madison. Character, James Davison Hunter has written, does not require religious faith. "But it does require a conviction of a truth made sacred, abiding as an authoritative presence within consciousness and life, reinforced by habits institutionalized within a moral community. Character, therefore, resists expedience; it defies hasty acquisition. This is undoubtedly why Søren Kierkegaard spoke of character as 'engraved,' deeply etched."[8]

VMI was an academically mediocre institution, and Marshall was not then a good student. But it held up heroes who were regarded as sacred. And the school certainly taught the habits of institutionalized self-discipline. Throughout his adult life, Marshall displayed a strong desire to be as close to flawless in all things as possible. Against the current advice, he absolutely did sweat the "small stuff."

VMI also taught renunciation, the ability to forgo small pleasures in order to enjoy great ones. VMI was a place where young men from mostly privileged backgrounds went to get toughened up, to renounce the luxuries they might have enjoyed at home and to acquire the hardness they would need to be worthy of the struggle of life. Marshall bought into the ascetic culture and its rigors. First-year students were compelled to sleep with their large dorm windows wide open, so that in winter they might awake covered in snow.

The week before he was due to arrive at the institute, Marshall was stricken with typhoid fever, and he was forced to show up a week after the other cadets. It was tough enough for the first-year students, and Marshall's sickly pallor and Northern accent drew unwanted attention from his seniors. He was called "Yankee rat" and "Pug" for his relatively snub-nosed appearance. "Rat" Marshall filled his days with undesirable chores, cleaning toilets a good deal. In his memory of the period, it did not occur to him to rebel or resent the treatment. "I think I was more philosophical about this sort of thing than a great many boys. It was part of the business, and the only thing to do was accept it as best you could."[9]

In one hazing ritual early in his rat tenure, Marshall was forced to squat naked over a bayonet that had been jammed into a hole in the floor. The ordeal was called "sitting on infinity," and it was a rite of passage. While a crowd of upperclassmen looked on, he strained to keep himself from collapsing onto the point. Finally he could take it no longer and fell. He did not fall straight down, but to one side, so he emerged with a deep but mendable wound to his right rear. Hazing that brutal was against regulations, even by the standards of the day, and the upperclassmen rushed him to the medical center, fearing what he might say. But Marshall did not report his tormentors, and he immediately won the regard of the corps for his staunch silence. One of his ex-classmates said, "By the time that episode was over nobody cared about his accent. He could have talked double Dutch and they'd have accepted it. He was in."[10]

Marshall still did not excel academically at VMI. But he excelled at drilling, neatness, organization, precision, self-control, and leadership. He mastered the aesthetic of discipline, having the correct posture, erect carriage, crisp salute, direct gaze, well-pressed clothing, and the way of carrying the body that is an outward manifestation of inner self-control. During one football game in his first or second year he badly tore a ligament in his right arm but refused to report the injury to a doctor. It would heal on its own (over the next two years)."[11] A day in the life of a VMI cadet is marked by the succession of saluting one does to one's superiors, and since Marshall could not lift his right arm above his elbow without pain, it must have been two years of discomfort.

This starchy formality is not in vogue today. We carry ourselves in ways that are more natural and relaxed. We worry about appearing artificial. But those in Marshall's military world were more likely to believe that great individuals are made, not born, and that they are made through training. Change happens from the outside in. It is through the exercise of drill that a person becomes self-regulating. It is through the expression of courtesy that a person becomes polite. It is through the resistance to fear that a person develops courage. It is through the control of facial expressions that one becomes sober. The act precedes the virtue.

The point of all this was to separate instant emotion from action, to reduce the power of temporary feelings. A person might feel fear, but he would not act on it. A person might desire sweets, but would be able to repress the urge to eat them. The stoic ideal holds that an emotion should be distrusted more often than trusted. Emotion robs you of agency, so distrust desire. Distrust anger, and even sadness and grief. Regard these things as one might regard fire: useful when tightly controlled, but a ravaging force when left unchecked.

People in this mold try to control emotion with the constant firebreaks of decorum. Hence all those strict Victorian manners. They policed emotional expression in order to reduce their vulnerability. Hence the elaborate formal way of addressing each other. People in this mold—and all his life, Marshall was one of them—were deliberately austere and undramatic. Marshall scorned the theatricality of a Napoleon or a Hitler or even the histrionic display of two generals who would work with him, Douglas MacArthur and George S. Patton.

"By means not always subtle," one of Marshall's biographers wrote, "the man whose mettle was fit for tempering grew from control to self-control, until in the end he imposed by his own desire those restraints upon himself which he could hardly brook when he first encountered them."[12]

Marshall was not funny or emotionally vibrant or self-reflective. He refused to keep a diary, because he thought the exercise might cause him to focus too much on himself and his own reputation, or on how others might view him in the future. Diary keeping, he told Robert E. Lee's biographer Douglas Southall Freeman in 1942, might unconsciously cause "self-deception or hesitation in reaching decisions" when, in war, he needed to focus objectively on "the business of victory."[13] Marshall never got around to writing his autobiography. *The Saturday Evening Post* once offered him more than $1 million to tell his story, but he turned it down. He did not want to embarrass himself or any of the other generals.[14]

The whole object of VMI training was to teach Marshall how to exercise controlled power. The idea was that power exaggerates the dispositions—making a rude person ruder and a controlling person more controlling. The higher you go in life, the fewer people there are to offer honest feedback or restrain your unpleasant traits. So it is best to learn those habits of self-restraint, including emotional self-restraint, at an early age. "What I learned at VMI was self-control, discipline, so that it was ground in," he would recall later.

In his last year at VMI, Marshall was named first captain, the Institute's highest rank. He completed his four years without a single demerit. He developed the austere commanding presence that would forever mark his personality. He excelled at anything to do with soldiering and was the unquestioned leader of his class.

A letter of recommendation from John Wise, the president of VMI, praised Marshall's accomplishment in the unique tone of the school: Marshall was "one of the fittest pieces of food for gunpowder turned out by this mill for many years."[15]

At an astonishingly early age, Marshall had constructed the sort of ordered mind that military men and women have generally admired. "That person then, whoever it may be," Cicero wrote in *Tusculan Disputations,* "whose mind is quiet through consistency and self-control, who finds contentment in himself, who neither breaks down in adversity nor crumbles in fright, nor burns with any thirsty need nor dissolves into wild and futile excitement, that person is the wise one we are seeking, and that person is happy."

The Service

THERE IS ALWAYS AN INTERESTING MOMENT IN THE LIVES OF SUCCESSFUL people when they first learn how to work. For Marshall, that moment came at VMI.

To get an appointment to the U.S. Army, he needed political support. He went to Washington and showed up at the White House without an appointment. He worked his way up to the second floor, where one of the ushers told him it was impossible for him just to burst in and see the president. But Marshall sneaked into the Oval Office with a larger group, and after they left, he stated his case to

President McKinley. Whether McKinley intervened is unclear, but in 1901, Marshall was permitted to take the army entrance exam, and in 1902 he received his commission.

Like Eisenhower, Marshall was a late bloomer. He worked professionally, he served other men, but he did not rise spectacularly. He was such a valuable aide, his superiors sometimes held him back from getting his own command. "Lt. Col. Marshall's special fitness is staff work," one general wrote. "I doubt that in this, whether it be teaching or practice, he has any equal in the army today."[16] He was such a genius at the dull, background work of military life, especially logistics, that he was not pushed forward to the fighting edge. By age thirty-nine, at the end of his service in World War I, he was still only a temporary lieutenant colonel, surpassed by younger men who had held combat commands. He suffered grievously with each disappointment.

But he was slowly acquiring skills. During postgraduate training at Fort Leavenworth, Marshall became an autodidact, compensating for his lamentable academic record. He was shuffled to the Philippines and across the American South and Midwest, serving as engineering officer, ordnance officer, post quartermaster, post commissary officer, and in other undistinguished staff positions. Each day passed to the rhythm of his daily chores and minor accomplishments. However, his attention to detail and endurance would serve him later on. As he later observed, "The truly great leader overcomes all difficulties, and campaigns and battles are nothing but a long series of difficulties to be overcome."[17]

He sublimated his ego: "The less you agree with the policies of your superiors, the more energy you must direct to their accomplishment." Biographers have scoured his life, and the most striking feature is what they don't find—any moment of clear moral failure. He made many poor decisions, but there is no clear moment when he committed adultery, betrayed his friends, told an egregious lie, or let himself and others down.

Though promotions did not come, Marshall began to develop a reputation as a legendary master of organization and administration. It was not exactly the glamor side of military life. In 1912, he organized maneuvers involving 17,000 officers and men in the United States. In 1914, during a training exercise in the Philippines, he effectively commanded an invading force of 4,800 men to tactically out-maneuver and defeat the defending force.

In World War I, Marshall served as an assistant to the chief of staff of the American Expeditionary Force (AEF) for the 1st Division in France. It was the first division ever fielded by the American Army in Europe, and, contrary to popular belief, Marshall saw more action and ducked more shot, shells, and gas attacks than many other Americans in the war. His assignment was to keep AEF headquarters informed about the frontline supplies, position, and morale of the men. Much of his time was spent on or near the front in France, jumping in and out of trenches, checking in with the soldiers, and taking note of what they most desperately needed.

The moment he returned safely to headquarters, he would report to the chief and begin mapping out logistics for the next massive movement of men to or from the line. In one operation, he organized the movement of 600,000 men and 900,000 tons of supplies and ammunition from one sector to another part of the front. It was the most complicated logistics problem of the war, and Marshall's performance became legendary, earning him the temporary nickname "Wizard."

During October 1917, Marshall's unit received a visit from General John "Blackjack" Pershing, the senior U.S. commander in the war. Pershing ripped into the unit for its poor training and performance, upbraiding Marshall's immediate commanding officer General William Sibert and Sibert's chief of staff, who had arrived only two days earlier. Marshall, then a captain, decided it was time for what he called a "sacrifice play." He stepped forward and attempted to explain the situation to the general. An already irate Pershing silenced Marshall and turned away. Marshall then did something that could have cost him his career. He placed his hand on Pershing's arm to prevent him from leaving. He vehemently countered the old man, overwhelming him with a torrent of facts about the failures of Pershing's own headquarters, about poor supplies, the misplacement of the troops, the lack of motor transport, and many other hurdles not to be overlooked.

There was a long silence and everyone stood amazed by Marshall's effrontery. Pershing looked at him narrowly and responded defensively, "Well, you have to appreciate the problems we have."

Marshall shot back, "Yes, General, but we have them every day and many a day, and we have to solve every one of them by night."

Pershing said nothing and stalked off angrily. Marshall's colleagues thanked him and told him his career was finished. Instead, Pershing remembered the younger man, hired him, and became his most important mentor.

Marshall was shocked by the letter he received summoning him to join the General Staff at its headquarters in Chaumont. He ached for a promotion that would position him to lead men into battle. However, he packed his bags immediately and said good-bye to the men he had known for more than a year. Tucked between war reports, Marshall wrote an uncharacteristically sentimental description of his departure:

> It was hard to preserve one's composure to these men with whom I had been so intimately associated for over a year in France. We had been prisoners and our trials and tribulations had seemed to bind us very close to one another. I can see them now—gathered in the broad doorway of the chateau. The friendly jests and affectionate farewells, as I got into the Cadillac, made a deep impression on my mind, and I drove off hardly daring to wonder when and where would be our next meeting.[18]

Six days later, the 1st Division joined the great counterattack that would lead to the retreat of the German army, and within seventy-two hours most of the men in that doorway, and every field officer, battalion commander, and the four lieutenants of the 1st Division, were casualties, either dead or wounded.

In 1918 in France, Marshall was close to being promoted to brigadier general. The war ended and it would take him eighteen long years to get his first star. He returned home, where he spent five years under Pershing in Washington doing paperwork. He served his superior officers but received few promotions for himself. Through it all, Marshall worked on his profession and served his institution, the U.S. Army.

Institutions

TODAY, IT IS UNUSUAL TO MEET SOMEONE WITH AN INSTITUTIONAL MIND-set. We live in an age of institutional anxiety, when people are prone to distrust large organizations. This is partly because we've seen the failure of these institutions and partly because in the era of the Big Me, we put the individual first. We tend to prize the freedom to navigate as we wish, to run our lives as we choose, and never to submerge our own individual identities in conformity to some bureaucracy or organization. We tend to assume that the purpose is to lead the richest and fullest individual life, jumping from one organization to the next as it suits our needs. Meaning is found in these acts of self-creation, in the things we make and contribute to, in our endless choices.

Nobody wants to be an Organization Man. We like start-ups, disruptors, and rebels. There's less prestige accorded to those who tend to the perpetual reform and repair of institutions. Young people are raised to think that big problems can be solved by a swarm of small, networked NGOs and social entrepreneurs. Big hierarchical organizations are dinosaurs.

This mentality has contributed to institutional decay. As the editor Tina Brown has put it, if everybody is told to think outside the box, you've got to expect that the boxes themselves will begin to deteriorate.

People who possess an institutional mindset, as Marshall did, have a very different mentality, which begins with a different historical consciousness. In this mindset, the primary reality is society, which is a collection of institutions that have existed over time and transcend generations. A person is not born into an open field and a blank social slate. A person is born into a collection of permanent institutions, including the army, the priesthood, the fields of science, or any of the professions, like being a farmer, a builder, a cop, or a professor.

Life is not like navigating through an open field. It is committing oneself to a few of the institutions that were embedded on the ground before you were born and will be here after you die. It is accepting the gifts of the dead, taking on the responsibility of preserving and improving an institution and then transmitting that institution, better, on to the next generation.

Each institution comes with certain rules, obligations, and standards of excellence. Journalism imposes habits that help reporters keep a mental distance from those they cover. Scientists have certain methods they use to advance and verify knowledge one step at a time. Teachers treat all their students equally and invest extra hours to their growth. In the process of subordinating ourselves to the institutions we inhabit, we become who we are. The customs of the institution structure the soul, making it easier to be good. They guide behavior gently along certain time-tested lines. By practicing the customs of an institution, we are not alone; we are admitted into a community that transcends time.

With this sense of scope, the institutionalist has deep reverence for those who came before and the rules he has temporarily taken delivery of. The rules of a profession or an institution are not like practical tips on how to best do something. They are deeply woven into the identities of the people who practice them. A teacher's relationship to the craft of teaching, an athlete's relationship to his or her sport, a doctor's commitment to the craft of medicine, is not an individual choice that can be easily renounced when the psychic losses exceed the psychic benefits. These are life-shaping and life-defining commitments. Like finding a vocation, they are commitments to something that transcends a single lifetime.

A person's social function defines who he or she is. The commitment between a person and an institution is more like a covenant. It is an inheritance to be passed on and a debt to be repaid.

The technical tasks of, say, being a carpenter are infused with a deep meaning that transcends the task at hand. There are long periods when you put more into your institutions than you get out of them, but service to the institution provides you with a series of fulfilling commitments and a secure place in the world. It provides you with a means to submerge your ego, to quiet its anxieties and its relentless demands.

Marshall conformed his life to the needs of his organization. Very few people in the course of the last century aroused as much reverence as Marshall did, even in his own lifetime, even among people who knew him well. There were also few people who felt entirely comfortable around him—Eisenhower included. The cost of his perfect self-denial and self-control was aloofness. While in uniform, he never let his hair down or allowed people into the intimacy of his own soul. He maintained his composure in all circumstances.

Love and Death

MARSHALL DID HAVE A PRIVATE LIFE. IT WAS STARKLY SEPARATED FROM HIS public role. Today we bring our work home, returning work emails on our phones. But for Marshall, these were two separate spheres, with different emotions and patterns of conduct. The home was a haven in a heartless world. Marshall's home life centered on his wife, Lily.

George Marshall wooed Elizabeth Carter Coles, known to her friends as Lily, while in his final year at VMI. They took long carriage rides, and at night he risked expulsion by sneaking off grounds to be with her. George was six years Lily's junior, and several other senior classmates and senior VMI graduates—including Marshall's older brother Stuart—had done their best to win her fancy. She was a striking, dark beauty and the reigning belle of Lexington. "I was much in love," he recalled, and it was for keeps.[19]

They married shortly after his graduation in 1902. He felt himself extraordinarily lucky to have won her, and he carried that gratitude with him forever after. His attitude toward Lily can be described as constant and extremely solicitous. Shortly after their marriage, he discovered that she suffered from a thyroid condition that gave her an extremely weak heart. She would have to be treated as a semi-invalid all her life. They could never risk having children. There would always be the possibility of sudden death by exertion. But Marshall's devotion and gratitude to his wife only deepened.

Marshall was pleased to put himself in her service, supplying her with little surprises, compliments, and comforts, always giving the greatest attention to the smallest details. She would never be allowed to rise to retrieve that needlepoint basket she had forgotten upstairs. Marshall was playing the role of the chivalric knight in service to his lady. Lily sometimes looked upon this with wry amusement. She was more rugged and capable than he thought, but it gave him such pleasure to look after her.

In 1927, when Lily was fifty-three, her heart condition worsened.

She was taken to Walter Reed Hospital, and on August 22 an operation was performed. Her recovery was slow but steady. Marshall was in his element, catering to her every need, and Lily seemed to be recovering. On September 15, she was told that she could return home the next day. She sat down to send her mother a note. She wrote the word "George," slumped over, and passed away. The doctors said it was her excitement over returning home that elevated her pulse irregularly.

Marshall was teaching classes at the War College in Washington at that moment. A guard interrupted his lecture and called him to the telephone. They went into a little office where Marshall took the call, listened for a few moments, and then put his head on his arms on the desk. The guard asked if there was any way he could be of assistance. Marshall replied with quiet formality. "No, Mr. Throckmorton, I just had word my wife, who was to join me here today, has just died."

The formality of that phrasing, the pause to remember the guard's name (Marshall was not good with names), perfectly captured his emotional self-control, his self-discipline at all times.

Marshall was stricken by his wife's death. He filled his home with photographs of her, so that she looked out at him from nearly every vantage point in every room. Lily had been not only his sweet wife but his most trusted confidante, and, it seemed, his only one. Only she had been privileged to see the burden he carried and help him bear it. Suddenly and brutally, he was alone and adrift.

General Pershing, who had lost a wife and three daughters, wrote a note of condolence. Marshall replied that he missed Lily desperately: "Twenty-six years of most intimate companionship, something I have never known since I was a mere boy, leave me lost in my best efforts to adjust myself to future prospects in life. If I had been given to club life or other intimacies with men outside of athletic diversion, or if there was a campaign on or other pressing duty that demanded concentrated effort, then I think I could do better. However, I will find a way."[20]

Lily's death changed Marshall. Once taciturn, he softened and became conversational, as if he could charm visitors into staying and filling the lonely hours. Over the years his letters became more thoughtful, more openly compassionate. Despite his commitment to the service, and several periods when work consumed him, Marshall had never been a workaholic. Careful not to strain his own health, he broke off work in late afternoon to garden, go horseback riding, or take a walk. Whenever possible, he encouraged, even ordered, his staff to do the same.

Privacy

MARSHALL WAS A PRIVATE MAN. THAT IS TO SAY, HE MADE A STRONGER DIS-tinction than many people today make between the private and public spheres, between those people he considered intimates and everybody else. He could be witty and tell long funny stories to people within the inner circle of his trust and affection, but his manner to the larger population was defined by courtliness and a certain reserved charm. Very rarely did he call anyone by their first name.

This code of privacy is different from the one that is common in the era of Facebook and Instagram. This privacy code, which he shared with Frances Perkins, is based on the notion that this zone of intimacy should be breached only gradually, after long reciprocity and trust. The contents of the private world should not instantly be shared online or in conversation; they should not be tweeted.

Marshall's polite social manner matched his polite inner makeup. The French philosopher André Comte-Sponville argues that politeness is the prerequisite for the great virtues: "Morality is like a politeness of the soul, an etiquette of inner life, a code of duties."[21] It is a series of practices that make you considerate of others.

Marshall was unfailingly considerate, but his formality made it hard for him to develop friendships. He strongly disapproved of gossip, he frowned at off-color stories, and he never enjoyed the garrulous relationships with men that Ike specialized in.

Marshall's early biographer, William Frye, wrote:

Marshall was one of those controlled and disciplined people who find both incentive and reward deep within themselves, who require neither urging nor applause from many men. Such people are terribly alone, without the release most find in the easy sharing of mind and heart with many people. For all their self-sufficiency, they are incomplete; and if they are fortunate, they find completion in one or two others. There are not more than two, usually—the heart opened to a lover, the mind to a friend.[22]

Reformer

MARSHALL FINALLY FOUND RESPITE FROM HIS GRIEF WITH AN ASSIGNMENT that consumed his energies. At the end of that year, he was asked to lead the Infantry School program at Fort Benning, Georgia. Marshall was conservative in manners, but he was not a traditionalist when it came to operations. All his life he pushed against what he regarded as the stifling traditionalism of the army way of doing things. In his four years there, he revolutionized officer training, and since many of the most important officers of World War II passed through Fort Benning during his time there, he revolutionized the U.S. Army, too.

The lesson plans he inherited were built on the ridiculous premise that in battle, officers would have complete information about their troops' positions and the enemy's. He sent them out on maneuvers without maps or with outdated ones, telling them that in a real war, the maps would be either absent or worse than useless. He told them the crucial issue is usually *when* a decision should be made as much as *what* the decision should be. He told them that mediocre solutions undertaken in time were better than perfect solutions undertaken too late. Until Marshall, professors wrote their lectures and simply read them out to the class. Marshall prohibited the practice. He cut the supply systems manual from 120 pages down to 12, to make training a citizen force easier and to allow greater discretion down the chain of command.

Even his success and reforms did not speed his promotions. The army had its own seniority system. But as the 1930s wore on and the Fascist threat became clearer, personal merit began to count for more. Eventually, Marshall received a series of large promotions, leapfrogging senior but less admired men, all the way to Washington and the centers of power.

The General

IN 1938, FRANKLIN ROOSEVELT HELD A CABINET MEETING TO DISCUSS STRATegy for an arms buildup. FDR argued that the next war would be largely determined by air and sea power, not ground troops. He went around the room, looking for agreement, and was met with general assent. Finally he turned to Marshall, the new deputy chief of staff, and asked, "Don't you think so, George?"

"I am sorry, Mr. President, but I don't at all." Marshall made the case for land forces. FDR looked startled and called the meeting to a close. It was the last time the president would presume to call Marshall by his first name.

In 1939, FDR had to replace the outgoing chief of staff, the top position in the U.S. military. Marshall at that time ranked thirty-fourth in seniority, but the contest came down to him and Hugh Drum. Drum was a talented general, but also a bit pompous, and he organized a lavish campaign for the job, lining up of letters of endorsement and organizing a series of positive articles in the press. Marshall refused to campaign and squashed efforts by others to campaign on his behalf. But he did have key friends in the White House, the most important of whom was Harry Hopkins, an FDR intimate who was an architect of the New Deal. FDR went with Marshall, though there was little personal warmth between them.

War is a series of blunders and frustrations. At the outset of the Second World War, Marshall understood he would have to ruthlessly cull the incompetent from their jobs. By this time he was married to his second wife, Katherine Tupper Brown, a glamorous former actress with a strong personality and an elegant manner who would become Marshall's constant companion. "I cannot afford the luxury of sentiment," he told her. "Mine must be cold logic. Sentiment is for others. I cannot allow myself to get angry, that would be fatal—it is too exhausting. My brain must be kept clear. I cannot afford to appear tired."[23]

The culling process was brutal. Marshall ended the careers of hundreds of colleagues. "He was once our dear friend, but he ruined my husband," a senior officer's wife observed after her husband had been shoved aside.[24] One evening he told Katherine, "I get so tired of saying

'No,' it takes it out of me." Organizing his department while war loomed, Marshall observed, "It is not easy to tell men where they have failed. . . . My days seem to be filled with situations and problems where I must do the difficult, the hard thing."[25]

A vintage Marshall performance was given at a meeting with the press in London in 1944. He entered the room without any papers and began by instructing each reporter to ask a question while he listened. After thirty-plus questions, Marshall explained in detail the situation of the war, addressing the larger visions, strategic goals, and technical details, shifting his eyes deliberately to a different face every few sentences. Then he finished, forty minutes later, and thanked the reporters for their time.

World War II had its share of cinematic generals, like MacArthur and Patton, but most, like Marshall and Eisenhower, were anticinematic. They were precise organizers, not flamboyant showmen. Marshall detested generals who screamed and pounded tables. He favored the simple, spare uniform rather than the more decorated uniform favored by generals today, with their placards of ribbons forming a billboard across their chests.

During this time Marshall developed an astounding reputation. The general view was summarized by the CBS war correspondent Eric Sevareid: "a hulking, homely man of towering intellect, the memory of an unnatural genius, and the integrity of a Christian saint. The atmosphere of controlled power he exuded made one feel oneself a physical weakling, and his selfless devotion to duty [was] beyond all influences of public pressure or personal friendship."[26] Speaker of the House Sam Rayburn said no other American had equal influence with Congress: "We are in the presence of a man who is telling the truth as he sees it." As Truman's secretary of state Dean Acheson put it, "the thing that stands out in everybody's recollection of General Marshall is the immensity of his integrity."

That integrity did not win him immediate favor with everybody. He held a soldier's contempt for politics and remembered his particular disgust when he once met with President Roosevelt to tell him that the plans for the North African invasion were ready. The president clapped his hands together in mock prayer and said, "Please make it before election day."[27] Marshall's deputy chief of staff, Tom Handy, later explained in an interview:

It's no use saying General Marshall was an easy man, because he wasn't. He could be extremely rigid. But he had a terrific influence and power, especially over the British and Congress. I think FDR envied him this. I think that the basis was that they knew, in Marshall's case, there was no underhanded or selfish motive. The British knew that he was not out to make American points or British points, but trying to win the war the best way. The Congress knew he was talking to them straight, with no politics involved.[28]

The quintessential Marshall moment came in the middle of the war. The Allies were planning Operation Overlord, the invasion of France, but still no overall commander had been selected. Marshall secretly craved the assignment and was widely accepted as the most qualified for it. This would be among the most ambitious military operations ever attempted, and whoever commanded it would be performing a great service to the cause and would go down in history as a result of it. The other Allied leaders, Churchill and Stalin, told Marshall that he would get the job. Eisenhower assumed Marshall would get the job. Roosevelt knew that if Marshall asked for the job, he would have to give it to him. He had earned it, and his stature was so high.

But Roosevelt relied on Marshall to be nearby in Washington, whereas the Overlord commander would go to London. FDR may also have had doubts about Marshall's austere personality. Commanding Overlord would mean managing political alliances, and a warm touch might come in handy. The controversy flared. Several senators argued that Marshall was needed in Washington and should not get the job. From his hospital bed, General Pershing pleaded with FDR to give Marshall a command in the field.

Still, everyone presumed that Marshall would command. In November 1943, Roosevelt visited Eisenhower in North Africa and nearly said as much: "You and I know who the Chief of Staff was during the last years of the Civil War, but practically no one else knows. . . . I hate to think that fifty years from now practically nobody will know who George Marshall was. That is one of the reasons why I want George to have the big command—he is entitled to establish his place in history as a great general."

Still Roosevelt had doubts. "It is dangerous to monkey with a winning team,"[29] he said. He sent Harry Hopkins to gauge Marshall's feelings about the appointment. Marshall would not be drawn in. He told Hopkins that he had served with honor. He would not ask for anything. He would "go along good-heartedly with whatever decision the president made."[30] In an interview with Forrest Pogue decades later, Marshall explained his behavior: "I was determined that I should not embarrass the President one way or the other—that he must be able to deal in this matter with a perfectly free hand in whatever he felt was the best interest [of the country]. . . . I was utterly sincere in the desire to avoid what had happened so much in other wars—the consideration of the feelings of the individual rather than the good of the country."[31]

FDR called Marshall into his office on December 6, 1943. Roosevelt beat around the bush for several awkward minutes, raising subjects of minor importance. Then he asked Marshall if he wanted the job. If Marshall had simply uttered the word "Yes," he presumably would have gotten the job. Still, Marshall refused to be drawn in. Marshall told Roosevelt to do what he thought best. Marshall insisted that his own private feelings should have no bearing on the decision. Again and again, he refused to express his preference one way or the other.

FDR looked at him. "Well, I didn't feel I could sleep at ease if you were out of Washington." There was a long silence. Roosevelt added, "Then it will be Eisenhower."[32]

Inwardly, Marshall must have been crushed. Somewhat gracelessly, Roosevelt asked him to transmit the decision to the Allies. As chief of staff, Marshall was compelled to write the order himself: "The immediate appointment of General Eisenhower to command of 'Overlord' operation has been decided on." He generously saved the slip of paper and sent it to Ike: "Dear Eisenhower. I thought you might like to have this as a memento. It was written very hurriedly by me as the final meeting broke up yesterday, the President signing it immediately. G.C.M."[33]

It was the greatest professional disappointment of Marshall's life, and it came about because he refused to express his own desires. But that, of course, was the code he lived by.

When the war in Europe was over, it was Eisenhower, not Marshall, who returned to Washington as the triumphant conqueror. Still, Marshall was overcome with pride. John Eisenhower remembered the scene of his father's return to Washington: "It was on that day that I saw General Marshall completely unbend. Standing behind Ike and eschewing the glare of the photographers, he beamed on Ike and Mamie with a kindly, fatherly expression. There was nothing of the normally aloof George Marshall in his demeanor that day. Then he faded into the background and let Ike take the stage for the rest of the day—a motorcade down the streets of Washington, a visit to the Pentagon."[34]

In a personal letter, Churchill wrote to Marshall, "It has not fallen to your lot to command the great armies. You have had to create them, organize them, and inspire them."[35] Outshone by the men he had promoted, Marshall had become known simply as the "organizer of victory."

Final Tasks

MARSHALL SPENT HIS POSTWAR LIFE TRYING TO RETIRE. ON NOVEMBER 26, 1945, there was a simple ceremony at the Pentagon and Marshall was released from duty as the army chief of staff. He drove to Dodona Manor, the home he and Katherine had bought in Leesburg, Virginia. They walked through the sunny yard, looking forward to years of leisure and retirement. Katherine went upstairs to rest before dinner and heard the phone ring as she climbed. An hour later, she came downstairs to find Marshall stretched out ashen-faced on a chaise longue listening to the radio. The news broadcast announced that the U.S. ambassador to China had just resigned and that George Marshall had accepted the president's request to take his place. The phone call had been President Truman asking Marshall to leave immediately. "Oh, George," she said, "how *could* you?"[36]

The job was thankless, but he and Katherine remained in China for fourteen months, trying to negotiate away an inevitable civil war between the Chinese Nationalists and Communists. On the return flight home from his first major failed mission, Marshall, now sixty-seven, was asked again by the president for another favor—to serve as secretary of state. Marshall accepted and hung up.[37] In his new position, he enacted the Marshall Plan—although he never called it anything but its official name, the European Recovery Plan—and President Roosevelt's wish that Marshall be long remembered by history came true.

There were other duties that followed: president of the American Red Cross, secretary of defense, chair of the U.S. delegation to the coronation of Elizabeth II. There were highs—winning the Nobel Prize—and lows—becoming the object of a hate campaign by Joe McCarthy and his allies. As each job was offered, Marshall felt the tug of obligation. He made some good decisions and some bad ones—he opposed the formation of the State of Israel. He was continually accepting assignments he did not want.

Some people seem to have been born into this world with a sense of indebtedness for the blessing of being alive. They are aware of the transmission of generations, what has been left to them by those who came before, their indebtedness to their ancestors, their obligations to a set of moral responsibilities that stretch across time.

One of the purest expressions of this attitude is a letter sent home by a Civil War soldier named Sullivan Ballou to his wife on the eve of the first battle of Bull Run, early in the war. Ballou, an orphan, knew the pain of growing up without a father. Nonetheless, he wrote to his wife, he was willing to die to pay the debt he owed to his ancestors:

> If it is necessary that I should fall on the battlefield for my country, I am ready. . . . I know how strongly American Civilization now leans upon the triumph of the government, and how great a debt we owe to those who went before us through the blood and suffering of the Revolution. And I am willing—perfectly willing—to lay down all my joys in this life, to help maintain this Government, to help pay that debt.
>
> But, my dear wife, when I know that with my own joys I lay down nearly all of yours, and replace them in this life with cares and sorrows—when, after having eaten for long years the bitter fruit of the orphanage myself, I must offer it as their only sustenance to my dear little children—is it weak or dishonorable, while the banner of my purpose floats calmly and proudly in the breeze, that my unbounded love for you, my darling wife and children, should struggle in fierce, though useless, contest with my love of country? . . .

Sarah, my love for you is deathless, it seems to bind me to you with mighty cables that nothing but Omnipotence could break; and yet my love of Country comes over me like a strong wind and bears me irresistibly on with all these chains to the battlefield. . . . I have, I know, but few and small claims upon Divine Providence, but something whispers to me—perhaps it is the wafted prayer of my little Edgar—that I shall return to my loved ones unharmed. If I do not, my dear Sarah, never forget how much I love you, and when my last breath escapes me on the battlefield it will whisper your name.

Of course, Ballou did fight the next day at Bull Run, and he did die. Like Marshall, he did have the sense that he couldn't find fulfill-ment outside of his obligations to community and country.

We live in a society that places great emphasis on personal happi-ness, defined as not being frustrated in the realization of your wants. But old moral traditions do not die. They waft down the centuries and reinspire new people in new conditions. Marshall lived in the world of airplanes and the nuclear bomb, but in many ways he was formed by the moral traditions of classical Greece and Rome. His moral make-up owed something to Homer, to the classical emphasis on courage and honor. It owed something to the Stoics, with their emphasis on moral discipline. But particularly later in life it also owed something to the ancient Athenian Pericles, who embodied the style of leadership that we call magnanimity, or great-souled.

The magnanimous leader of Greece's golden age had a high but ac-curate view of his own virtue. He put himself in a different category from most people around him, understanding that he had been blessed by unusual good fortune. This understanding strained his relations with those around him. He could seem solitary and detached, reserved and dignified, except with a few close friends. He navigated the world with a qualified friendliness, genial to people but never quite exposing his inner feelings, thoughts, and fears.[38] He hid his vulnerabilities and detested the thought that he might be dependent on others. As Rob-ert Faulkner writes in *The Case for Greatness,* he is not a joiner, a team player, or a staffer: "He does not put his shoulder to any ordinary wheel, especially if he must take a secondary role. Neither is he eager for reciprocity."[39] He is fond of granting favors but ashamed to receive them. He was, as Aristotle put it, "Not capable of leading his life to suit anyone else."[40]

The magnanimous leader does not have a normal set of social relations. There is a residual sadness to him, as there is in many grandly ambitious people who surrender companionship for the sake of their lofty goals. He can never allow himself to be silly or simply happy and free. He is like marble.

The magnanimous leader is called upon by his very nature to perform some great benefit to his people. He holds himself to a higher standard and makes himself into a public institution. Magnanimity can only really be expressed in public or political life. Politics and war are the only theaters big enough, competitive enough, and consequential enough to call forth the highest sacrifices and to elicit the highest talents. The man who shelters himself solely in the realms of commerce and private life is, by this definition, less consequential than one who enters the public arena.

By the time of Pericles, the great-souled leader was supposed to carry himself with steadiness and sobriety. He was supposed to be more judicious and self-disciplined than the hot-tempered Homeric heroes. Most of all, he was supposed to provide some public benefit on a grand scale. He was supposed to save his people in a time of peril or transform them to fit the needs of a new age.

The great-souled man may not be a good man—he may not always be kind, compassionate, considerate, and pleasant—but he is a great man. He wins great honors because he is worthy of them. He achieves a different style of happiness, defined by the popularizer of Greek thought, Edith Hamilton, as "the exercise of vital powers along lines of excellence in a life affording them scope."

Death

IN 1958, MARSHALL CHECKED IN TO WALTER REED HOSPITAL FOR THE removal of a cyst on his face. His goddaughter, Rose Wilson, came to visit, stunned at how old he suddenly looked.

"I have so much time to remember now," he told her, recalling a time when as a boy he went tobogganing with his father in Uniontown. "Colonel Marshall," she replied, "I'm sorry your father didn't live long enough to know what a great son he had. He would have been very proud of you."

"Do you think so?" Marshall answered. "I'd like to believe he would have approved of me."

Marshall continued to weaken. Every corner of the earth seemed to respond to the general's illness. Messages arrived from Winston Churchill and General Charles de Gaulle, Mao Tse-tung and Chiang Kai-shek, Joseph Stalin and General Dwight Eisenhower, Marshal Tito and Field Marshal Bernard Montgomery.[41] Thousands of letters from ordinary people poured in. President Eisenhower came to visit three times. Truman visited. Winston Churchill, then eighty-four, also visited. Marshall was in a coma by then, and Churchill could do no more than stand in the doorway weeping as he looked at the small body of the man he had once known.

He died on October 16, 1959, just shy of his eightieth birthday. General Tom Handy, his old deputy chief of staff, had once asked him about the arrangements for his funeral but Marshall cut him off. "You don't have to worry about it. I've left all the necessary instructions."[42] These instructions were opened after his death. They were remarkable: "Bury me simply, like any ordinary officer of the U.S. Army who has served his country honorably. No fuss. No elaborate ceremonials. Keep the service short, confine the guest-list to the family. And above everything, do it quietly."[43]

At his express order, there was no state funeral. There was no lying in state in the Capitol rotunda. His body lay in state at the Bethlehem Chapel of the National Cathedral for twenty-four hours so friends could pay their respects. In attendance at the funeral were family, a few colleagues, and his old wartime barber, Nicholas J. Totalo, who had cut the general's hair in Cairo, Teheran, Potsdam, and later at the Pentagon.[44] Then there was a short, plain service at Fort Myer in Arlington, Virginia, using the standard Order for the Burial of the Dead from the Book of Common Prayer, with no eulogy.

CHAPTER 6

DIGNITY

THE MOST PROMINENT CIVIL RIGHTS LEADER IN AMERICA AT THE TIME *Command Performance* aired was A. Philip Randolph. He was the African American leader who organized and called for marches, who met with the president, and whose fame and moral authority helped shape the movement.

Randolph was born in 1899, near Jacksonville, Florida. His father was a minister in an African Methodist Episcopal church, but the church paid so little that he made most of his income as a tailor and butcher, while his wife worked as a seamstress.

Randolph, who was not a religious person, recalled, "My father preached a racial religion. He spoke to the social condition of his flock, and always reminded them that the AME church was the first black militant institution in America."[1] The elder Randolph also took his two boys to political meetings run by blacks. He introduced them to successful black men. And he told and retold the stories of black exemplars throughout history: Crispus Attucks, Nat Turner, Frederick Douglass.

The family lived lives of highly respectable poverty. The home was kept impeccably neat. They followed a code of old-fashioned propriety, discipline, and etiquette. Randolph's parents practiced perfect elocution and taught their son to pronounce every syllable of each word so that throughout his life, words like "responsibility" came out as a long, stately procession: "re-spons-a-bil-i-tay."

Confronted by humiliating racism, they hewed to a code of moral refinement and gentlemanly conduct that jarred with their material circumstances. The elder Randolph, the biographer Jervis Anderson wrote, "was, very simply, a self-made gentleman, one who was guided by the values of civility, humility, and decency, inspired by religious and social service, and utterly devoted to the idea of dignity."[2]

At school, Randolph was taught by two white New England schoolmarms who had come south to educate black underprivileged children, and whom Randolph would later call "two of the finest teachers who ever lived." Miss Lillie Whitney taught Randolph Latin and math, while Miss Mary Neff taught him literature and drama. Tall and athletic, Randolph excelled at baseball, but he developed a love of Shakespeare and drama that would last. In the final decades of his wife's life, when she was confined to a wheelchair, Randolph would read Shakespeare to her each day.

Most people are the product of their circumstances, but Randolph's parents, his teachers, and he himself created a moral ecology that transcended circumstances, a way of behaving that was always slightly more elevated, slightly more formal, and much more dignified than that of the world around him. Throughout his life, Randolph's carriage was always proper and upright. C. L. Dellums, a colleague and labor leader, remembered, "Randolph learned to sit erect and walk erect. You almost never saw him leaning back, reclining. No matter how enjoyable the occasion, you look around and there's Randolph just as straight as if there was a board in his back."[3]

His voice was soft, deep, and serene. He had an accent that people described as a cross between upper-class Boston and West Indian. He spoke in biblical cadences and used archaic words like "verily" and "vouchsafe."[4]

He fought any tendency toward looseness or moral laziness with constant acts of self-mastery, whether small acts of personal conduct or large acts of renunciation. His staff marveled at the way women threw themselves at him during his travels and the gentle way he turned them aside. "I don't think a man ever lived who women begged and chased more than that man," Dellums would recall to a biographer, "They tried everything but rape. Webster and I had a joke between us that we followed the chief around to handle the overflow. And they were the most beautiful women. . . . It was always depressing having to get out of there. I've seen women try everything, plead with him to come up to their hotel room, for a nightcap or something. He would just say, 'Sorry, I'm tired. I had a hard day. We better call it a night.' Sometimes I'd say to him, 'Chief? You kidding me?' "[5]

He did not believe in self-exposure. Outside of his writing, which could be tough and polemical, he did not often criticize others. His formality often kept people from feeling that they really knew him; even Bayard Rustin, one of his closest colleagues, always called him "Mr. Randolph." He was not interested in money and suspected that personal luxury was morally corrupting. Even when he was an old man and globally famous, he rode the bus home from work every day. One day he was mugged in the hallway of his building. The muggers found $1.25 on him, but no watch or jewelry of any kind. When some donors tried to raise money for him, to enhance his lifestyle, he shut them down, saying, "I am sure you know that I have no money and, at the same time, don't expect to get any. However, I would not think of having a movement started to raise money for me and my family. It is the lot of some people to be poor and it is my lot, which I do not have any remorse about."[6]

These qualities—his incorruptibility, his reticent formality, and above all his dignity—meant it was impossible to humiliate him. His reactions and internal state were determined by himself, not by the racism or even by the adulation that later surrounded him. Randolph's significance was in establishing a certain model for how to be a civil rights leader. He exuded self-mastery and, like George C. Marshall, left a string of awed admirers in his wake. "It is hard to make anyone who has never met him believe that A. Philip Randolph must be the greatest man who has lived in the U.S. this century," the columnist Murray Kempton wrote. "But it is harder yet to make anyone who has ever known him believe anything else."

Public-Spiritedness

THE CHIEF CHALLENGES OF RANDOLPH'S LIFE WERE: HOW DO YOU TAKE IM-perfect people and organize them into a force for change? How do you amass power while not being corrupted by power? Even in the midst of one of the noblest enterprises of the century, the civil rights movement, leaders like Randolph were filled with self-suspicion, feeling they had to be on the lookout for their own laxity, their own sinfulness, feeling that even in the midst of fighting injustice it is still possible to do horrible wrong.

There's a reason the civil rights leaders were transfixed by the book of Exodus. The Israelites in that book were a divided, shortsighted, and petulant people. They were led by a man, Moses, who was meek, passive, and intemperate and who felt himself inadequate to the task. The leaders of the movement had to tackle the insoluble dilemmas of Mosaic leadership: how to reconcile passion with patience, authority with power sharing, clarity of purpose with self-doubt.[7]

The solution was a certain sort of public-spiritedness. Today, when we use the phrase "public-spirited," we tend to mean someone who gathers petitions, marches and protests, and makes his voice heard for the public good. But in earlier eras it meant someone who curbed his own passions and moderated his opinions in order to achieve a larger consensus and bring together diverse people. We think of public-spiritedness as self-assertion, but historically it has been a form of self-government and self-control. The reticent and sometimes chilly George Washington exemplified this version of public-spiritedness.[8] Randolph exemplified it, too. He combined political radicalism with personal traditionalism.

Sometimes his advisers would get fed up with his unfailing politeness. "Every now and then," Bayard Rustin told Murray Kempton, "I think he permits good manners to get in the way. . . . Once I complained about that and he answered, 'Bayard, we must with good manners accept everyone. Now is the time for us to learn good manners. We will need them when this is over, because we must show good manners after we have won.'"[9]

The Genteel Radical

RANDOLPH BEGAN HIS CAREER BY MOVING FROM FLORIDA TO HARLEM, ARriving in April, 1911, a month after the Triangle factory fire. He became active in theater groups, and with his elocution and presence seemed on the verge of becoming a Shakespearean actor until his parents squelched the idea. He briefly attended City College, where he

read Karl Marx voraciously. He helped start a series of racial magazines, bringing Marxism to the black community. In one editorial he
called the Russian Revolution "the greatest achievement of the twentieth century." He opposed U.S. entry into World War I, believing
the war only served the interests of munitions makers and other in-
dustrialists. He crusaded against Marcus Garvey's Back-to-Africa
movement. In the middle of that fight some anonymous enemy sent
Randolph a box containing a threatening note and a severed human
hand.

At the same time he was getting arrested for violating antisedition
legislation, his personal life became even more bourgeois and upstand-
ing. Randolph married a genteel woman from a prominent Harlem
family. On Sunday afternoons they enjoyed taking part in the weekly
promenades. People got dressed up in their finest clothes—gaiters,
canes, boutonnieres, spats, and fancy hats—and strolled down Lenox
Avenue or 135th Street, exchanging greetings and pleasantries with
neighbors along the way.

By the early 1920s, Randolph had begun to move into labor organizing. He helped start a half dozen small trade unions, organizing
waiters, waitresses, and other disaffected groups. In June 1925, Randolph was approached by a few Pullman car porters who were looking for a charismatic, educated leader who could build a union for
them. The Pullman Company provided luxury railway sleeping cars
that were leased to railroads. The patrons were served by squads of
liveried black men who shined shoes, changed linens, and brought
food. After the Civil War, the founder, George Pullman, had hired
ex-slaves to do this work, believing they would be a docile labor force.
The porters had tried to unionize as early as 1909, but had always been
beaten back by the company.

Randolph accepted the challenge and spent the next twelve years
trying to create a porters' union and win concessions from the company. He traveled around the country trying to persuade porters to
join the union, at a time when the slightest whiff of union activity
could cost them their job or get them beaten. Randolph's primary
tool was his manner. As one union member would recall, "He gripped
you. You would have to be without feeling to pull yourself away from
him. You felt by him the way the disciples felt by the Master. You may
not know it right then, but when you got home to yourself, and got

to thinking what he had said, you would just have to be a follower of him, that's all."[10]

The work was slow, but over the next four years the union grew to nearly seven thousand members. Randolph learned that the rank and file didn't like it when he criticized the company, to which they still felt loyal. They did not share his more general critique of capitalism, so he changed tactics. He made it a fight for dignity. Randolph also decided he would reject all donations from sympathetic whites. This would be a victory blacks would organize and win on their own.

Then the Depression hit, and the company struck back, firing or threatening any employee who voted to strike. By 1932, union membership was down to 771. Offices had closed in nine cities. Randolph and the headquarters staff were evicted for failure to pay rent. Randolph's salary, which had been ten dollars a week, fell to nothing. Always a polished, sharp-dressed man, his clothes became tattered and worn. Union activists were beaten in cities from Kansas City to Jacksonville. In 1930 an Oakland loyalist named Dad Moore wrote a determined letter a month before his death:

> My back is against the wal but I will Die before I will Back up one inch. I am fiting not for myself but for 12,000 porters and maids, and there children. . . . I has bin at Starvasion Door but it had not change my mind, for just as the night folows the Day we are gointer win. Tell all the men in your Dist that they should folow Mr. Randolph as they would follow Jes Christ.[11]

Nonviolent Resistance

THE BLACK PRESS AND THE BLACK CHURCHES TURNED AGAINST THE UNION for being overly aggressive. In New York, Mayor Fiorello La Guardia offered Randolph a city job paying $7,000 a year, but Randolph turned it down.

The tide turned in 1933 with the election of Franklin Roosevelt and a change in the labor laws. Still, company executives had trouble wrapping their minds around the fact that to settle the labor dispute they would have to sit down as equals with the black porters and their representatives. It wasn't until July 1935 that the company and union leadership met in a room in Chicago to begin negotiations. An agreement was finally reached two years later. The company agreed to a reduction in the work month from 400 to 240 hours and agreed to increase the company's total pay package by $1,250,000 a year. Thus ended one of the longest and most bitter labor fights of the twentieth century.

By this time Randolph was the most famous African American organizer in the country. Having broken decisively with the Marxism of his youth, he spent the next years in a series of brutal fights to purge Soviet-dominated organizations from the labor movement. Then, in the early 1940s, with the country mobilizing for war, a new injustice pressed down on the black community. The factories were hauling in workers in droves to build planes, tanks, and ships, but they were not hiring blacks.

On January 15, 1941, Randolph issued a statement calling for a giant march on Washington if this discrimination was allowed to continue. "We loyal Negro American citizens demand the right to work and fight for our country," he declared. He formed the March on Washington Committee and realistically expected they could bring ten thousand or perhaps twenty or thirty thousand blacks together for a protest march on the Mall.

The prospect of the march alarmed the nation's leadership. Roosevelt asked Randolph to come see him for a meeting at the White House.

"Hello, Phil," the president said when they were together. "Which class were you in at Harvard?"

"I never went to Harvard, Mr. President," Randolph responded.

"I was sure you did. Anyway, you and I share a kinship in our great interest in human and social justice."

"That's right, Mr. President."

Roosevelt launched into a series of jokes and political anecdotes, but Randolph eventually cut him off.

"Mr. President, time is running on. You are quite busy, I know. But what we want to talk with you about is the problem of jobs for Negroes in defense industries."

Roosevelt offered to call some company heads and urge them to hire blacks.

"We want you to do more than that," Randolph replied. "We want something concrete. . . . We want you to issue an executive order making it mandatory that Negroes be permitted to work in these plants."

"Well, Phil, you know I can't do that. If I issue an executive order for you, then there'll be no end of other groups coming here and asking me to issue executive orders for them, too. In any event I couldn't do anything unless you called off this march of yours. Questions like this can't be settled with a sledgehammer."

"I'm sorry, Mr. President, the march cannot be called off." Randolph, bluffing a bit, vowed to bring a hundred thousand marchers.

"You can't bring a hundred thousand Negroes to Washington," Roosevelt protested, "somebody might get killed."

Randolph insisted. The impasse lasted until Mayor La Guardia, who was at the meeting, jumped in. "It is clear Mr. Randolph is not going to call off the march, and I suggest we all begin to seek a formula."[12] Six days before the march was due to take place, Roosevelt signed Executive Order 8802, banning discrimination in the defense industries. Randolph called off the march, amid much opposition from civil rights leaders who wanted to use it to push other causes such as discrimination in the armed forces themselves.

After the war, Randolph pushed more broadly for worker rights and desegregation. His great power, as always, derived from his obvious moral integrity, his charisma, his example as an incorruptible man in service to a cause. He was, however, not a meticulous administrator. He had trouble concentrating his energies on a single cause. The unabashed admiration he inspired in the people around him could threaten organizational effectiveness. "There is, especially in the National Office, an unhealthy degree of leader-worship of Mr. Randolph," one outside analyst of the 1941 March on Washington organization observed, "which paralyzes action and prevents an intelligent working out of policy."[13]

But Randolph had one more important contribution to make to the civil rights movement. In the 1940s and 1950s he was among those who championed nonviolent resistance as a tactic to advance the civil rights cause. Influenced by Mahatma Gandhi and some of the early labor movement tactics, he helped form the League of Non-Violent Civil Disobedience Against Military Segregation in 1948.[14] Against most of the established civil rights groups, which advocated education and reconciliation over confrontation and contention, Randolph argued for restaurant sit-ins and "prayer protests." As he told the Senate Armed Services Committee in 1948, "Ours would be [a movement] of non-resistance. . . . We would be willing to absorb the violence, absorb the terrorism, to face the music and to take whatever comes."

This tactic of nonviolence relied on intense self-discipline and renunciation of the sort Randolph had practiced his entire life. One of the aides who influenced Randolph and was influenced by him was Bayard Rustin. A few decades younger, Rustin shared many qualities with his mentor.

Rustin

BAYARD RUSTIN GREW UP IN WEST CHESTER, PENNSYLVANIA, AND WAS raised by his grandparents. He was well into boyhood before he learned that the person he thought was his older sister was actually his mother. His father, who suffered from alcoholism, lived in the town but had no role in Rustin's life.

Rustin remembered his grandfather as having "the most erect carriage of any person you have ever seen. None of us can remember a single unkindness in him." His grandmother had been raised a Quaker and was one of the first black women in the county to receive a high school education. She impressed upon Bayard the need for calm, dignity, and relentless self-control. "One just doesn't lose one's temper" was one of her favorite maxims. His mother also ran a summer Bible camp, with emphasis on the book of Exodus, which Bayard attended every day. "My grandmother," he recalled, "was thoroughly convinced that when it came to matters of the liberation of black people, we had much more to learn from the Jewish experience than we had to learn out of Matthew, Mark, Luke and John."[15]

In high school Rustin was a good athlete and wrote poetry. Like Randolph, he spoke in a proper, almost British accent, which could appear haughty to those who first met him. His classmates teased him for his excessive dignity. One high school classmate recalled, "He spoke biblical poetry. And Browning. He would tackle you and then get up and recite a poem."[16] As a freshman he became the first black student in forty years to win his high school's oratory prize. By senior year he made the all-county football team, and he was a class valedictorian. He developed a passion for opera, Mozart, Bach, and Palestrina, and George Santayana's novel *The Last Puritan* was one of his favorite books. On his own he also read Will and Ariel Durant's *The Story of Civilization,* which, he testified, was like "taking a whiff of something that simply opens your nostrils except that it happened in my brain."[17]

Rustin went off to college at Wilberforce University in Ohio and then Cheney State in Pennsylvania. While in college he realized he was gay. The realization did not induce too much emotional turmoil—he had been raised in a tolerant family and was to live more or less openly as a homosexual for his entire life—but it did cause him to move to New York, where there was at least an underground gay culture and a bit more acceptance.

Once in Harlem, he went in multiple directions at once, joining leftist organizations and also volunteering to help organize Randolph's March on Washington effort. He joined a Christian pacifist organization, the Fellowship of Reconciliation (FOR), and quickly emerged as a rising star of the movement. Pacifism was a way of life for Rustin. It provided him with both a path to inner virtue and a strategy for social change. The path to inner virtue meant suppressing personal anger and the violent tendencies inside. "The only way to reduce ugliness in the world is to reduce it in yourself," Rustin would say.[18] As a strategy for change, pacifism, he later wrote in a letter to Martin Luther King, "rests upon two pillars. One is resistance, continuous military resistance. The evildoer is subjected to pressure so that he never is permitted to rest. Second it projects good-will against ill-will. In this way, nonviolent resistance is a force against apathy in our own ranks."[19]

Throughout his late twenties, Rustin traveled for FOR, electrifying audiences around the country. He staged constant acts of civil disobedience, which quickly became legendary in pacifist and civil rights circles. In 1942 in Nashville he insisted upon riding in the white section of a public bus. The driver called the police. Four officers arrived and beat him while Rustin maintained a passive, Gandhian demeanor. As David McReynolds, a member of FOR, later recalled,

"Not only was he the Fellowship's most popular lecturer but he was also a genius at tactical matters. Bayard was being groomed by FOR to become an American Gandhi."[20]

In November 1943, when he received his draft notice, Rustin decided he would take a stance of noncooperation and go to jail rather than serve in one of the rural labor camps as a conscientious objector. At that time, one out of every six inmates in federal prison was a prisoner of conscience. These inmates thought of themselves as the shock troops of pacifism and civil rights. Locked away, Rustin aggressively defied the prison's segregationist policies. He insisted upon eating in the Whites Only part of the dining hall. During free time he stationed himself in the Whites Only part of the cell block. Sometimes his agitation got him in trouble with the other prisoners. On one occasion a white prisoner went after him, bashing him with a mop handle, landing blows on Rustin's head and body. Once again, Rustin went into a Gandhian pose of nonresistance. He simply repeated over and over again, "You can't hurt me." Eventually the mop handle snapped. Rustin suffered a broken wrist and bruises across his head.

Word of Rustin's exploits soon spread beyond prison walls, to the wider press and activist circles. In Washington, officials at the Federal Bureau of Prisons, under the leadership of James Bennett, classified Rustin as a "notorious offender," in the same category as Al Capone. As his biographer John D'Emilio put it, "Throughout Rustin's 28-month imprisonment, Bennett was plagued by letters from subordinates who pleaded for advice on what to do about Rustin, and from Rustin's supporters on the outside who kept an eye on his treatment."[21]

Promiscuity

RUSTIN BEHAVED HEROICALLY, BUT THERE WAS ALSO AN ARROGANCE AND an anger and sometimes a recklessness in his behavior that was not in keeping with his stated beliefs. On October 24, 1944, he felt compelled to send a letter to the warden apologizing for his behavior at a disciplinary hearing. "I am quite ashamed that I lost my temper and behaved rudely," he wrote.[22] There was also a recklessness to his sexual life. Rustin was gay at a time when gay life was pushed underground, when there was no public affirmation for gays and lesbians. But there was a relentlessness to Rustin's search for partners that even his lovers found disturbing. His speaking tours before and after prison involved constant rounds of seduction. One long-term lover complained that "coming home one day and finding him in bed with somebody else was not my idea of fun."[23] In prison he was flagrant about his sexual interests and was several times caught performing fellatio on other prisoners.

The prison authorities eventually convened a disciplinary hearing. At least three prisoners testified that they had seen Rustin performing oral sex. At first Rustin lied, vehemently denying the charges. When authorities announced they were putting him in a separate part of the prison as punishment, he wrapped his arms and legs around a swivel chair, resisted the guards, and ended up in isolation.

News of the incident spread across activist circles nationwide. Some of his supporters were upset to learn he was gay, but Rustin had never really hidden that. Mostly they were upset because his sexual activities undermined the example he had been setting as a disciplined, heroic resister. In a movement that called upon its leaders to be peaceful, self-restrained, and self-purifying, Rustin had been angry, arrogant, lax, and self-indulgent. A. J. Muste, the leader of FOR and Rustin's mentor, wrote him a harsh letter:

> You have been guilty of gross misconduct, especially reprehensible in a person making the claims to leadership and—in a sense—moral superiority which you were making. Furthermore, you have deceived everybody, including your own comrades and most devoted friends. . . . You are still far from facing reality in yourself. In the self that has been and still is you, there is nothing to respect, and you must ruthlessly cast out *everything* in you, which prevents you from facing that. Only so can your true self come to birth—through fire, anguish complete and child-like humility. . . . You remember Psalm 51: "Have mercy upon me, O God, according to thy loving kindness—wash me thoroughly from mine iniquities and cleanse me from my sin. . . . against thee only have I sinned and done this evil in thy sight. . . . Create me a clean heart, O God, and renew a right spirit within me."[24]

In a later letter, Muste made it clear that it was not Rustin's homosexuality he was objecting to, but his promiscuity: "How utterly horrible and cheap where there is no discipline, no form in the relationship." Just as an artist with the freest vision, the most powerful creative urge, submits to the severest discipline, so, too, must a lover tame his impulses in order to reach "the discipline, the control, the effort to understand the other."

With promiscuity, Muste continued, "we come close to the travesty and denial of love, for if love means depth, means understanding above the ordinary . . . means exchange of life blood, how can that happen among an indefinite number of people?"

Rustin initially resisted Muste's harsh judgment, but eventually, after weeks in isolation, he surrendered, writing a long, heartfelt letter in reply:

> When success was imminent in our racial campaign my behavior stopped progress. . . . I have misused the confidence that negroes here had in my leadership; I have caused them to question the moral basis of non-violence; I have hurt and let down my friends over the country. . . . I am a traitor (by our means of thought) just as surely as an army captain who willfully exposed military positions during a battle. . . . I have really been dedicated to my "ego." I have thought in terms of my power, my time, my energy and of giving them to the great struggle. I have thought in terms of my voice, my ability, my willingness to go into the non-violent vanguard. I have not humbly accepted God's gifts to me. . . . [This] has led, I now see, first to arrogance and pride and then to weakness, to artificiality and failure.[25]

A few months later Rustin was permitted to travel home, with an accompanying guard, to visit his dying grandfather. While on the way home, Rustin met up with Helen Winnemore, a fellow activist and an old friend. Winnemore told Rustin she loved him and wanted to be his life companion, to give him the heterosexual relationship, or at least cover, so that he could continue his work. In a letter to his longtime male lover, Davis Platt, Rustin summarized the offer Winnemore had made, paraphrasing her words:

Now since I believe that once redeemed your power for service and redemption of others will be vast, and since I believe your greatest immediate need is for real love, real understanding, and confidence, I tell you without shame of the love I have for you, of my desire to be with you thru light and darkness, to give all that I possess that the goodness within you shall live and flower. Men must see the goodness that potentially is yours and glorify your creator. This, Bayard, she went on to say in effect, this [is the] love I have for you and I offer it joyfully not for myself or for you alone, but for all mankind, which would profit by what your integration would mean—and then for a long time we were silent.[26]

Rustin was touched by Winnemore's offer. "Never had I heard such unselfish love speak in a woman. Never had I sensed a more simple and complete offering." He did not take Winnemore up on her offer, but he regarded it as a sign from God. The memory of their conversation brought him "a joy that is almost beyond understanding—a flash of light in the right direction—a new hope . . . a sudden reevaluation . . . a light on the road I know I should travel."[27]

Rustin vowed to curb his arrogance, the spirit of anger that had marred his pacifist activities. He also rethought his sex life. He fundamentally accepted Muste's critique of his promiscuity. Rustin worked on his relationship with his longtime lover Davis Platt, exchanging a series of long, searching letters with him in the hopes that one truly loving relationship would serve as a barricade against lust and promiscuity.

Rustin remained in prison until June 1946. Upon his release he immediately became active again in the civil rights movement. In North Carolina, he and some fellow activists sat at the front of a segregated bus and were beaten and nearly lynched. In Reading, Pennsylvania, he extracted an apology from a hotel manager after a clerk denied him a room. In St. Paul, Minnesota, he conducted a sit-in until he was given a room. On a train from Washington to Louisville he sat in the middle of the dinner car from breakfast straight through lunchtime as the waiters refused to serve him.

When A. Philip Randolph called off a resistance campaign, Rustin harshly criticized his mentor for issuing a statement that was nothing more than a "weasel worded, mealy mouthed sham."[28] He was quickly ashamed of himself, and he avoided Randolph for the next two years. When they finally met again, "I was so nervous I was shaking, waiting for his wrath to descend upon me." Randolph laughed it off and resumed their relationship.

Rustin went on speaking tours around the world, a star once again. He also continued to seduce men at every stop. Eventually Platt threw him out of their apartment. Then, in 1953, while on a speaking engagement in Pasadena, he was arrested at just after three in the morning. He was performing oral sex on two men in a car when two county police officers approached and arrested him for lewd vagrancy.

He was sentenced to sixty days in jail, and his reputation would never fully recover. He had to dissociate himself from his activist organizations. He tried unsuccessfully to get a job as a publicist for a publishing house. A social worker suggested he get a job cleaning bathrooms and hallways in a hospital.

Backstage

SOME PEOPLE TRY TO RECOVER FROM SCANDAL BY STARTING WHERE THEY were and simply continuing through life. Some people strip themselves down and start again from the bottom. Rustin eventually understood that his new role was to serve his good cause, but in the background.

Rustin slowly recommitted himself to the civil rights movement. Instead of being the star speaker, leader, and organizer, he would forever after be mostly in the shadows, working behind the scenes, receiving no credit, shifting the glory to others, like his friend and protégé, Martin Luther King, Jr. Rustin wrote for King, spread ideas through King, introduced King to labor leaders, pushed him to talk about economic as well as civil rights issues, tutored him on nonviolent confrontation and the Gandhian philosophy, and organized one action after another on King's behalf. Rustin was a significant player in the Montgomery bus boycott. King wrote a book about the boycott, but Rustin asked him to take out all references to his own role.

When asked to sign some public statement on behalf of this or that stand, he generally refused.

Even this backstage role was fragile. In 1960, Adam Clayton Powell, the pastor and then congressman from New York City, let it be known that if King and Rustin did not bow to his demands on a certain tactical matter, he would accuse them of having a sexual affair. Randolph urged King to stand by Rustin, since the charge was so obviously bogus. King hesitated. Rustin handed in his resignation from the Southern Christian Leadership Conference in the hope that King would reject it. Instead, King quietly accepted it, much to Rustin's dismay. King dropped Rustin personally as well, no longer calling upon him for advice, sending the occasional bland note as a cover for his decision to cut him off.

In 1962, Rustin turned fifty, largely unknown. Of all the major civil rights leaders, Randolph was the one who had stuck by him most steadfastly. One day, as they were sitting around in Harlem, Randolph began reminiscing about the World War II era march on Washington that never took place. Rustin sensed immediately that it was time to complete that dream and organize a "mass descent" on the nation's capital. The marches and protests across the South had begun to shake the foundations of the old order, Rustin believed. The election of John F. Kennedy made Washington once again relevant. It was time to force federal action through mass confrontation.

At first, the major civil rights organizations such as the Urban League and the NAACP were skeptical or completely hostile. They did not want to offend legislators or members of the administration. A confrontational march might reduce their access to those in power and lessen their ability to exercise influence from the inside. In addition, there had long been a basic difference of outlook within the civil rights movements that involved not just a debate about strategy but also a deep difference of opinion about morality and human nature.

As David L. Chappell argues in his book *A Stone of Hope,* there were really two civil rights movements. The first was northern and highly educated. People in this group tended to have an optimistic view of history and human nature. Without thinking much about it, they perceived the arc of history as a gradual ascent, a steady accumulation of more scientific and psychological knowledge, a steady achievement of greater prosperity, a steady growth of progressive legislation, and a gentle rise from barbarism to decency.

They believed that racism was such a clear violation of America's founding documents that the main job for the civil rights activist was to appeal to reason and the better angels of people's nature. As education levels increased, as consciousness was raised, as prosperity and economic opportunity spread, then more and more people would gradually see that racism was wrong, that segregation was unjust, and they would rise to combat it. Education, prosperity, and social justice would rise together. All good things are compatible and mutually reinforcing.

People in this camp tended to believe in conversation over confrontation, consensus over aggression, and civility over political force.

There was a second camp, Chappell argues, that emerged from the biblical prophetic tradition. Its leaders, including King and Rustin, cited Jeremiah and Job. In this world, they argued, the just suffer while the unjust prosper. Being right does not necessarily lead to being victorious. Man is a sinner at the core of his being. He will rationalize the injustices that benefit him. He will not give up his privileges even if you can persuade him they are unjust. Even people on the righteous side of a cause can be corrupted by their own righteousness, can turn a selfless movement into an instrument to serve their own vanity. They can be corrupted by whatever power they attain and corrupted by their own powerlessness.

Evil, King declared, is "rampant" in the universe. "Only the superficial optimist who refuses to face the realities of life fails to see this patent fact."[29] People in this realist camp, who were mostly southern and religious, had contempt for the northern faith in gradual natural progress. "This particular sort of optimism has been discredited by the brutal logic of events," King continued. "Instead of assured progress in wisdom and decency, man faces the ever present possibility of swift relapse not merely to animalism, but into such calculated cruelty as no other animal can practice."[30]

The optimists, members of this camp argued, practice idolatry. They worship man and not God, and when they do worship God it is a God who merely possesses human qualities in extreme form. As a result they overestimate the power of human goodwill, idealism, and compassion and their own noble intentions. They are too easy on themselves, too complacent about their own virtue, and too naïve about the resolve of their opponents.

Randolph, King, and Rustin had this more austere view of their struggle. The defenders of segregation would not lie down, and people of goodwill would not be persuaded to act if there was any risk to themselves. The civil rights activists themselves could not rely on their own goodwill or their own willpower, because very often they would end up perverting their own cause. If there was to be any progress, it was necessary not just to be engaged, one had to utterly surrender to the movement, at the cost of one's own happiness and fulfillment and possibly life. This attitude of course fueled a fierce determination, which many of their more optimistic secular allies could not match. As Chappell put it, "Civil rights activists drew from illiberal sources to supply the determination that liberals lacked, but needed."[31] The biblical lens didn't protect the realists from pain and suffering, but it explained that pain and suffering were inevitable and redemptive.

One consequence of this attitude was that the prophetic realists were much more aggressive. They took it as a matter of course that given the sinful nature of man, people could not be altered merely by education, consciousness raising, and expanded opportunity. It was wrong to put one's faith in historical processes, human institutions, or human goodness. As Rustin put it, American blacks look "upon the middle class idea of long term educational and cultural changes with fear and mistrust."[32]

Instead, change comes through relentless pressure and coercion. That is to say, these biblical realists were not Tolstoyan, they were Gandhian. They did not believe in merely turning the other cheek or trying to win people over with friendship and love alone. Nonviolence furnished them with a series of tactics that allowed them to remain on permanent offense. It allowed them to stage relentless protests, marches, sit-ins, and other actions that would force their opponents to do things against their own will. Nonviolence allowed the biblical realists to aggressively expose the villainy of their foes, to make their enemies' sins work against them as they were exposed in ever more brutal forms. They compelled their foes to commit evil deeds because they themselves were willing to absorb evil. Rustin endorsed the idea that extreme behavior was required to make the status quo crumble. He saw Jesus as "this fanatic whose insistence on love thrust at the very pillars of a stable society."[33] Or, as Randolph put it, "I feel morally obligated to disturb and keep disturbed the conscience of Jim Crow America."[34]

Even in the midst of these confrontations, Randolph, Rustin, and the other civil rights activists were in their best moments aware that they were in danger of being corrupted by their own aggressive actions. In their best moments they understood that they would become guilty of self-righteousness because their cause was just; they would become guilty of smugness as their cause moved successfully forward; they would become vicious and tribal as group confronted group; they would become more dogmatic and simplistic as they used propaganda to mobilize their followers; they would become more vain as their audiences enlarged; their hearts would harden as the conflict grew more dire and their hatred for their enemies deepened; they would be compelled to make morally tainted choices as they got closer to power; the more they altered history, the more they would be infected by pride.

Rustin, who had been so undisciplined in his sexual life, saw nonviolence as a means a protester could use to discipline himself against these corruptions. Nonviolent protest in this view is different from normal protest. It demands relentless self-control. The Gandhian protester must step into race riots without ever striking out, must face danger while remaining calm and communicative, must confront with love those who deserve to be hated. This requires physical self-discipline, marching into danger slowly and deliberately, keeping one's arms curled around one's head as the blows rain down. It requires emotional discipline, resisting the urge to feel resentment, maintaining a spirit of malice toward none and charity toward all. It requires above all the ability to absorb suffering. As King put it, the people who had suffered for so long had to endure more suffering if they were to end their oppression: "Unearned suffering is redemptive."[35]

The nonviolent path is an ironic path: the weak can triumph by enduring suffering; the oppressed must not fight back if they hope to defeat their oppressor; those on the side of justice can be corrupted by their own righteousness.

This is the inverted logic of people who see around them a fallen world. The midcentury thinker most associated with this ironic logic is Reinhold Niebuhr. People like Randolph, Rustin, and King thought along Niebuhrian lines, and were influenced by him. Niebuhr argued that, beset by his own sinful nature, man is a problem to himself. Human actions take place in a frame of meaning too large for human comprehension. We simply can't understand the long chain of consequences arising from what we do, or even the origins of our own impulses. Neibuhr argued against the easy conscience of modern man, against moral complacency on every front. He reminded readers that we are never as virtuous as we think we are, and that our motives are never as pure as in our own accounting.

Even while acknowledging our own weaknesses and corruptions, Niebuhr continued, it is necessary to take aggressive action to fight evil and injustice. Along the way it is important to acknowledge that our motives are not pure and we will end up being corrupted by whatever power we manage to attain and use.

"We take and must continue to take morally hazardous actions to preserve our civilization," Niebuhr wrote in the middle of the Cold War. "We must exercise our power. But we ought neither to believe that a nation is capable of perfect disinterestedness in its exercise nor become complacent about particular degrees of interest and passion which corrupt the justice by which the exercise of power is legitimized."[36]

Behaving in this way, he continued, requires the innocence of a dove and the shrewdness of a serpent. The ultimate irony is that in any struggle "we could not be virtuous if we were really as innocent as we pretended to be."[37] If we were truly innocent we couldn't use power in the ways that are necessary to achieve good ends. But if you adopt a strategy based on self-doubt and self-suspicion, then you can achieve partial victories.

Culmination

AT FIRST RUSTIN AND RANDOLPH HAD TROUBLE RALLYING CIVIL RIGHTS leaders around the idea of a March on Washington. But the violent protests in Birmingham, Alabama, during the spring of 1963 changed the mood. The whole world saw the Birmingham police force setting dogs on teenage girls, unleashing water cannons, and hurling boys into walls. The images mobilized the Kennedy administration to prepare civil rights legislation, and they persuaded nearly everybody in the civil rights movement that the time was right for a mass descent on the nation's capital.

Rustin, as the chief organizer of the march, expected to be named the official director. But at a crucial meeting, Roy Wilkins of the NAACP objected: "He's got too many scars." King vacillated and finally Randolph stepped in, saying he would himself serve as director of the march. This would give him the right to appoint a deputy, and he would appoint Rustin, who would be director in all but name. Wilkins was outmaneuvered.

Rustin oversaw everything from the transportation systems to the toilet facilities to the speaker lineup. To avoid confrontation with the D.C. police he organized a corps of black off-duty policemen and gave them training in nonviolence. They were to surround the marchers and prevent clashes.

Two weeks before the march, the segregationist senator Strom Thurmond went on the Senate floor and lambasted Rustin for being a sexual pervert. He introduced the Pasadena police booking slip into the Congressional Record. As John D'Emilio points out in his outstanding biography *Lost Prophet,* Rustin instantly and inadvertently became one of the most visible homosexuals in America.

Randolph leaped to Rustin's defense: "I am dismayed there are in this country men who, wrapping themselves in the mantle of Christian morality, would mutilate the most elementary conceptions of human decency, privacy and humility in order to persecute other men."[38] Since the march was only two weeks away, the other civil rights leaders had no choice but to defend Rustin as well. Thurmond ended up doing Rustin a great favor.

The Saturday before the march, Rustin issued a final statement that summed up his policy of tightly controlled aggression. The march, he declared, "will be orderly, but not subservient. It will be proud, but not arrogant. It will be non-violent but not timid."[39] On the day, Randolph spoke first. Then John Lewis brought the gigantic crowd to full roar with a fiery, aggressive speech. Mahalia Jackson sang and King delivered his "I have a dream" speech.

He ended with the refrain from the old spiritual, "Free at last! Free at last! Thank God Almighty we are free at last!" Then Rustin, playing a master of ceremonies role, mounted the podium and reintroduced Randolph. Randolph led the crowd in a pledge to continue the struggle: "I pledge that I will not relax until victory is won. . . . I will pledge my heart and my mind and my body unequivocally and without regard to personal sacrifice, to the achievement of social peace through social justice."

After the march, Rustin and Randolph found each other. As Rustin would later recall, "I said to him, 'Mr. Randolph, it looks like your dream has come true.' And when I looked into his eyes, tears were streaming down his cheeks. It is the one time I can recall that he could not hold back his feelings."[40]

In the final decades of his life, Rustin cut his own path, working hard to end apartheid in South Africa, bucking the civil rights establishment in New York City during a crucial teachers' strike in 1968, defending the ideal of integration against more nationalist figures like Malcolm X. In those final years, he did find personal peace, in the form of a long-term relationship with a man named Walter Naegle. Rustin almost never spoke about his private life in public, but he did tell an interviewer, "The most important thing is that after many years of seeking, I've finally found a solid, ongoing relationship with one individual with whom I have everything in common, everything. . . . I spent years looking for exciting sex instead of looking for a person who was compatible."

THE STORY OF A. Philip Randolph and Bayard Rustin is the story of how flawed people wield power in a fallen world. They shared a worldview based on an awareness of both social and personal sin, the idea that human life is shot through with veins of darkness. They learned, Randolph instantly and Rustin over a lifetime, to build an inner structure to contain the chaotic impulses within. They learned that sinfulness is battled obliquely through self-giving, by directing life away from the worst tendencies. They were extremely dignified in their bearing. But this same sense made them aggressive in their outward strategy. They knew that dramatic change, when it is necessary, rarely comes through sweet suasion. Social sin requires a hammering down of the door by people who are simultaneously aware that they are unworthy to be so daring.

This is a philosophy of power, a philosophy of power for people who combine extreme conviction with extreme self-skepticism.

CHAPTER 7

LOVE

"A HUMAN LIFE, I THINK," GEORGE ELIOT WROTE, "SHOULD BE WELL rooted in some spot of native land, where it may get the love of tender kinship for the face of the earth, for the labors men go forth to, for the sounds and accents that haunt it, for whatever will give that early home a familiar unmistakable difference amidst the future widening of knowledge."[1]

Eliot's native spot was in Warwickshire, in the middle of England, a gentle, soft, unremarkable landscape. From her home she could see both the ancient rolling farmland and also the new and grimy coal mines, the economic clash that gave the Victorian era its special intensity. She was born with the name Mary Anne Evans on November 22, 1819.

Her father began as a carpenter but rose through self-discipline and an eye for opportunity and ended up as a very successful land agent. He supervised other people's properties and became moderately rich in the process. She adored him. When she became a novelist, she would use his traits—practical knowledge, unlettered wisdom, a loyal devotion to his work—as the basis for several of her more admirable characters. After he died she kept his wire-rimmed glasses as a reminder of his watchful eyes and his perspective on the world.

Her mother, Christiana, was in ill health through most of Mary Anne's girlhood. She lost twin boys eighteen months after Mary Anne's birth, and she sent her surviving children away to boarding schools to spare herself the physical effort of raising them. Mary Anne seems to have felt the loss of her mother's affection acutely, responding with what one biographer, Kathryn Hughes, calls "an infuriating mix of attention-seeking and self-punishing behavior."[2] She was, on the surface, a precocious, strong-willed, somewhat awkward girl, more comfortable in the company of adults than with other children, but there was something deeply needy about her.

Hungry for affection and terrified of being abandoned, she turned her attention, as a young girl, to her older brother, Isaac. When he returned on visits from school she followed him about, badgering him with questions about every particular of his life. For a time he returned her love, and they enjoyed "little spots of time," perfect days playing in the grass and streams. But then he grew older, got a pony, and lost interest in the bothersome little girl. She was left weeping and abandoned. This was a pattern—her desperate need for love and some man's exasperated refusal—that would dominate the first thirty years of her life. As her final husband, John Cross, would put it, "In her moral development she showed, from the earliest years, the trait that was most marked in her all through life—namely the absolute need of some one person who should be all in all to her, and to whom she should be all in all."[3]

In 1835 her mother fell ill with breast cancer. Mary Anne, who had been sent away to boarding school at age five to spare her mother's health, was called back at age sixteen to tend to it. There's no record that she suffered any great grief when her mother finally succumbed to the disease, but her formal education was over, and she took over the role of supervising the household, almost as her father's surrogate wife.

In her famous preface to *Middlemarch,* Eliot writes about the crisis of vocation that many young women feel. They experience a great yearning inside, she wrote, a spiritual ardor to devote their energies in some substantial, heroic, and meaningful direction. They are propelled by moral imagination, the urge to do something epic and righteous with their life. These young women, "fed from within," soared after some "illimitable satisfaction, some object which would never justify weariness, which would reconcile self-despair with the rapturous consciousness of life beyond self." And yet Victorian society provided so few avenues for their energy that their "loving heartbeats and sobs after an unattainable goodness tremble off and are dispersed among hindrances, instead of centering in some long-recognizable deed."

Mary Anne was driven by that moral ardor, that spiritual perfectionism. In her late teens and early twenties, she became something of a religious nut. She came of age in a time when society was in great religious tumult. Science was beginning to expose cracks in the Church's description of human creation. The spread of unbelief made morality a problem; many Victorians clung more ferociously to stern moral precepts even as their doubts about the existence of God increased. Among the faithful, there were efforts to make the church more vibrant and more spiritual. John Henry Newman and the Oxford Movement tried to return Anglicanism to its Catholic roots, tried to restore a sense of reverence for tradition and medieval ritual. The evangelicals democratized the faith, creating more charismatic services and emphasizing individual prayer, individual conscience, and each individual's direct relationship with God.

During her teenage years, Mary Anne was caught up in the religious fervor and, in her self-centered immaturity, came to embody many of religion's most priggish and unattractive aspects. Her faith was long on self-admiring renunciation and short on delight or humane sympathy. She gave up reading fiction, believing that a morally serious person should focus on the real world and not imaginary ones. She forswore wine and as manager of her household forced those around her into abstinence as well. She adopted a severe and puritanical mode of dress. Music, which had once been a source of great joy, was now, she decided, permissible only when it accompanied worship. At social events she could be counted on to disapprove of the vulgar humanity and then to fall into fits of weeping. At one party, she wrote a friend, "the oppressive noise that accompanied the dancing" made it impossible for her to "maintain the Protestant character of a True Christian."[4] She developed a headache, slipped into hysterics, and vowed to reject "all invitations of a dubious character."

D. H. Lawrence once wrote, "It was really George Eliot who started it all. It was she who started putting the action inside." In her teenage years, Mary Anne lived melodramatically and narcissistically, full of solitary internal anguish, struggle, and resignation. She was trying to lead a life of martyrdom and surrender. But she was artificially narrowing herself, amputating every humane and tender piece that didn't fit into a rigid frame. Her behavior was filled with affectation, less about being a saint than about getting herself admired for being a saint. There was a painful and ostentatious self-consciousness in her letters from this period, and even in her bad early poetry: "Oh Saint! Oh would that I could claim / The privileg'd, the honored name / And confidently take my stand / Though lowest in a saintly band!" One biographer, Frederick R. Karl, sums up the common view: "Except for her high intelligence, Mary Ann, in 1838, at close to nineteen, sounds intolerable."[5]

Fortunately, her roving mind couldn't be contained for long. She was too intelligent not to be able to observe herself accurately. "I feel that my besetting sin is the one of all others most destroying, as it is the fruitful parent of them all, Ambition, a desire insatiable for the esteem of my fellow creatures," she wrote in a letter. "This seems the center whence all my actions proceed."[6] At some level she understood that her public righteousness was just a play for attention. Furthermore, she was just too curious to stay in a self-imposed mental straitjacket for very long. She was too hungry for knowledge. Her reading could not be contained within narrow banks.

She was still reading biblical commentary, but she was also learning Italian and German, reading Wordsworth and Goethe. Her reading stretched to include the Romantic poets, including Shelley and Byron, whose lives certainly did not conform to the strictures of her faith.

Soon she was reading widely in the sciences, including John Pringle Nichol's *The Phenomena and Order of the Solar System* and Charles Lyell's *Principles of Geology,* a book that paved the way for Darwin's account of evolution. Christian writers were rising up to defend the biblical account of creation. She read their books, too, but they backfired with her. They were so unpersuasive in rebutting the findings of the new science that they only served to reinforce Mary Anne's growing doubts.

She was profoundly influenced by a book titled *An Inquiry Concerning the Origin of Christianity* by Charles Hennell, which she bought in 1841 at the age of twenty-one. Hennell parsed through each of the Gospels, trying to determine what could be established as fact and what was later embellishment. He concluded that there was insufficient evidence to prove that Jesus was divinely born, or that he had performed any miracles, or that he had been resurrected from the dead. Hennell concluded that Jesus was a "noble minded reformer and sage, martyred by crafty priests and brutal soldiers."[7]

For most of this time, Mary Anne had nobody close to her intellectual level with whom she could discuss what she was reading. She invented a word to describe her condition: "non-impartitive." She received information but could not digest it through conversation.

But then she learned that Hennell's youngest sister, Cara, lived nearby. Cara's husband, Charles Bray, was a successful ribbon merchant who had written his own religious tract, "The Philosophy of Necessity." It held that the universe was governed by unchanging rules ordained by God, but that God was not active in the world. It was man's duty to discover these rules and improve the world along their lines. Bray believed people should spend less time praying and more time involved in social reform. The Brays were bright, intellectual, unconventional thinkers who would go on to lead unconventional lives. Though they remained married, Charles fathered six children with their cook, and Cara had a close and possibly sexual friendship with Edward Noel, a relative of Lord Byron, who had three children of his own and an estate in Greece.

Mary Anne was introduced to the Brays by a mutual friend, perhaps in order to bring the Brays back into the fold of orthodox Christianity. If that was her intent, it didn't work. By the time Mary Anne settled into their lives, she herself was already drifting away from the faith. The Brays immediately recognized her as a kindred spirit. She began socializing with them more and more, delighted to have found intellectual peers at last. They did not cause her defection from Christianity, but they catalyzed it.

It was dawning on Mary Anne that her growing disbelief would cause her no end of trouble. It would mean a rupture with her father, the rest of her family, and polite society generally. It would make it very hard for her to find a husband. In the society of her time, agnosticism meant ostracism. But she pushed on bravely toward what her heart and head told her was truth. "I wish to be among the ranks of that glorious crusade that is seeking to set Truth's Holy Sepulcher free from usurped domination," she wrote in a letter to a friend.[8]

As that sentence indicates, Mary Anne was not renouncing the spirit of religion even while she was coming to renounce Christianity.

She discounted Christian teaching, and the divinity of Jesus, but she did not doubt, especially at this age, the existence of God. She rejected Christianity on realist grounds, out of distaste for anything abstract or fantastical. She did it after exhaustive reading, but she did not do it coldly or by the use of dry reason. Rather, she loved life with such an earthy passion that she had trouble accepting the idea that this world was subsidiary to some other world that obeyed different laws. She came to feel she could achieve a state of grace not through surrender but through her own moral choices, by living a virtuous and rigorous life. With this philosophy Mary Anne put a heavy burden on herself, and on her own conduct.

In January 1842, Mary Anne told her father that she would no longer accompany him to church. His response was to withdraw into what one biographer called a cold and sullen rage. Mary Anne was not only defying her father and God, as he saw it; she was also choosing to dishonor her family and to cast it into social disgrace. On the first Sunday after her refusal, Mary Anne's father went to church, but he noted simply and coldly in his diary, "Mary Anne did not go."

The next few weeks were spent in what Mary Anne called a "Holy War." She lived at home at loggerheads with her father. He broke off contact with her but fought back in different ways. He enlisted friends and relatives to come plead with her to attend church, if only on prudence grounds. If she continued on this path, they warned, she would spend her life poor, cast out, isolated. These very plausible predictions had no effect on her. Her father also asked clergy and other knowledgeable scholars to come and persuade her by force of reason that Christianity was the true doctrine. They came, they argued, they were defeated. Mary Anne had already read every book they cited to make their case, and she had her responses.

Finally, her father decided to relocate the family. If Mary Anne was going to make herself unmarriageable, there was no use keeping the big house that had been rented to catch her a husband.

Mary Anne tried to reopen conversation with her father by writing him a letter. First, she made clear why she could no longer be a Christian. She said she regarded the Gospels as "histories consisting of mingled truth and fiction, and while I admire and cherish much of what I believe to have been the moral teaching of Jesus himself, I consider the system of doctrines built upon the facts of his life . . . to be most dishonorable to God and most pernicious in its influence on individual and social happiness."

It would be rank hypocrisy, she told him, to appear to worship in the home of a doctrine she thought pernicious. She wrote that she would like to go on living with her father, but if he wanted her to leave, "I can cheerfully do it if you desire it and shall go with deep gratitude for all the tenderness and rich kindness you have never been tired of showing me. So far from complaining I shall joyfully submit if as a proper punishment for the pain I have most unintentionally given you, you determine to appropriate any provision you may have intended to make for my future support to your other children whom you may consider more deserving."

At the first dawn of her adulthood, Mary Anne was not only renouncing the faith of her family. She was willing to go out into the world without a home, without an inheritance, without a husband, and without prospects. She concluded with a declaration of love: "As a last vindication of herself from one who has no one to speak for her I may be permitted to say that if ever I loved you I do so now, if ever I sought to obey the laws of my Creator and to follow duty wherever it may lead me I have that determination now and the consciousness of this will support me though every being on earth were to frown on me."

This letter, remarkable for a woman so young, shows many of the traits the world would later come to see in George Eliot: an intense intellectual honesty, an arduous desire to live according to the strictures of her conscience, an amazing bravery in the face of social pressure, a desire to strengthen her character by making the necessary hard choices, but also a bit of egotism, a tendency to cast herself as the star of her own melodrama, an intense desire for the love of men even as she puts that love at risk.

After a few months, they compromised. Mary Anne agreed to accompany her father to church, so long as he and everybody else understood that she was not a Christian and a believer in the doctrines of the faith.

It looks like a capitulation, but it wasn't entirely. Mary Anne's father must have realized the cruelty in his rejection of his daughter. He bent. Meanwhile, Mary Anne came to see and regret the thick vein of self-aggrandizement that was running through her protest. She came to see that she was taking a secret delight in being the center of a town scandal. She regretted the pain she was causing her father.

Moreover, she knew there was something self-indulgent in the way she had taken an uncompromising stance. Within a month she was writing a friend saying that she deplored her "impetuosity both of feeling and judging." Later she said she deeply regretted this collision with her father, which might have been avoided with a little subtlety and management. Yes, she had an obligation to follow her individual conscience, she concluded, but it was her moral duty to mute her own impulses by considering their effect on others and on the social fabric of the community. By the time Mary Anne Evans became the novelist George Eliot, she was an avowed enemy of that kind of stark grandstanding. By middle age, she was a meliorist and a gradualist, believing that people and society were best reformed by slow stretching, not by sudden rupture. She was capable of making brave and radical moves in line with her own convictions, as we shall see, but she also believed in the importance of social niceties and conventions. She believed that society is held together by a million restraints on individual will, which enmesh the individual within a common moral world. When people behave on the basis of uncompromising individual desire, she came to believe, they might set off a selfish contagion in those around them. She cloaked her own radical path in all the trappings of respectability. She became a courageous freethinker with a faith in ritual, habit, and convention. The Holy War with her father was important in teaching her that lesson.

Within a few months, Mary Anne and her father were reconciled. Her admiration for him and moral dependence upon him was expressed in a letter she wrote shortly after his death seven years after the Holy War: "What shall I be without my Father? It will seem as if part of my moral nature were gone. I had a horrid vision of myself last night becoming earthly sensual and devilish for want of that purifying restraining influence."

Neediness

INTELLECTUALLY, MARY ANNE WAS MATURE. THE INTENSIVE READING SHE had done throughout her adolescence produced an impressive depth of knowledge and a capacity for observation and judgment. At the level of the mind, Mary Anne was well on the central journey of her life, the transformation that would take her from a self-absorbed adolescent to an adult whose maturity was measured by an unsurpassed ability to enter into other people's feelings.

Emotionally, though, she was still something of a basket case. By the time she was twenty-two it became a joke in her circle that Mary Anne fell in love with everyone she met. These relationships followed a general pattern. Desperate for affection, she would throw herself at some man, usually a married or otherwise unavailable one. Dazzled by her conversation, he would return her attention. Mistaking his intellectual engagement for romantic love, she would become emotionally embroiled, hoping their love would fill some void in herself. Finally he would reject her or flee, or his wife would force her out of the picture. Mary Anne would be left awash in tears, or crippled by migraines.

Mary Anne's romantic forays might have been successful if she had been conventionally pretty, but as Henry James, then a young and handsome man, reported, she was "magnificently ugly—deliciously hideous." A series of men simply couldn't get around her heavy jaw and plain horselike features, though finer spirits eventually came to see the beauty within. In 1852, an American visitor, Sara Jane Lippincott, described the effect her conversation had on her appearance: "Miss Evans certainly impressed me at first as exceedingly plain, with her aggressive jaw and her evasive blue eyes. Neither nose, nor mouth nor chin were to my liking; but, as she grew interested and earnest in conversation, a great light flashed over or out of her face, till it seemed transfigured, while the sweetness of her rare smile was something quite indescribable."[9]

Men came. Mary Anne fell. Men went. She had an infatuation with a music instructor and with Charles Hennell, the author. She became entangled with a young man named John Sibree who was studying for the ministry. Sibree didn't return her affection, but after conversations with her, he gave up his clerical career, though he had nothing else to fall back on.

Later she attached herself with disturbing intensity to a married, four-foot-tall, middle-aged artist named François d'Albert Durade. Once, and for about a day, she developed an infatuation with a man who was actually single, but she lost interest in him by the morrow.

Friends would invite Mary Anne to stay in their homes. Before long she'd be involved in some sort of passionate intimacy with the father of the family. Dr. Robert Brabant was a much older, cultivated doctor who gave Mary Anne access to his library and asked her to come live with his family. Before long they were completely entwined. "I am in a little heaven here, Dr. Brabant being its archangel," she wrote in a letter to Cara; "time would fail me to tell of all his charming qualities. We read, walk and talk together, and I am never weary of his company." Before long Dr. Brabant's wife put her foot down. Either Mary Anne would leave the house or she would. Mary Anne had to flee in disgrace.

The oddest imbroglio happened in the home of John Chapman, publisher of the *Westminster Review,* which Mary Anne would eventually write for and edit. Chapman was already living with his wife and a mistress when Mary Anne moved in. Before long the three women were competing for Chapman's affections. As the Eliot biographer Frederick R. Karl puts it, the situation had all the makings of a country house farce, with slammed doors, couples sneaking out for walks, hurt feelings, and tearful, angry scenes. If there was too much calm one day, Chapman would stir the drama by showing a love letter from one woman to one of the others. Eventually the wife and the mistress formed an alliance against Mary Anne. Once again she had to flee amid whispers of scandal.

Biographers generally argue that the absence of maternal love created a hole at the center of Mary Anne's being, which she desperately tried to fill for the rest of her life. But there was also some narcissism here, the love of her own love, the love of her own nobility, of feeling the sweep of one's own passion. She made a drama of herself and indulged in it, enjoying the attention, luxuriating in her own capacity for emotional depth, and savoring the sense of her own epic importance. People who see themselves as the center of their solar system, often get enraptured by their own terrible but also delicious suffering. People who see themselves as a piece of a larger universe and a longer story rarely do.

She would later write, "to be a poet is to have a soul so quick to discern, that no shade of quality escapes it, and so quick to feel, that discernment is but a hand playing with finely ordered variety of chords of emotion—a soul in which knowledge passes instantaneously into feeling, and feeling flashes back as a new organ of knowledge." Mary Anne had that kind of soul. Feeling and action and thought were the same thing. But she had no person to attach her passion to, and no work to give it discipline and shape.

Agency

IN 1852, AT AGE THIRTY-TWO, MARY ANNE FELL IN LOVE WITH THE PHILOSO-pher Herbert Spencer, the only one of the men thus far in her life who was close to her intellectual equal. They went to the theater together and talked constantly. Spencer liked her company but could not overcome his own narcissism and her ugliness. "The lack of physical attraction was fatal," Spencer would write decades later. "Strongly as my judgment prompted, my instincts would not respond."

In July she wrote him a letter that was both pleading and bold. "Those who have known me best have already said that if ever I loved any one thoroughly my whole life must turn upon that feeling, and I find they said truly," she declared. She asked him not to forsake her: "If you become attached to someone else, then I must die, but until then I could gather courage to work and make life valuable, if only I had you near me. I do not ask you to sacrifice anything—I would be very glad and cheerful and never annoy you. . . . You will find that I can be satisfied with very little, if I am delivered from the dread of losing it."

Finally, she added a climactic flourish: "I suppose no woman ever before wrote such a letter as this—but I am not ashamed of it, for I am conscious in the light of reason and true refinement I am worthy of your respect and tenderness, whatever gross men or vulgar-minded women might think of me."[10]

This letter represents a pivotal moment in Eliot's life, with its mixture of pleading vulnerability and strong assertion. After the years of disjointed neediness, the iron was beginning to enter her soul and she became capable of that declaration of her own dignity. You might say that this moment was Eliot's agency moment, the moment when she began the process by which she would stop being blown about by her voids and begin to live according to her own inner criteria, gradually developing a passionate and steady capacity to initiate action and drive her own life.

The letter didn't solve her problems. Spencer still rejected her. She remained insecure, especially about her writing. But her energies were roused. She exhibited growing cohesion and at times amazing courage.

This agency moment can happen, for many people, surprisingly late in life. Sometimes you see lack of agency among the disadvantaged. Their lives can be so blown about by economic disruption, arbitrary bosses, and general disruption that they lose faith in the idea that input leads to predictable output. You can offer programs to improve their lives, but they may not take full advantage of them because they don't have confidence that they can control their own destinies.

Among the privileged, especially the privileged young, you see people who have been raised to be approval-seeking machines. They may be active, busy, and sleepless, but inside they often feel passive and not in control. Their lives are directed by other people's expectations, external criteria, and definitions of success that don't actually fit them.

Agency is not automatic. It has to be given birth to, with pushing and effort. It's not just the confidence and drive to act. It's having engraved inner criteria to guide action. The agency moment can happen at any age, or never. Eliot began to display signs of emotional agency when she was with Spencer, but it came to mature fruition only after she met George Lewes.

One True Love

THE STORY OF GEORGE ELIOT'S LOVE FOR GEORGE LEWES IS ALMOST ALways told from her perspective, as the great passion that gave coherence to her soul, that took her from a self-absorbed and desperate girl and provided her with the love she craved and the emotional support and security she required. But the story can equally well be told from Lewes's perspective, as the central element in his journey from fragmentation to integrity.

Lewes came from a long lineage of family chaos. His grandfather was a comic actor who was married three times. His father was married to one woman in Liverpool and had four children by her, then left and set up a new household with another woman in London with whom he had three boys before he disappeared forever to Bermuda.

Lewes grew up moderately poor and educated himself by going to Europe and schooling himself in the leading Continental authors such as Spinoza and Comte, who were then largely unknown in England. He returned to London and supported himself with his pen, writing on any subject for anybody who would pay. In an age that was beginning to favor specialization and earnestness, he was slighted as a superficial journeyman writer.

The American feminist Margaret Fuller met Lewes at a party at Thomas Carlyle's house and called him a "witty, French, flippant sort of man" who possessed a "sparkling shallowness." Most biographers have followed this line, slighting him as a bit of an adventurer and opportunist, as a facile but shallow and not entirely reliable writer.

The biographer Kathryn Hughes persuasively takes a more appreciative view. Lewes, she writes, was witty and effervescent in a society that tended toward dour self-importance. He was knowledgeable about French and German life in a society that was often suspicious of anything that wasn't British. He had a genuine passion for ideas and for bringing neglected thinkers to public view. He was freethinking and romantic in a society that was in a stringent, buttoned-up Victorian phase.

Lewes was famously ugly (notoriously, the only major London figure who was even less attractive than George Eliot), but he could talk comfortably and sensitively with women, and this served him well. He married a beautiful young woman named Agnes when he was twenty-three and she was nineteen. They had a modern, freethinking marriage, mostly faithful for the first nine years and then mostly unfaithful after that. Agnes had a long-running affair with a man named Thornton Hunt. Lewes sanctioned this affair so long as she didn't have any children by Hunt. When she did, he adopted them as his own in order to spare them the disgrace of illegitimacy.

By the time he met Mary Anne, Lewes was living apart from Agnes (though he seems to have believed that someday he would move back, and their marriage would remain legally intact for the rest of his life). He was in what he regarded as a "very dreary wasted period of my life. I had given up all ambition whatever, lived from hand to mouth, and thought the evil of each day sufficient."[11]

Mary Anne, for her part, was also lonely, but maturing. She wrote to Cara Bray, "My troubles are purely psychical—self-dissatisfaction and despair of achieving anything worth doing." In her journal she embraced the sentiment that was first written by the feminist author Margeret Fuller: "I shall always reign through the intellect, but the life! The life! O my god! Shall that never be sweet?"[12]

But by this stage, in her midthirties, she was less frantic about herself: "When we are young we think our troubles a mighty business—that the world is spread out expressly as a stage for the particular drama of our lives and that we have a right to rant and foam at the mouth if we are crossed. I have done enough of that in my time. But we begin at last to understand that these things are important only to one's own consciousness, which is but as a globule of dew on a rose-leaf that at midday there will be no trace of. This is no high flown sentimentality, but a simple reflection which I find useful to me every day."[13]

Lewes and Mary Anne met at a bookshop on October 6, 1851. By this time she had moved to London and had established herself as an anonymous contributor to (and eventually the editor of) the *Westminster Review*. They traveled in the same circles. They both had a close friendship with Herbert Spencer.

She was unimpressed at first, but before long she was writing to friends that she found Lewes "genial and amusing" and reporting that he has "quite won my liking, in spite of myself." On his part, Lewes seemed to understand the quality of the woman he was getting to know. Flitting and peripatetic in other spheres of life, Lewes was completely solid and dependable when it came to his service to the woman who would become George Eliot.

None of their letters to each other survive. That is in part because they didn't write very many (they were often together) and also because Eliot did not want later biographers raking over her private life and exposing the vulnerable heart that underlay the formidable novels. So we don't know exactly how their love grew. But we know that Lewes was gradually winning her over. On April 16, 1853, she wrote to a friend, "Mr. Lewes, especially, is kind and attentive, and has quite won my regard, after having had a good deal of my vituperation. Like a few other people in the world, he is much better than he seems. A man of heart and conscience, wearing a mask of flippancy."

At some point Lewes would have told her about his broken marriage and his messy private life. This probably wouldn't have shocked Mary Anne, who was familiar with complex living arrangements. But they also would have talked a great deal about ideas. They were interested in the same authors: Spinoza, Comte, Goethe, Ludwig Feuerbach. Around this time Mary Anne was translating Feuerbach's *The Essence of Christianity*.

Feuerbach was arguing that even if the age had lost faith in Christianity, it was still possible to retain the essence of its morality and ethics, and this could be done through love. He maintained that through love and sex with someone you loved, human beings could achieve transcendence, and defeat the sinfulness in their own nature. He wrote:

> Now by what means does man deliver himself from this state of disunion between himself and the perfect being, from the painful consciousness of sin, from the distracting sense of his own nothingness? How does he blunt the fatal sting of sin? Only by this; that he is conscious of love as the highest, the absolute power and truth, that he regards the Divine Being not only as a law, as a moral being of the understanding; but also as a loving tender even subjective human being (that is, having sympathy even with the individual man.)[14]

Mary Anne and Lewes fell in love over ideas. In the years before they met they had been drawn to the same writers, often at the same time. They composed essays on overlapping subjects. They both took the search for truth with the same earnest intensity, and both subscribed to the idea that human love and sympathy could serve as the basis for their own morality as a substitute for a Christianity they could not actually believe in.

Intellectual Love

WE DON'T HAVE ACCESS TO THE EXACT SCENE IN WHICH THEIR HEARTS BE-
came inflamed with each other, but we do have access to the process
by which similar sorts of people fell in love, and they give one the
flavor of what Mary Anne and Lewes must have felt. One famous passion of this sort occurred between the British philosopher Isaiah Berlin and the Russian poet Anna Akhmatova. Their meeting of the
minds took on a special drama, because it happened all in one night.

The scene took place in Leningrad in 1945. Twenty years older than
Berlin, Akhmatova had been a great prerevolutionary poet. Since 1925
the Soviets had allowed her to publish nothing. Her first husband had
been executed on false charges in 1921. In 1938, her son was taken prisoner. For seventeen months, Akhmatova had stood outside his prison,
vainly seeking news of him.

Berlin didn't know much about her, but he was visiting Leningrad
and a friend offered to make an introduction. Berlin was taken to her
apartment and met a woman still beautiful and powerful, but wounded
by tyranny and war. At first their conversation was restrained. They
talked about war experiences and British universities. Other visitors
came and went.

By midnight they were alone, sitting on opposite ends of her room.
She told him about her girlhood and marriage and her husband's ex-
ecution. She began to recite Byron's *Don Juan* with such passion that
Berlin turned his face to the window to hide his emotion. She began
reciting some of her own poems, breaking down as she described how
they had led the Soviets to execute one of her colleagues.

By four in the morning they were talking about the greats. They
agreed about Pushkin and Chekhov. Berlin liked the light intelligence
of Turgenev, while Akhmatova preferred the dark intensity of Dostoyevsky.

Deeper and deeper they went, baring their souls. Akhmatova confessed her loneliness, expressed her passions, spoke about literature
and art. Berlin had to go to the bathroom but didn't dare break the
spell. They had read all the same things, knew what the other knew,
understood each other's longings. That night, his biographer Michael
Ignatieff writes, Berlin's life "came as close as it ever did to the still

perfection of art." He finally pulled himself away and returned to his hotel. It was eleven o'clock in the morning. He flung himself on the bed and exclaimed, "I am in love, I am in love."[15]

The night Berlin and Akhmatova spent together stands as the beau ideal of a certain sort of communication. It's communication between people who think that the knowledge most worth attending to is found not in data but in the great works of culture, in humanity's inherited storehouse of moral, emotional, and existential wisdom. It's a communication in which intellectual compatibility turns into emotional fusion. Berlin and Akhmatova could experience that sort of life-altering conversation because they had done the reading. They believed you have to grapple with the big ideas and the big books that teach you how to experience life in all its richness and how to make subtle moral and emotional judgments. They were spiritually ambitious. They had the common language of literature written by geniuses who understand us better than we understand ourselves.

The night also stands as the beau ideal of a certain sort of bond. This sort of love depends on so many coincidences that it happens only once or twice in a lifetime, if ever. Berlin and Akhmatova felt all the pieces fitting amazingly into place. They were the same in many ways. There was such harmony that all the inner defenses fell down in one night.

If you read the poems Akhmatova wrote about that night, you get the impression that they slept together, but according to Ignatieff, they barely touched. Their communion was primarily intellectual, emotional, and spiritual, creating a combination of friendship and love. If friends famously confront the world side by side and lovers live face to face, Berlin and Akhmatova seemed somehow to embody both postures at once. They shared and also augmented each other's understanding.

For Berlin this night was the most important event of his life. Akhmatova was stuck in the Soviet Union, suffering under a regime of manipulation, fear, and lies. The regime decided that she had consorted with a British spy. She was expelled from the Writers' Union. Her son was in prison. She was desolated but remained grateful for Berlin's visit, speaking of him fervently and writing movingly about the numinous magic of that night.

The love Eliot felt for Lewes had some of that intellectual and emotional intensity. They, too, experienced love as a moral force that deepens a person, organizing human minds around other souls and lifting them so they are capable of great acts of service and devotion.

And indeed, if we look at love in its most passionate phase, we see that love often does several key things to reorient the soul. The first thing it does is humble us. It reminds us that we are not even in control of ourselves. In most cultures and civilizations, love is described in myth and story as an external force—a god or a demon—that comes in and colonizes a person, refashioning everything inside. It is Aphrodite or Cupid. Love is described as a delicious madness, a raging fire, a heavenly frenzy. We don't build love; we *fall* in love, out of control. It is both primordial and also something distinctly our own, thrilling and terrifying, this galvanic force that we cannot plan, schedule, or determine.

Love is like an invading army that reminds you that you are not master of your own house. It conquers you little by little, reorganizing your energy levels, reorganizing your sleep patterns, reorganizing your conversational topics, and, toward the end of the process, rearranging the objects of your sexual desire and even the focus of your attention. When you are in love, you can't stop thinking about your beloved. You walk through a crowd and think you see her in a vaguely familiar form every few yards. You flip from highs to lows and feel pain at slights that you know are probably trivial or illusory. Love is the strongest kind of army because it generates no resistance. When the invasion is only half complete, the person being invaded longs to be defeated, fearfully, but utterly and hopelessly.

Love is a surrender. You expose your deepest vulnerabilities and give up your illusions of self-mastery. This vulnerability and the desire for support can manifest itself in small ways. Eliot once wrote, "There is something strangely winning to most women in that offer of the firm arm; the help is not wanted physically at the moment, but the sense of help, the presence of strength that is outside them and yet theirs, meets a continual want of imagination."

Love depends on the willingness of each person to be vulnerable and it deepens that vulnerability. It works because each person exposes their nakedness and the other rushes to meet it. "You will be loved the day when you will be able to show your weakness without the person using it to assert his strength," the Italian novelist Cesar Pavese wrote.

Next, love decenters the self. Love leads you out of your natural state of self-love. Love makes other people more vivid to you than you are to yourself.

The person in love may think she is seeking personal happiness, but that's an illusion. She is really seeking fusion with another, and when fusion contradicts happiness, she will probably choose fusion. If the shallow person lives in the smallness of his own ego, a person in love finds that the ultimate riches are not inside, they are out there, in the beloved and in the sharing of a destiny with the beloved. A successful marriage is a fifty-year conversation getting ever closer to that melding of mind and heart. Love expresses itself in shared smiles and shared tears and ends with the statement, "Love you? I am you."

Many observers have noticed that love eliminates the distinction between giving and receiving. Since the selves of the two lovers are intermingled, scrambled, and fused, it feels more delicious to give to the beloved than to receive. Montaigne writes that the person in love who receives a gift is actually giving her lover the ultimate gift: the chance to experience the joy of giving to her. It doesn't make sense to say that a lover is generous or altruistic, because a lover in the frenzy of love who gives to her beloved is giving to a piece of herself.

In his famous essay on friendship, Montaigne described how a deep friendship or a love can rearrange the boundaries of self:

> Such a friendship has no model but itself, and can only be compared to itself. It was not one special consideration, nor two, nor three, nor four, nor a thousand; it was some mysterious quintessence of all this mixture which possessed itself of my will, and led it to plunge and lose itself in his, which possessed itself of his whole will, and led it, with a similar hunger and a like impulse, to plunge and lose itself in mine. I may truly say lose, for it left us with nothing that was our own, nothing that was either his or mine.

Next, love infuses people with a poetic temperament. Adam I wants to live according to a utilitarian calculus—to maximize pleasant experiences, to guard against pain and vulnerability, to maintain control. Adam I wants you to go through life as a self-contained unit, coolly weighing risks and rewards and looking out for your own interests.

Adam I is strategizing and calculating costs and benefits. He wants you to keep the world at arm's length. But to be in love is to lose your mind a bit, to be elevated by magical thinking.

To be in love is to experience hundreds of small successive feelings that you never quite experienced in that way before, as if another half of life has been opened up to you for the first time: a frenzy of admiration, hope, doubt, possibility, fear, ecstasy, jealousy, hurt, and so on and so on.

Love is submission, not decision. Love demands that you make a poetic surrender to an inexplicable power without counting the cost. Love asks you to discard conditional thinking and to pour out your love in full force and not measure it by tablespoons. It crystallizes your vision so that, as Stendhal put it, your beloved shimmers like a sparkling jewel. To you she possesses magic that others don't see. To you the historic spots where love first bloomed take on a sacred meaning that others can't perceive. The dates on the calendar when the crucial first kisses and words were exchanged assume the aura of holy days. The emotions you feel cannot quite be captured in prose, but only in music and poetry, looks and touches. The words you exchange are so silly and overwrought that they have to be kept private. They would sound insane if they were bandied about with your friends in the daylight world.

You don't fall in love with the person who might be of most use to you—not the richest, most popular, most well-connected person, not the one with the best career prospects. Adam II falls for the distinct person, for no other reason than some inner harmony, inspiration, joy, and uplift, because he is he and she is she. Moreover, love doesn't seek the efficient path, the sure thing; for some perverse reason, love feeds on roadblocks and is not usually won by prudence. You might have tried to warn two people in love that they should be wary of marrying because their union will not be a happy one. But lovers caught up in magical thinking don't see what others see, and they probably wouldn't change their course even if they could because they would rather be unhappy together than happy apart. They are in love, not buying a stock, and the poetic temperament—part thinking, part brilliant emotion—guides their decisions. Love is a state of poetic need; it exists on both a higher and a lower plane than logic and calculation.

In this way, love opens up the facility for spiritual awareness. It is an altered state of consciousness that is intense and overwhelming but at the same time effervescent. In that state, many people are likely to have mystical moments when they feel an awareness of some wordless mystery beyond the human plane. Their love gives them little glimmerings of pure love, love detached from this or that particular person but emanating from some transcendent realm. These sensations come in fleeting moments. They are intense and effervescent mystical experiences, glimpses into an infinity beyond what can be known for sure.

In his masterpiece, *My Bright Abyss,* the poet Christian Wiman writes,

> In any true love—a mother's for her child, a husband's for his wife, a friend's for a friend—there is an excess energy that always wants to be in motion. Moreover, it seems to move not simply from one person to another but through them toward something else. ("All I know now / is the more he loved me the more I loved the world"—Spencer Reece.) That is why we can be so baffled and overwhelmed by such love (and I don't mean merely when we fall in love; in fact, I'm talking more of other, more durable relationships): it wants to be more than it is; it cries out inside of us to make it more than it is."[16]

For many people, religious and nonreligious, love provides a glimpse of some realm beyond the edge of what we know. It also in a more practical sense enlarges the heart. This act of yearning somehow makes the heart more open and more free. Love is like a plow that opens up hard ground and allows things to grow. It cracks open the crust that Adam I depends on and exposes the soft fertile soil of Adam II. We notice this phenomenon all the time: one love leads to another, one love magnifies the capacity for another.

Self-control is like a muscle. If you are called upon to exercise self-control often in the course of a day, you get tired and you don't have enough strength to exercise as much self-control in the evening. But love is the opposite. The more you love, the more you can love. A person who has one child does not love that child less when the second and third child come along. A person who loves his town does not love his country less. Love expands with use.

In this way love softens. We all know people who were brittle and armored up for life before they fell in love. But in the midst of that sweet and vulnerable state of motivation their manner changed. Behind their back we tell each other that they are aglow with love. The lobster shell has been peeled away, exposing flesh. This has made them more frightened, and more open to damage, but also kinder, more capable of living life as an offering. Shakespeare, the inevitable authority on this subject, wrote, "The more I give to thee / The more I have, for both are infinite."[17]

And so, finally, love impels people to service. If love starts with a downward motion, burrowing into the vulnerability of self, exposing nakedness, it ends with an active upward motion. It arouses great energy and desire to serve. The person in love is buying little presents, fetching the glass from the next room, bringing a tissue when there's flu, driving through traffic to pick the beloved up at the airport. Love is waking up night after night to breastfeed, living year after year to nurture. It is risking and sacrificing your life for your buddy's in a battle. Love ennobles and transforms. In no other state do people so often live as we want them to live. In no other commitment are people so likely to slip beyond the logic of self-interest and unconditional commitments that manifest themselves in daily acts of care.

Occasionally you meet someone with a thousand-year heart. The person with the thousand-year heart has made the most of the passionate, tumultuous phase of love. Those months or years of passion have engraved a deep commitment in their mind. The person or thing they once loved hotly they now love warmly but steadily, happily, unshakably. They don't even think of loving their beloved because they want something back. They just naturally offer love as a matter of course. It is gift-love, not reciprocity-love.

This is the kind of love that George Lewes had for Mary Anne Evans. They were both transformed and ennobled by their love for each other, but Lewes's was in many ways the greater and more ennobling transformation. He celebrated her superior talent. He encouraged, elicited, and nurtured it. With a thousand letters and gestures, he put himself second and her uppermost in his mind.

The Decision

THE DECISION TO BE TOGETHER WAS A PROFOUND AND LIFE-ALTERING one. Even though he and his wife were living in separate households and Agnes was bearing children by another man, Lewes was officially a married man. If Eliot and Lewes became a couple they would be committing brazen adultery in the eyes of the world. Polite society would be closed to them. Family would cut them off. They would be outcasts, especially Eliot. As Eliot's biographer Frederick R. Karl puts it, "The men who kept mistresses were called philanderers, but the women who were kept were called whores."[18]

And yet by the winter of 1852–53, Eliot seems to have recognized that Lewes was her soul mate. During the spring of 1853 they began to contemplate breaking with society to be with each other. In April, Lewes collapsed with dizziness, headaches, and ringing in the ears. Eliot spent these months translating Feuerbach. He argued that in its true definition, a marriage is not fundamentally a legal arrangement, it is a moral arrangement, and reading his thoughts on the subject would have helped Eliot conclude that the love she and Lewes shared was a truer and higher thing than the arrangement he had with his legal and separated wife.

Ultimately she had to make a decision about what sort of ties meant the most to her, and she decided that love must triumph over social connections. As she later wrote, "Light and easily broken ties are what I neither desire theoretically nor could live for practically. Women who are satisfied with such ties do not act as I have done."

With her genius for judging character, Eliot decided to put her faith in Lewes, even though at this point he had not fully committed himself to her. As she put it in a letter, "I have counted the cost of the step that I have taken and am prepared to bear, without irritation or bitterness, renunciation by all my friends. I am not mistaken in the person to whom I have attached myself. He is worthy of the sacrifice I have incurred, and my only anxiety is that he should be rightly judged."

All love is narrowing. It is the renunciation of other possibilities for the sake of one choice. In a 2008 wedding toast to Cass Sunstein and Samantha Power, Leon Wieseltier put it about as well as possible:

Brides and grooms are people who have discovered, by means of love, the local nature of happiness. Love is a revolution in scale, a revision of magnitudes; it is private and it is particular; its object is the specificity of this man and that woman, the distinctness of this spirit and that flesh. Love prefers deep to wide, and here to there; the grasp to the reach. . . . Love is, or should be, indifferent to history, immune to it—a soft and sturdy haven from it: when the day is done, and the lights are out, and there is only this other heart, this other mind, this other face, to assist in repelling one's demons or in greeting one's angels, it does not matter who the president is. When one consents to marry, one consents to be truly known, which is an ominous prospect; and so one bets on love to correct for the ordinariness of the impression, and to call forth the forgiveness that is invariably required by an accurate perception of oneself. Marriages are exposures. We may be heroes to our spouses but we may not be idols.

Eliot's mind at that juncture seems to have been in a state of convulsive change. She was aware that her life was about to take an irreversible new form. She seems to have concluded that her life up to this moment had been based on a series of faulty choices and it was time to bet all on one true choice. She took the leap W. H. Auden described in his famous poem "Leap Before You Look":

> The sense of danger must not disappear:
> The way is certainly both short and steep,
> However gradual it looks from here;
> Look if you like, but you will have to leap.
>
> Tough-minded men get mushy in their sleep
> And break the by-laws any fool can keep;
> It is not the convention but the fear
> That has a tendency to disappear. . . .
>
> The clothes that are considered right to wear
> Will not be either sensible or cheap,
> So long as we consent to live like sheep
> And never mention those who disappear. . . .

A solitude ten thousand fathoms deep
Sustains the bed on which we lie, my dear:
Although I love you, you will have to leap;
Our dream of safety has to disappear.

On July 20, 1854, Eliot went to a dock near the Tower of London and boarded a ship, the *Ravensbourne,* bound for Antwerp. She and Lewes would begin their life together abroad. She wrote some letters to a few friends informing them of her choice, trying to soften the blow. They considered this journey together something of a trial cohabitation, but in reality they were about to begin the rest of their lives. For both, it was an amazing act of courage, and an amazing commitment to mutual love.

Life Together

THEY CHOSE WELL. THE CHOICE OF EACH REDEEMED BOTH OF THEIR LIVES. They traveled around Europe together, mostly in Germany, where they were welcomed by the leading writers and intellectuals of the day. Mary Anne loved living openly as Mrs. Lewes: "I am happier every day and find my domesticity more and more delightful and beneficial to me."[19]

Back in London, however, their relationship unleashed a storm of vituperation that would define Eliot's social life forever after. Some people took pleasure in thinking the worst of her, calling her a husband stealer, a homewrecker, and a sex maniac. Others understood that Lewes was effectively unmarried, understood the love that drew them together, but still could not sanction this relationship because it might loosen morals for others. One former acquaintance, who had conducted a phrenological examination of Eliot's head, declared, "We are deeply mortified and distressed; and I should like to know whether there is insanity in Miss Evans' family; for her conduct, with her brain, seems to me like a morbid mental aberration."[20]

Eliot was unwavering in her choice. She insisted on being known as Mrs. Lewes because even though her decision to be with Lewes had been an act of rebellion, she believed in the form and institution of traditional marriage. Circumstances had compelled her to do something extreme, but morally and philosophically she believed in the conventional path. They lived as traditional husband and wife. And they complemented each other. She could be gloomy, but he was a bright and funny social presence. They took walks together. They worked together. They read books together. They were exclusive, ardent, self-composed and self-completing. "What greater thing is there for two human souls," Eliot would later write in *Adam Bede,* "than to feel they are joined for life—to strengthen each other in all labor, to rest on each other in all sorrow, to minister to each other in all pain, to be one with each other in silent unspeakable memories at the moment of last parting."

Her bond with Lewes cost her many friendships. Her family renounced her, most painfully her brother, Isaac. But the scandal was also productive in furnishing them with deeper insights into themselves and the world. They were forever on edge, looking for signs of insult or affirmation. Because they were cutting against the grain of social convention, they had to pay extra attention to what they were doing, to exercise special care. The shock of public hostility served as a stimulant. It made them acutely conscious of how society functioned.

Eliot had always been a sensitive observer of other people's emotional lives. She had always devoured books, ideas, and people. People had always found her scarily perceptive—as if she was some sort of witch with magical powers. But now there was something more orderly about her thought processes. In the months after her scandalous departure with Lewes, she seems to have finally come to terms with her exceptional gifts. Everything was hardening into a distinct worldview, a settled way of seeing the world. Maybe it is simply that she could finally approach the world with a sense of self-confidence. After all her flailing about in life, Eliot had finally gotten the big thing right. She had taken a chance on Lewes. She had paid a fearsome price. She had endured a baptism of fire. But she was able slowly to come out the other side. The prize of a fulfilling love was worth the cost. As she put it in *Adam Bede,* "Doubtless a great anguish may do the work of years, and we may come out from that baptism of fire with a soul full of new awe and new pity."

Novelist

LEWES HAD LONG ENCOURAGED ELIOT TO WRITE FICTION. HE WASN'T SURE she could come up with plots, but he knew she had a genius for description and characterization. Plus, fiction paid better than non-fiction, and the Lewes family was always hard up for cash. He urged her to just try her hand: "You must try to write a story." One morning in September 1856, she was fantasizing about writing fiction when a title popped into her head: *The Sad Fortunes of the Reverend Amos Barton*. Lewes was immediately enthusiastic. "Oh what a capital title!" he blurted.

A week later she read to him the first part of what she had written. He knew immediately that Eliot was a gifted writer. Eliot wrote in her journal, "We both cried over it, and then he came up to me and kissed me, saying, 'I think your pathos is better than your fun.'" They both realized that Mary Anne would be a successful novelist. She would be George Eliot, the name she took to hide (for a time) her scandalous identity. The skill that he doubted most—whether she could write dialogue—was actually the area where her talent was most obvious. Lewes still wondered if she could create action and movement in her tales, but he knew she had all the other tools.

Before long he was her consultant, agent, editor, publicist, psychotherapist, and general counselor. He understood quickly that her talent was vastly above his own, and he seems to have felt nothing but selfless delight in the way she was bound to overshadow him.

By 1861, her brief diary entries make it clear how intimately involved Lewes was in the development of her plots: She would write during the day and then read what she had written to Lewes. Judging by her letters and diary entries over the years, he was an encouraging audience: "I read the . . . opening scenes of my novel, and he expressed great delight in them. . . . After this record I read aloud what I had written of Part IX to George and he, to my surprise, entirely approved of it. . . . When I read aloud my manuscript to my dear, dear husband, he laughed and cried alternately and then rushed to me to kiss me. He is the prime blessing that has made all the rest possible to me, given me a response to everything I have written."

Lewes shopped her novels around, negotiating with different

editors. In the early years, he lied about who the true author of the George Eliot novels was, claiming it was a clergyman friend who wished to remain anonymous. After the truth got out, he protected his wife from criticism. Even after she was celebrated as one of the greatest writers of her day, he would get to the newspapers first and cut out and discard any article that might mention her with anything but the most fulsome praise. Lewes's rule was simple: "Never tell her anything that other people say about her books, for good or evil. . . . Let her mind be as much as possible fixed on her art and not the public."

Arduous Happiness

GEORGE AND MARY ANNE CONTINUED TO SUFFER FROM ILLNESSES AND bouts of depression, but they were generally happy together. The letters and diary entries they wrote during their years together bubble forth with assertions of joy and love. In 1859, Lewes wrote to a friend, "I owe Spencer another and deeper debt. It was through him that I learned to know Marian—to know her was to love her—and since then my life has been a new birth. To her I owe all my prosperity and my happiness. God bless her!"

Six years later Eliot wrote, "In each other we are happier than ever. I am more grateful to my dear husband for his perfect love, which helps me in all good and checks me in all evil—more conscious that in him I have the greatest of blessings."

Her masterpiece, *Middlemarch,* is mostly about unsuccessful marriages, but there are glimpses in her books of happy marriages, and marital friendship, such as she enjoyed. "I should never like scolding any one else so well; and that is a point to be thought of in a husband," one of her characters declares. She wrote in a letter to a friend, "I am happier every day, and find my domesticity more and more delightful and beneficial to me. Affection, respect and intellectual sympathy deepen, and for the first time in my life I can say to the moments, 'Let them last, they are so beautiful.'"

Eliot and Lewes were happy, but they were not content. In the first place, life did not cease happening. One of Lewes's sons from his earlier marriage came to them, terminally ill, and they nursed him until his death. Their frequent periods of ill health and depression were marked by migraines and dizzy spells. But through it all, they were impelled by their own need to cultivate themselves morally, to be deeper and wiser. Capturing this mixture of joy and ambition, Eliot wrote in 1857, "I am very happy—happy in the highest blessing life can give us, the perfect love and sympathy of a nature that stimulates my own healthy activity. I feel, too, that all the terrible pain I have gone through in past years, partly from the defects of my own nature, partly from outward things, has probably been a preparation for some special work that I may do before I die. That is a blessed hope, to be rejoiced in with trembling."

Eliot would write, "Adventure is not outside man; it is within."

As she aged, her affections grew stronger and were less perturbed by the egoism of youth. Writing for her remained an agonizing process. She fell into fits of anxiety and depression with each book. She despaired. Recovered hope. Then despaired again. Her genius as a writer derives from the fact that she was capable of the deepest feeling but also of the most discerning and disciplined thought. She had to feel and suffer through everything. She had to transform that feeling into meticulously thought-through observation. The books had to be pushed out of her like children, painfully and amid exhaustion. Like most people who write, she had to endure the basic imbalance of the enterprise. The writer shares that which is intimate and vulnerable, but the reader is far away, so all that comes back is silence.

She had no system. She was antisystem. As she wrote in *The Mill on the Floss,* she despised "men of maxims," because the "complexity of our life is not to be embraced by maxims, and that to lace ourselves up in formulas of that sort is to repress all the divine promptings and inspirations that spring from growing insight and sympathy."

She didn't use her books to set forth an argument or make points so much as to create a world that readers could dip into at different times of life and derive different lessons each time. Rebecca Mead writes, "I think *Middlemarch* has disciplined my character. I know it has become part of my own experience and my own endurance. *Middlemarch* inspired me when I was young, and chafing to leave home; and now, in middle life, it suggests to me what else home might mean, beyond a place to grow up and grow out of."[21]

Eliot creates her own interior landscape. She was a realist. She was not concerned with the lofty and the heroic. She wrote about the workaday world. Her characters tend to err when they reject the grubby and complex circumstances of everyday life for abstract and radical notions. They thrive when they work within the rooted spot, the concrete habit, the particular reality of their town and family. Eliot herself believed that the beginning of wisdom was the faithful and attentive study of present reality, a thing itself, a person herself, unfiltered by abstract ideas, mists of feeling, leaps of imagination, or religious withdrawals into another realm.

In her early novel *Adam Bede,* she writes, "There are few prophets in the world; few sublimely beautiful women; few heroes. I can't afford to give all my love and reverence to such rarities: I want a great deal of those feelings for my every-day fellow-men, especially for the few in the foreground of the great multitude, whose faces I know, whose hands I touch, for whom I have to make way with kindly courtesy."

She ended her later and perhaps greatest novel, *Middlemarch,* with a flourish celebrating those who lead humble lives: "But the effect of her being on those around her was incalculably diffusive: for the growing good of the world is partly dependent on unhistoric acts; and that things are not so ill with you and me as they might have been, is half owing to the number who live faithfully a hidden life, and rest in unvisited tombs."

Sympathy lay at the heart of Eliot's moral vision. After a self-absorbed adolescence, she went on to develop an amazing capacity to enter the minds of others and observe them from different points of view and with sympathetic understanding. As she put it in *Middlemarch,* "There is no general doctrine which is not capable of eating out our morality if unchecked by a deep-seated habit of direct fellow-feeling with individual fellow-men."

She became, as she aged, an attentive listener. Because she registered other people with such emotional intensity, the facts and feelings of their lives lodged in her memory. She was one of those people on whom nothing is lost. Even though she was herself in a happy marriage, she wrote her greatest book about a series of unhappy marriages, and could describe them from the inside with concrete intensity.

"Every limit is a beginning as well as an ending," she writes in

Middlemarch. She sympathizes with even her least sympathetic characters, such as Edward Casaubon, the dreary, narcissistic pedant whose talent isn't as great as he thinks it is and who slowly comes to realize this fact. Under her perceptive pen, the inability to sympathize and the inability to communicate, especially within families, is revealed as the great moral poison in many of her stories.

The Inner Adventure

ELIOT WAS A MELIORIST. SHE DID NOT BELIEVE IN BIG TRANSFORMATIONAL change. She believed in the slow, steady, concrete march to make each day slightly better than the last. Character development, like historic progress, best happens imperceptibly, through daily effort.

Her books were aimed to have a slow and steady effect on the internal life of her readers, to enlarge their sympathies, to refine their ability to understand other people, to give them slightly wider experiences. In that sense her father, and the humble ideal he represented, lived in her all her life. In *Adam Bede,* she celebrated the local man:

> They make their way upward, rarely as geniuses, most commonly as painstaking, honest men, with the skill and conscience to do well the tasks that lie before them. Their lives have no discernible echo beyond the neighborhood where they dwelt, but you are almost sure to find some good piece of road, some building, some application of mineral produce, some improvement in farming practice, some reform of parish abuses, which their names are associated by one or two generations after them.

Many of her characters, and especially her magnetic character, Dorothea Brooke in *Middlemarch,* begin their adulthood with an ardent moral ambition. They want to achieve some great good, like a Saint Teresa, but they don't know what it is or what their vocation might be or just how to go about it. Their attention is fixed on some pure ideal, some distant horizon. Eliot was a Victorian; she believed in moral improvement. But she used her novels to critique such lofty and otherworldly moral goals. They are too abstract, and they can easily, as in Dorothea's case, be unrealistic and delusional. The best moral reform, she counters, is tied to the here and now, directed by honest feelings for this or that individual rather than for humanity as a whole. There's power in the particular and suspicion of the general. For Eliot, holiness isn't in the next world but is embedded in a mundane thing like a marriage, which ties one down but gives one concrete and daily opportunities for self-sacrifice and service. Holiness is inspired by work, the daily task of doing some job well. She takes moral imagination—the sense of duty, the need to serve, the ardent desire to quell selfishness—and she concretizes it and makes it useful.

There are limits, she teaches, in how much we can change other people or how quickly we can change ourselves. So much of life is lived in a state of tolerance—tolerating other people's weaknesses and our own sins, even as we try to have some slow, loving effect. "These fellow mortals, every one," she wrote in *Adam Bede,* "must be accepted as they are: you can neither straighten their noses nor brighten their wit nor rectify their dispositions; and it is these people—amongst whom your life is passed—that it is needful you should tolerate, pity, and love: it is these more or less ugly, stupid, inconsistent people whose movement of goodness you should be able to admire—for whom you should cherish all possible hopes, all possible patience." This posture is at the essence of her morality. It is easy to say but hard to enact. She sought to be tolerant and accepting, but also rigorous, earnest, and demanding. She loved but she also judged.

The word most associated with Eliot's work is "maturity." Hers is, as Virginia Woolf said, literature for grown-ups—seeing life from a perspective both more elevated and more immediate, both wiser and more generous. "People glorify all sorts of bravery except the bravery they might show on behalf of their nearest neighbor," she wrote—a mature sentiment if ever there was one.[22]

A woman named Bessie Rayner Parkes met Eliot when she was still a young woman. She wrote later to a friend saying that she didn't yet know if she would come to like this creature, still known then as Mary Anne Evans. "Whether you or I should ever love her, as a friend, I don't know at all. There is as yet no high moral purpose in the impression she makes, and it is that alone which commands love. I think she will alter. Large angels take a long time unfolding their wings, but when they do, soar out of sight. Miss Evans either has no wings, or which I think is the case, they are coming budding."[23]

Mary Anne Evans took a long road to become George Eliot. She had to grow out of self-centeredness into generous sympathy. But it was a satisfying maturation. She never overcame her fits of depression and her anxieties about the quality of her own writing, but she could think and feel her way into other people's minds and hearts to exercise what she called "the responsibility of tolerance." From disgrace she rose, by the end of her life, to be celebrated as a large angel.

The crucial event in that long journey was her love for George Lewes, which stabilized, lifted, and deepened her. The fruits of their love are embodied in the inscriptions she put in each of her works:

Adam Bede (1859): To my dear husband, George Henry Lewes, I give the MS of a work which would never have been written but for the happiness which his love has conferred on my life.

The Mill on the Floss (1860): To my beloved husband, George Henry Lewes, I give this MS of my third book, written in the sixth year of our life together.

Romola (1863): To the Husband whose perfect love has been the best source of her insight and strength, this manuscript is given by his devoted wife, the writer.

Felix Holt (1866): From George Eliot to her dear Husband, this thirteenth year of their united life, in which the deepening sense of her own imperfectness has the consolation of their deepening love.

The Spanish Gypsy (1868): To my dear—every day dearer—Husband.

Middlemarch (1872): To my dear Husband, George Henry Lewes, in this nineteenth year of our blessed union.

CHAPTER 8

ORDERED LOVE

AUGUSTINE WAS BORN IN THE YEAR 354 IN THE TOWN OF THAGASTE in what is now Algeria. He was born at the tail end of the Roman Empire, at a time when the empire was collapsing but still seemed eternal. His hometown was near the edge of that empire, two hundred miles from the coast, in a culture that was a messy mix of Roman paganism and fervent African Christianity. He lived, for the first half of his life, caught in the tension between his personal ambitions and his spiritual nature.

Augustine's father, Patricius, a minor town counselor and tax collector, headed a family that was somewhere in the upper end of the middle class. Patricius was materialistic and spiritually inert, and he hoped that his brilliant son would one day have the glittering career he had missed out on. One day he saw his pubescent son in the public baths and wounded Augustine with a lewd crack about his pubic hair or penis size or something. "He saw in me only hollow things," Augustine would write, dismissively.

Augustine's mother, Monica, has always riveted the attention of historians—and psychoanalysts. On the one hand, she was an earthy, unlettered woman, raised in a church that was dismissed, at the time, as primitive. She devoutly attended services each morning, ate meals on the tombs of the dead, and consulted her dreams as omens and guides. On the other hand, she had a strength of personality, and a relentlessness in her convictions about her views, that makes your jaw drop. She was a force in the community, a peacemaker, above gossip, formidable, and dignified. She was capable, as the magnificent biographer Peter Brown notes, of dismissing the unworthy with biting sarcasm.[1]

Monica ran the household. She corrected her husband's errors, waited out and rebuked his infidelities. Her love for her son, and her hunger to run his life, were voracious and at times greedy and unspiritual. Much more than most mothers, Augustine admitted, she longed to have him by her side and under her dominion. She warned him away from other women who might snare him into marriage. She organized her adult life around the care of his soul, doting on him when he tended toward her version of Christianity, weeping and exploding in a delirium of rage when he deviated. When Augustine joined a philosophic sect she disapproved of, she banished him from her presence.

At twenty-eight, when Augustine was already a successful adult, he had to trick her so he could get on a boat to leave Africa. He told her that he was going to the harbor to see a friend off and then slipped aboard a vessel with his mistress and son. As he sailed away, he saw her weeping and gesticulating on the shore, consumed, as he put it, by "a frenzy of grief." She followed him to Europe, of course, prayed for him, got rid of his mistress, and set up an arranged marriage with a ten-year-old heiress that she hoped would force Augustine to receive the rites of baptism.

Augustine understood the possessive nature of her love, but he could not dismiss her. He was a sensitive boy, terrified of her disapproval, but even in adulthood he was proud of her spirit and commonsense wisdom. He was delighted when he found she could keep conversational pace with scholars and philosophers. He understood that she suffered for him even more than he suffered for himself, or more than she could suffer for herself. "I have no words to express the love she had for me; and how much more anguish she was now suffering during the pangs of birth for my spiritual state than when she had given birth to me physically."[2] Through it all, she would love him fiercely and stalk his soul. For all her overbearing harshness, some of the sweetest moments of Augustine's life were moments of reconciliation and spiritual communion with his mother.

Ambition

AUGUSTINE WAS A SICKLY CHILD WHO GREW SERIOUSLY ILL WITH CHEST pains at seven and looked prematurely old in middle age. As a schoolboy, he was brilliant and sensitive, but uncooperative. He was bored by the curriculum and detested the beatings that were a constant feature of school discipline. When possible, he skipped school to see the pagan bear fights and cockfights that were put on in the town arena.

Even as a young boy, Augustine was caught between the competing ideals of the classical world and the Judeo-Christian world. As Matthew Arnold writes in *Culture and Anarchy,* the primary idea of Hellenism is spontaneity of consciousness, while the governing idea of what he calls Hebraism is strictness of conscience.

That is to say, a person in a Hellenistic frame of mind wants to see things as they really are and explore the excellence and good she finds in the world. A person in this frame of mind approaches the world in a spirit of flexibility and playfulness. "To get rid of one's ignorance, to see things as they are, and by seeing them as they are to see them in their beauty, is the simple and attractive ideal which Hellenism holds out before human nature."[3] The Hellenistic mind has an "aerial ease, clearness and radiancy." It is filled with "sweetness and light."

Hebraism, by contrast, "seizes upon certain plain, capital intimations of the universal order, and rivets itself, one may say, with unequalled grandeur of earnestness and intensity on the study and observance of them."[4] So while the person in a Hellenistic frame of mind is afraid of missing any part of life and is really directing her own life, the person in a Hebraic frame of mind is focusing on the higher truth and is loyal to an immortal order: "Self-conquest, self-devotion, the following not of our own individual will, but the will of God, obedience, is the fundamental idea of this form."[5]

The person in the Hebraic frame of mind, unlike the Hellenist, is not at ease in this world. She is conscious of sin, the forces in herself that impede the passage to perfection. As Arnold puts it, "To a world stricken with moral enervation, Christianity offered the spectacle of an inspired self-sacrifice; to men who refused themselves nothing, it shows one who refused himself everything."[6]

Augustine lived nominally under the rule of the semidivine emperors, who had by then become remote, awe-inspiring figures and were celebrated by courtly sycophants as "Ever-Victorious" and "Restorers of the World."[7] He was taught the philosophy of the Stoics, with their ideal lives of calm, emotion-suppressing self-sufficiency. He memorized Virgil and Cicero. "My ears were inflamed for Pagan myths, and the more they were scratched the more they itched," he would later recall.[8]

By the time he hit his teenage years, Augustine seems to have established himself as something of a golden boy. "I was called a promising lad," he recalled. He attracted the attention of a local grandee, Romanianus, who agreed to sponsor the young man's education and send him away to centers of learning. Augustine hungered for recognition and admiration and hoped to fulfill the classical dream of living forever in the mouths of posterity.

At seventeen, Augustine went to Carthage to continue his studies. In his spiritual memoir, the *Confessions,* he makes it sound as if he was consumed by lust. "I came to Carthage," he says of his student days, "where the cauldron of illicit loves leapt and boiled about me." Augustine's presence didn't exactly calm things down. He describes himself as a tumultuous young man, his blood boiling with passions, lusts, jealousies, and desires:

> I was not yet in love, but I was in love with love, and from the depths of my need, I hated myself. . . . What I needed most was to love and to be loved, but most of all when I obtained the enjoyment of the body of the person who loved me . . . I rushed headlong into love, eager to be caught. . . . Happily I wrapped those painful bonds around me, and sure enough I would be lashed with red-hot iron rods of jealousy, by suspicion and fear, by bursts of anger and quarrels.

Augustine was apparently history's most high-maintenance boyfriend. His language is precise. He is not in love with another human being, he is in love with the prospect of being loved. It's all about him. And in his memoir he describes how his disordered lusts fed on themselves. In book 8 of the *Confessions,* Augustine includes an almost clinical description of how his emotional neediness was an addiction:

I was bound not by an iron imposed by anyone else but by the iron of my own choice. The enemy had a grip on my will and so made a chain for me to hold me prisoner. The consequence of a distorted will is passion. By servitude to passion, habit is formed, and habit to which there is no resistance becomes necessity. By these links . . . connected one to another . . . a harsh bondage held me under constraint.

Augustine was forced to confront, in a very direct way, the fact that he was divided against himself. Part of him sought the shallow pleasures of the world. Part of him disapproved of these desires. His desires were out of harmony with his other faculties. He can imagine a purer way of living, but can't get there. He was restless, unaligned.

In this most fevered writing, Augustine makes it sound like he was some sort of sex-obsessed Caligula. And throughout the centuries many people have read the *Confessions* and concluded that Augustine was really just writing about sex. In fact, it's not exactly clear how wild Augustine really was. If you look at what he accomplished during these years, he seems to have been a studious and responsible young man. He excelled at university. He became a teacher in Carthage and rose up the ladder from one good job to the next. Then he moved to Rome and eventually got a job in Milan, the real center of power, at the court of the emperor Valentinian II. He had a common-law wife, conventional in that day, for about fifteen years. He had one child by this woman and did not cheat on her. He studied Plato and Cicero. His sins, such as they were, seem to have consisted mostly of going to the theater to see plays, and occasionally checking out the women he saw at church. All in all, he seems like a contemporary version of a successful young Ivy Leaguer, a sort of normal meritocrat of the late Roman Empire. In Adam I career terms, Augustine's life was something of a model of upward mobility.

As a young man, Augustine belonged to a strict philosophic sect called the Manichees. This was a little like joining the Communist Party in Russia at the start of the twentieth century. It was joining a group of smart, committed young people who believed they had come into possession of an all-explaining truth.

Manichaeans believed the world is divided into a Kingdom of Light and a Kingdom of Darkness. They believed there is an eternal conflict between all that is good and all that is evil, and that in the course of this conflict, bits of good get trapped within the darkness. Pure spirit can be trapped in mortal flesh.

As a logical system, Manichaeism has several advantages. God, who is on the side of pure good, is protected from the faintest suspicion that he is responsible for evil.[9] Manichaeism also helps excuse individuals from the evils they perform: it wasn't me, I am essentially good, it was the Kingdom of Darkness working through me. As Augustine put it, "It gave joy to my pride to be above guilt, and when I did an evil deed, not to confess that I myself had done it." Finally, once you accepted its premises, Manichaeism was a very rigorous logical system. Everything in the universe could be explained through neat rational steps.

The Manichaeans found it easy to feel superior to everyone else. Plus, they had fun together. Augustine would remember "conversation and laughter and mutual deferrings; shared readings of sweetly phrased books, facetious alternating with serious, heated arguing, to spice our general agreement with dissent; teaching and being taught by turns; the sadness at anyone's absence, and the joy of return."[10] They also practiced asceticism to purify themselves of evil matter. They were celibate and ate only certain foods. They avoided contact with the flesh as much as possible and were served by "hearers" (including Augustine) who did soiling chores for them.

Classical culture placed great emphasis on winning debates, on demonstrations of rhetorical prowess. Augustine, living a life more of head than heart, found he could use Manichaean arguments to easily win debates: "I always used to win more arguments than was good for me, debating with unskilled Christians who had tried to stand up for their faith in argument."[11]

Inner Chaos

ALL IN ALL, AUGUSTINE WAS LIVING THE ROMAN DREAM. BUT AUGUSTINE was unhappy. Inside he felt fragmented. His spiritual energies had nothing to attach to. They dissipated, evaporated. His Adam II life was a mess. "I was tossed to and fro," he writes in the *Confessions,* "I poured myself out, was made to flow away in all directions and boiled off."

At a phenomenally young age, he won the ultimate mark of success. He was given a chance to speak before the imperial court. He found that he was a mere peddler of empty words. He told lies and people loved him for it so long as the lies were well crafted. There was nothing in his life he could truly love, nothing that deserved the highest form of devotion: "I was famished within, deprived of inner food." His hunger for admiration enslaved him rather than delighting him. He was at the whim of other people's facile opinions, sensitive to the slightest criticism, always looking for the next rung on the golden ladder. This frantic pursuit of the glittering vices killed tranquillity.

Augustine's feeling of fragmentation has its modern corollary in the way many contemporary young people are plagued by a frantic fear of missing out. The world has provided them with a superabundance of neat things to do. Naturally, they hunger to seize every opportunity and taste every experience. They want to grab all the goodies in front of them. They want to say yes to every product in the grocery store. They are terrified of missing out on anything that looks exciting. But by not renouncing any of them they spread themselves thin. What's worse, they turn themselves into goodie seekers, greedy for every experience and exclusively focused on self. If you live in this way, you turn into a shrewd tactician, making a series of cautious semicommitments without really surrendering to some larger purpose. You lose the ability to say a hundred noes for the sake of one overwhelming and fulfilling yes.

Augustine found himself feeling increasingly isolated. If you organize your life around your own wants, other people become objects for the satisfaction of your own desires. Everything is coldly instrumental. Just as a prostitute is rendered into an object for the satisfaction of orgasm, so a professional colleague is rendered into an object for the purpose of career networking, a stranger is rendered into an object for the sake of making a sale, a spouse is turned into an object for the purpose of providing you with love.

We use the word "lust" to refer to sexual desire, but a broader, better meaning is selfish desire. A true lover delights to serve his beloved. But lust is all incoming. The person in lust has a void he needs filled by others. Because he is unwilling to actually serve others and build a full reciprocal relationship, he never fills the emotional emptiness inside. Lust begins with a void and ends with a void.

At one point Augustine called his fifteen-year relationship with his lower-class common-law wife "a mere bargain of lustful love." Still, their relationship could not have been entirely empty. It is hard to imagine a person who lived at Augustine's intense emotional register taking a fifteen-year intimate relationship lightly. He loved the child they had together. He indirectly celebrated his wife's steadfastness in a tract titled "What Is Good in Marriage." When Monica intervened and got rid of the woman so Augustine could marry a rich girl of an appropriate social class, he seems to have suffered: "She was an obstacle to my marriage, the woman I lived with for so long was torn out of my side. My heart, to which she had been grafted, was lacerated, wounded, shedding blood."

Augustine sacrificed this woman for his social standing. The unnamed woman was sent back to Africa without her son, where we are told she vowed to remain celibate the rest of her life. The person chosen to be Augustine's official wife was just ten years old, two years below the legal age of marriage, so Augustine took another concubine to satisfy his cravings in the interim. This is what he was doing in all phases of his life at this point: shedding sacrificial commitments in favor of status and success.

One day, while walking in Milan, he observed a beggar who had clearly just finished a good meal and had a few drinks. The man was joking and joyful. Augustine realized that though he himself toiled and worked all day, fraught with anxieties, the beggar, who did none of these things, was happier than he was. Maybe he was suffering because he was shooting for higher goals, he considered. No, not really, he was seeking the same earthly pleasures as that beggar, but he was finding none of them.

By his late twenties Augustine had become thoroughly alienated. Here he was living an arduous life and it was providing him with none of the nourishment he needed. He had desires that didn't lead to happiness and yet he still followed his desires. What on earth was going on?

Self-Knowledge

AUGUSTINE RESPONDED TO THIS CRISIS BY LOOKING WITHIN HIMSELF. You'd think that somebody who has become appalled by his own self-centeredness would immediately head in the direction of self-forgetfulness. His advice would be simple: ignore yourself, pay attention to other people. But Augustine's first step was to undertake an almost scientific expedition into his own mind. It is hard to think of another character in Western history up to that time who did such a thorough excavation of his own psyche.

Looking in, he saw a vast universe beyond his own control. He sees himself with a depth and complexity almost no one had observed before: "Who can map out the various forces at play in one soul, the different kinds of love. . . . Man is a great depth, O Lord; you number his hairs . . . but the hairs of his head are easier by far to count than his feelings, the movements of his heart." The vast internal world is dappled and ever-changing. He perceives the dance of small perceptions and senses great depths below the level of awareness.

Augustine was fascinated, for example, by memory. Sometimes painful memories pop into the mind unbidden. He was amazed by the mind's ability to transcend time and space. "Even while I dwell in darkness and silence, in my memory I can produce colors if I will. . . . Yea, I discern the breath of the lilies from violets, though smelling nothing. . . ."[12] The very scope of a person's memories amazed him:

> Great is the force of memory, excessive great, O my God; a large and boundless chamber; whoever sounded the bottom thereof? Yet is this a power of mine and belongs to my nature; nor do I myself comprehend all that I am. Therefore is the mind too straight to contain itself. And where should that be, which containeth not itself? Is it without it and not within? And how then does it not comprehend itself? A wonderful admiration surprises me, amazement seizes me upon this.

At least two great conclusions arose from this internal expedition. First, Augustine came to realize that though people are born with magnificent qualities, original sin had perverted their desires. Up until this point in his life Augustine had fervently desired certain things, like fame and status. These things didn't make him happy. And yet he kept on desiring them.

Left to ourselves, we often desire the wrong things. Whether it's around the dessert tray or in the late-night bar, we know we should choose one thing but end up choosing another. As the Bible says in Romans, "For the good that I would I do not: but the evil which I would not, that I do."

What sort of mysterious creature is a human being, Augustine mused, who can't carry out his own will, who knows his long-term interest but pursues short-term pleasure, who does so much to screw up his own life? This led to the conclusion that people are a problem to themselves. We should regard ourselves with distrust: "I greatly fear my hidden parts,"[13] he wrote.

Small and Petty Corruptions

IN THE *CONFESSIONS*, AUGUSTINE USED AN IDLE TEENAGE PRANK FROM HIS own past to illustrate this phenomenon. One boring evening when he was sixteen, Augustine was hanging out with his buddies and they decided to steal some pears from a nearby orchard. They didn't need the pears. They weren't hungry. They weren't particularly nice pears. They just stole them wantonly and threw them to some pigs for sport.

Looking back, Augustine was astounded by the pointlessness and the tawdriness of the act. "I lusted to thieve, and did it, compelled by no hunger, nor poverty, but through a cloyedness of well-doing, and pamperedness of iniquity. . . . It was foul, and I loved it; I loved to perish, I loved mine own fault, not that for which I was faulty, but my fault itself. Foul soul, falling from Thy firmament to utter destruction; not seeking aught through the shame, but the shame itself."

Casual readers of the *Confessions* have always wondered why Augustine got so worked up over a childhood prank. I used to think that the theft of the pears was a stand-in for some more heinous crime the teenage boys committed that night, like molesting a girl or some such thing. But for Augustine, the very small purposelessness of the crime is part of its rotten normality. We commit such small perversities all the time, as part of the complacent order of life.

His larger point is that the tropism toward wrong love, toward sin, is at the center of the human personality. People not only sin, we have a weird fascination with sin. If we hear that some celebrity has committed some outrageous scandal, we're kind of disappointed when it turns out the rumor isn't really true. If you leave sweet children to their own devices with nothing to do, before long they will find a way to get into trouble. (The British writer G. K. Chesterton once observed that the reality of sin can be seen on a lovely Sunday afternoon when bored and restless children start torturing the cat.)

Even sweet institutions, like camaraderie and friendship, can be distorted if they are unattached to a higher calling. The story of the stealing of the pears is also the story of a rotten friendship. Augustine realizes he probably wouldn't have done it if he had been alone. It was the desire for camaraderie, for mutual admiration, that egged the boys on into doing what they did. We so fear exclusion from the group that we are willing to do things that we would find unconscionable in other circumstances. When unattached to the right ends, communities can be more barbarous than individuals.

God's Presence

THE SECOND LARGE OBSERVATION THAT FLOWS FROM AUGUSTINE'S INTERnal excavation is that the human mind does not contain itself, but stretches out toward infinity. It's not only rottenness Augustine finds within, but also intimations of perfection, sensations of transcendence, emotions and thoughts and feelings that extend beyond the finite and into another realm. If you wanted to capture Augustine's attitude here, you might say that his thoughts enter and embrace the material world, but then fly up and surpass it.

As Reinhold Niebuhr put it, Augustine's study of memory led him to the "understanding that the human spirit in its depth and heights reaches into eternity and that this vertical dimension is more important for the understanding of man than merely his rational capacity for forming general concepts."[14]

The path inward leads upward. A person goes into himself but finds himself directed toward God's infinity. He senses the nature of God and his eternal creation even in his own mind, a small piece of creation. Centuries later, C. S. Lewis would make a related observation: "In deepest solitude there is a road right out of the self, a commerce with something which, by refusing to identify itself with any object of the senses, or anything whereof we have biological or social need, or anything imagined, or any state of our minds, proclaims itself purely objective." We are all formed within that eternal objective order. Our lives cannot be understood individually, abstracted from it. Sin—the desire to steal the pears—seems to flow from the past through human nature and each individual. At the same time, the longing for holiness, the striving upward, the desire to live a life of goodness and meaning, are also universal.

The result is that people can understand themselves only by looking at forces that transcend themselves. Human life points beyond itself. Augustine looks inside himself and makes contact with certain universal moral sentiments. He is simultaneously aware that he can conceive of perfection, but it is also far beyond his powers to attain. There must be a higher power, an eternal moral order.

As Niebuhr put it, "man is an individual but he is not self-sufficing. The law of his nature is love, a harmonious relation of life to life in obedience to the divine center and source of his life. This law is violated when man seeks to make himself the center and source of his own life."

Reform

AUGUSTINE BEGAN TO REFORM HIS LIFE. HIS FIRST STEP WAS TO QUIT THE Manichees. It no longer seemed true to him that the world was neatly divided into forces of pure good and pure evil. Instead, each virtue comes with its own vice—self-confidence with pride, honesty with brutality, courage with recklessness, and so on. The ethicist and theologian Lewis Smedes, expressing an Augustinian thought, describes the mottled nature of our inner world:

> Our inner lives are not partitioned like day and night, with pure light on one side of us and total darkness on the other. Mostly, our souls are shadowed places; we live at the border where our dark sides block our light and throw a shadow over

our interior places. . . . We cannot always tell where our light ends and our shadow begins or where our shadow ends and our darkness begins.[15]

Augustine also came to believe that the Manichees were infected with pride. Having a closed, all-explaining model of reality appealed to their vanity; it gave them the illusion that they had intellectually mastered all things. But it made them cold to mystery and unable to humble themselves before the complexities and emotions that, as Augustine put it, "make the heart deep." They possessed reason, but no wisdom.

Augustine hung between worlds. He wanted to live a truthful life. But he wasn't ready to give up his career, or sex, or some of his worldly pursuits. He wanted to use the old methods to achieve better outcomes. That is to say, he was going to start with the core assumption that had always been the basis for his ambitious meritocratic life: that you are the prime driver of your life. The world is malleable enough to be shaped by you. To lead a better life you just have to work harder, or use more willpower, or make better decisions.

This is more or less how many people try to rearrange their life today. They attack it like a homework assignment or a school project. They step back, they read self-help books like *The Seven Habits of Highly Effective People*. They learn the techniques for greater self-control. They even establish a relationship with God in the same way they would go after a promotion or an advanced degree—by conquest: by reading certain books, attending services regularly, practicing spiritual disciplines such as regular prayer, doing their spiritual homework.

Pride

BUT EVENTUALLY AUGUSTINE CAME TO BELIEVE THAT YOU CAN'T GRADU-ally reform yourself. He concluded that you can't really lead a good life by using old methods. That's because the method is the problem. The crucial flaw in his old life was the belief that he could be the driver of his own journey. So long as you believe that you are the captain of your own life, you will be drifting farther and farther from the truth.

You can't lead a good life by steering yourself, in the first place, because you do not have the capacity to do so. The mind is such a vast, unknown cosmos you can never even know yourself by yourself. Your emotions are so changeable and complex you can't order your emotional life by yourself. Your appetites are so infinite you can never satisfy them on your own. The powers of self-deception are so profound you are rarely fully honest with yourself.

Furthermore, the world is so complex, and fate so uncertain, that you can never really control other people or the environment effectively enough to be master of your own destiny. Reason is not powerful enough to build intellectual systems or models to allow you to accurately understand the world around you or anticipate what is to come. Your willpower is not strong enough to successfully police your desires. If you really did have that kind of power, then New Year's resolutions would work. Diets would work. The bookstores wouldn't be full of self-help books. You'd need just one and that would do the trick. You'd follow its advice, solve the problems of living, and the rest of the genre would become obsolete. The existence of more and more self-help books is proof that they rarely work.

The problem, Augustine came to believe, is that if you think you can organize your own salvation you are magnifying the very sin that keeps you from it. To believe that you can be captain of your own life is to suffer the sin of pride.

What is pride? These days the word "pride" has positive connotations. It means feeling good about yourself and the things associated with you. When we use it negatively, we think of the arrogant person, someone who is puffed up and egotistical, boasting and strutting about. But that is not really the core of pride. That is just one way the disease of pride presents itself.

By another definition, pride is building your happiness around your accomplishments, using your work as the measure of your worth. It is believing that you can arrive at fulfillment on your own, driven by your own individual efforts.

Pride can come in bloated form. This is the puffed-up Donald Trump style of pride. This person wants people to see visible proof of his superiority. He wants to be on the VIP list. In conversation, he boasts, he brags. He needs to see his superiority reflected in other people's eyes. He believes that this feeling of superiority will eventually bring him peace.

That version is familiar. But there are other proud people who have low self-esteem. They feel they haven't lived up to their potential. They feel unworthy. They want to hide and disappear, to fade into the background and nurse their own hurts. We don't associate them with pride, but they are still, at root, suffering from the same disease. They are still yoking happiness to accomplishment; it's just that they are giving themselves a D– rather than an A+. They tend to be just as solipsistic, and in their own way as self-centered, only in a self-pitying and isolating way rather than in an assertive and bragging way.

One key paradox of pride is that it often combines extreme self-confidence with extreme anxiety. The proud person often appears self-sufficient and egotistical but is really touchy and unstable. The proud person tries to establish self-worth by winning a great reputation, but of course this makes him utterly dependent on the gossipy and unstable crowd for his own identity. The proud person is competitive. But there are always other people who might do better. The most ruthlessly competitive person in the contest sets the standard that all else must meet or get left behind. Everybody else has to be just as monomaniacally driven to success. One can never be secure. As Dante put it, the "ardor to outshine / Burned in my bosom with a kind of rage."

Hungry for exaltation, the proud person has a tendency to make himself ridiculous. Proud people have an amazing tendency to turn themselves into buffoons, with a comb-over that fools nobody, with golden bathroom fixtures that impress nobody, with name-dropping stories that inspire nobody. Every proud man, Augustine writes, "heeds himself, and he who pleases himself seems great to himself. But he who pleases himself pleases a fool, for he himself is a fool when he is pleasing himself."[16]

Pride, the minister and writer Tim Keller has observed, is unstable because other people are absentmindedly or intentionally treating the proud man's ego with less reverence than he thinks it deserves. He continually finds that his feelings are hurt. He is perpetually putting up a front. The self-cultivator spends more energy trying to display the fact that he is happy—posting highlight reel Facebook photos and all the rest—than he does actually being happy.

Augustine suddenly came to realize that the solution to his problem would come only after a transformation more fundamental than any he had previously entertained, a renunciation of the very idea that he could be the source of his own solution.

Elevation

AUGUSTINE LATER WROTE THAT GOD SPRINKLED BITTERNESS AND DISCON-tent over his life to draw him toward God. "The greater I got in age, the worse I got in emptiness, as I could not conceive of any substance except the kind I saw with these eyes." Or, as he most famously put it, "our hearts are restless until we rest in Thee."

Augustine's pain during his years of ambition, at least as he describes it later, is not just the pain of someone who is self-centered and unstable. It is the pain of someone who is self-centered and unstable but who has a deep sensation that there is a better way to live, if only he could figure out what it is. As other converts have put it, they are so rooted in God that even when they haven't found God they feel the lack. They are aware of a divine absence, which picks at them from the inside, and that absence is evidence of a presence. Augustine had an inkling of what he needed in order to feel peace, but still, perversely, was unmotivated to actually travel there.

To move from a fragmentary life to a cohesive one, from an opportunistic life to a committed life, it is necessary to close off certain possibilities. Augustine, like most of us in this situation, didn't want to close his options and renounce the things that made him feel good. His natural inclination was to think his anxieties could be solved if he got more of what he desired, not less. So he hung on an emotional precipice between a religious life he was afraid to sacrifice for and a secular one he detested but would not renounce. He commanded himself to decenter himself and put God at the center of his life. But he refused to obey himself.

He worried about his reputation. He worried he'd have to give up sex, sensing that for him, celibacy would be a necessary part of a religiously devoted life. "This controversy in my heart was self against self only." Looking back, he recalled, "I was in love with the idea of the happy life, but I feared to find it in its true place and I sought for it by running away from it."

His general solution was to delay. Make me virtuous—but not yet.

In the *Confessions,* Augustine paints the scene when the delay finally ended. He was sitting in a garden talking with a friend, Alypius, who told him some stories about monks in Egypt who gave up everything to serve God. Augustine was amazed. The people who were not part of the elite educational system were out doing amazing things while the graduates of that system lived for themselves. "What ails us?" Augustine cried. "The unlearned start up and take heaven by force and we, with this our learning, but without heart, wallow in flesh and blood."

In this fever of doubt and self-reproach, Augustine stood up and strode away while Alypius gazed on in stunned silence. Augustine began pacing around the garden, and Alypius got up and followed him. Augustine felt his bones crying out to end this self-divided life, to stop turning and tossing this way and that. He tore at his hair, beat his forehead, locked his fingers and hunched over, clasping his knee. It seemed as if God was beating on his insides, inflicting a "severe mercy," redoubling the lashes of fear and shame that afflicted him. "Be it done now, be it done now," he cried to himself.

But his worldly desires would not give up so easily. Thoughts jumped into his head. It was as if they were plucking at his garments. "Are you going to cast us off? You'll never experience our pleasures ever again?" Augustine hesitated, wondering, "Do I really think I can live without these pleasures?"

Then there appeared in his mind a thought, the ideal of dignified chastity and self-control. In the *Confessions,* he dresses up this thought in metaphorical terms, as a vision of a woman, Lady Continence. He does not describe her as an ascetic, puritanical goddess. On the contrary, she is an earthy, fecund woman. She's not renouncing joy and sensuality; she's offering better versions. She describes all the young men and women who have already renounced the pleasures of the world for the pleasures of the faith. "Can't you do what they did?" she asks. "Why are you standing apart in yourself?"

Augustine blushed, still undecided. "There arose a mighty storm, bringing a mighty shower of tears." He got up and walked away from

Alypius again, wanting to be alone with his weeping. This time Alypius didn't follow but let Augustine go. Augustine cast himself down under a fig tree, giving way to his tears. Then he heard a voice, which sounded like the voice of a boy or a girl from another house neighboring the garden. It said, "Take up and read. Take up and read." Augustine felt a sense of immediate resolve. He opened up a nearby Bible and read the first passage on which his eyes fell: "Not in rioting and drunkenness, not in chambering and wantonness, not in strife and envying; but put ye in the Lord Jesus Christ, and make not provision for the flesh, in concupiscence."

Augustine had no need to read any further. He felt a light flooding his heart and erasing every shadow. He felt a sudden turning of his will, a sudden desire to renounce worldly, finite pleasures and to live for Christ. It felt all the sweeter to be without shallow sweet things. What he had once been so terrified of losing was now a delight to dismiss.

Naturally, he went to Monica straightaway and told her what had happened. We can imagine her screams of joy, her praises to God for answering a lifetime of prayers. As Augustine put it, "thou had convertest me unto Thyself. . . . And Thou didst convert her mourning into joy, much more plentiful than she had desired, and in a much more precious and purer way than she required, by having grandchildren of my body."

The scene in the garden is not really a conversion scene. Augustine was already a Christian of a sort. After the garden he does not immediately have a fully formed view of what a life in Christ means. The scene in the garden is an elevation scene. Augustine says no to one set of desires and pleasures and rises to a higher set of joys and pleasures.

Agency

THIS ELEVATION IS NOT ONLY A RENUNCIATION OF SEX—THOUGH IN AUGUS-tine's case it seemed to involve that. It's a renunciation of the whole ethos of self-cultivation. The basic formula of the Adam I world is that effort produces reward. If you work hard, play by the rules, and take care of things yourself, you can be the cause of your own good life.

Augustine came to conclude that this all was incomplete. He didn't withdraw from the world. He spent the rest of his life as a politically active bishop, engaging in brutal and sometimes vicious public controversies. But his public work and effort was nestled in a total surrender. He came to conclude that the way to inner joy is not through agency and action, it's through surrender and receptivity to God. The point, according to this view, is to surrender, or at least suppress, your will, your ambition, your desire to achieve victory on your own. The point is to acknowledge that God is the chief driver here and that he already has a plan for you. God already has truths he wants you to live by.

What's more, God has already justified your existence. You may have the feeling that you are on trial in this life, that you have to work and achieve and make your mark to earn a good verdict. Some days you provide evidence for the defense that you are a worthwhile person. Some days you provide evidence for the prosecution that you are not. But as Tim Keller put it, in Christian thought, the trial is already over. The verdict came in before you even began your presentation. That's because Jesus stood trial for you. He took the condemnation that you deserve.

Imagine the person you love most in the world getting nailed to wood as penalty for the sins you yourself committed. Imagine the emotions that would go through your mind as you watched that. This is, in the Christian mind, just a miniature version of the sacrifice Jesus made for you. As Keller puts it, "God imputes Christ's perfect performance to us as if it were our own, and adopts us into His family."[17]

The problem with the willful mindset is, as Jennifer Herdt put it in her book *Putting On Virtue,* "God wants to give us a gift, and we want to buy it."[18] We continually want to earn salvation and meaning through work and achievement. But salvation and meaning are actually won, in this way of living, when you raise the white flag of surrender and allow grace to flood your soul.

The implied posture here is one of submission, arms high, wide open and outstretched, face tilted up, eyes gazing skyward, calm with patient but passionate waiting. Augustine wants you to adopt this sort of surrendered posture. That posture flows from an awareness of need, of one's own insufficiency. Only God has the power to order your inner world, not you. Only God has the power to orient your desires and reshape your emotions, not you. [19]

This posture of receptiveness, for Augustine and much Christian thought since, starts with the feeling of smallness and sinfulness one gets next to the awesome presence of God. Humility comes with daily reminders of your own brokenness. Humility relieves you of the awful stress of trying to be superior all the time. It inverts your attention and elevates the things we tend to look down on.

Throughout his early life, Augustine had been climbing upward, getting out of Thagaste, moving to Carthage, Rome, and Milan in search of more prestigious circles, more brilliant company. He lived, as we do today, in a thoroughly class-driven society, striving upward. But in Christianity, at least in its ideal form, the sublime is not in the prestigious and the lofty but in the everyday and the lowly. It is in the washing of feet, not in triumphal arches. Whoever exalts himself shall be humbled. Whoever humbles himself shall be exalted. One goes down in order to rise up. As Augustine put it, "Where there's humility, there's majesty; where there's weakness, there's might; where there's death, there's life. If you want to get these things, don't disdain those."[20]

The hero of this sort of humble life is not averse to the pleasures of praise, but the petty distinctions you earn for yourself do not really speak to your essential value as a human being. God possesses talents so all-encompassing that in relation to them, the difference between the most brilliant Nobel laureate and the dimmest nitwit are simply a matter of degree. Every soul is equal in the most important sense.

Augustinian Christianity demands a different tone of voice, not the peremptory command of the master to the servant but the posture of coming in under, coming to each relationship from below, and hoping to serve upward. It's not that worldly achievement and public acclaim are automatically bad, it's just that they are won on a planet that is just a resting place for the soul and not our final destination. Success here, acquired badly, can make ultimate success less likely, and that ultimate success is not achieved through competition with others.

It's not quite right to say that Augustine had a low view of human nature. He believed that each individual is made in God's image and possesses a dignity that merits the suffering and death of Jesus. It's more accurate to say that he believed human beings are incapable of living well on their own, as autonomous individuals—incapable of ordering their desires on their own. They can find that order, and that proper love, only by submitting their will to God's. It's not that human beings are pathetic; it's just that they will be restless until they rest in Him.

Grace

AUGUSTINE'S THOUGHT, AND MUCH CHRISTIAN TEACHING GENERALLY, challenges the code of the self-cultivator in one more crucial way. In Augustine's view, people do not get what they deserve; life would be hellish if they did. Instead people get much more than they deserve. God offers us grace, which is his unmerited love. God's protection and care comes precisely because you do not deserve it and cannot earn it. Grace doesn't come to you because you've performed well on your job or even made great sacrifices as a parent or as a friend. Grace comes to you as part of the gift of being created.

One of the things you have to do in order to receive grace is to renounce the idea that you can earn it. You have to renounce the meritocratic impulse that you can win a victory for God and get rewarded for your effort. Then you have to open up to it. You do not know when grace will come to you. But people who are open and sensitive to it testify that they have felt grace at the oddest and at the most needed times.

Paul Tillich puts it this way in his collection of essays, *Shaking the Foundations:*

> Grace strikes us when we are in great pain and restlessness. It strikes us when we walk through the dark valley of a meaningless and empty life. . . . It strikes us when our disgust for our own being, our indifference, our weakness, our hostility, and our lack of direction and composure have become intolerable to us. It strikes us when, year after year, the longed-for perfection of life does not appear, when the old compulsions reign within us as they have for decades, when despair destroys all joy and courage. Sometimes at that moment a wave of light breaks into our darkness and it is as though a voice were saying: "You are accepted. *You are accepted,* accepted by that which is greater than you, and the name of which you do not know. Do not ask for the name now; perhaps you will find it later. Do not try to do

anything now; perhaps later you will do much. Do not seek for anything; do not perform anything; do not intend anything. *Simply accept the fact that you are accepted.*" If that happens to us, we experience grace. After such an experience we may not be better than before and we may not believe more than before. But everything is transformed. In that moment, grace conquers sin, and reconciliation bridges the gulf of estrangement. And nothing is demanded of this experience, no religious or moral or intellectual presupposition, nothing but acceptance.[21]

Those of us in mainstream culture are used to the idea that people get loved because they are kind, or funny, or attractive, or smart, or attentive. It's surprisingly difficult to receive a love that feels unearned. But once you accept the fact that you are accepted, there is a great desire to go meet this love and reciprocate this gift.

If you are passionately in love with a person, you naturally seek to delight her all the time. You want to buy her presents. You want to stand outside her window singing ridiculous songs. This is a replica of the way those who feel touched by grace seek to delight God. They take pleasure in tasks that might please him. They work tirelessly at tasks that they think might glorify him. The desire to rise up and meet God's love can arouse mighty energies.

And as people rise up and seek to meet God, their desires slowly change. In prayer, people gradually reform their desires so that more and more they want the things they believe will delight God rather than the things they used to think would delight themselves.

The ultimate conquest of self, in this view, is not won by self-discipline, or an awful battle within self. It is won by going out of self, by establishing a communion with God and by doing the things that feel natural in order to return God's love.

This is the process that produces an inner transformation. One day you turn around and notice that everything inside has been realigned. The old loves no longer thrill. You love different things and are oriented in different directions. You have become a different sort of person. You didn't get this way simply by following this or that moral code, or adopting a drill sergeant's discipline or certain habits. You did it instead because you reordered your loves, and as Augustine says again and again, you become what you love.

Humble Ambition

WE HAVE ARRIVED, THEREFORE, AT A DIFFERENT THEORY OF MOTIVATION. To recapitulate the Augustinian process, it starts with the dive inside to see the vastness of the inner cosmos. The inward dive leads outward, toward an awareness of external truth and God. That leads to humility as one feels small in contrast to the almighty. That leads to a posture of surrender, of self-emptying, as one makes space for God. That opens the way for you to receive God's grace. That gift arouses an immense feeling of gratitude, a desire to love back, to give back and to delight. That in turn awakens vast energies. Over the centuries many people have been powerfully motivated to delight God. This motivation has been as powerful as the other great motivations, the desire for money, fame, and power.

The genius of this conception is that as people become more dependent on God, their capacity for ambition and action increases. Dependency doesn't breed passivity; it breeds energy and accomplishment.

The Old Loves

AFTER HIS "CONVERSION" IN THE GARDEN, AUGUSTINE DID NOT LIVE A tranquil, easy life. He enjoyed an initial burst of optimism, but then came the thudding realization that his own sinfulness was still there. His own false loves had not magically died away. As his biographer Peter Brown puts it, "The past can come very close: its powerful and complex emotions have only recently passed away; we can still feel their contours through the thin layer of new feeling that has grown over them."[22]

When Augustine writes the *Confessions,* which is in some sense a memoir of his early manhood, he is not writing them as genial reminiscences. He is writing them as a necessary reassessment occasioned by hard times. As Brown writes, "He must base his future on a different view of himself: and how could he gain this view, except by reinterpreting just that part of his past, that had culminated in the conversion, on which he had until recently placed such high hopes?"[23]

Augustine is reminding believers that the center of their lives is not

in themselves. The material world is beautiful and to be sa
enjoyed, but the pleasures of this world are most delicious wɪ
are savored in the larger context of God's transcendent love. A
tine's prayers and meditations are filled with celebrations of the w ɪd
that surpass the world. In one of his most beautiful meditations, for
example, Augustine asks, "What do I love when I love my God?"

> It is not physical beauty or temporal glory or the brightness of
> light dear to earthy eyes, or the sweet melodies of all kinds of
> songs, or the gentle odor of flowers and ointments and perfumes,
> or manna or honey, or limbs welcoming the embraces of the
> flesh; it is not these I love when I love my God. Yet there is a
> light I love, and a food, and a kind of embrace when I love my
> God—a light, voice, odor, food, embrace of my innerness, where
> my soul is floodlit by light which space cannot contain, where
> there is sound that time cannot seize, where there is a perfume
> which no breeze disperses, where there is a taste for food no
> amount of eating can lessen, where there is a bond of union that
> no satiety can part. That's what I love when I love my God.

This is living life in a broader context. As the theologian Lisa Ful-
lam has put it, "Humility is a virtue of self-understanding in context,
acquired by the practice of other centeredness."

Hush

AFTER HIS RENUNCIATION IN THE GARDEN, AUGUSTINE DRAGGED HIMSELF
through the end of the school term, teaching the rhetoric he no longer believed in. Then he, his mother, his son, and a group of friends
went to stay for five months at the villa of a Milanese friend of theirs
whose wife was Christian. The villa was in Cassiciacum, twenty miles
north of Milan. The party engaged in a series of colloquia, which have
the feel of a group of scholars meditating together on deep things.
Augustine was delighted that Monica had enough native smarts to
keep up with and even lead the conversations. Then Augustine decided to return home to Africa, where he could live a secluded life of
prayer and contemplation with his mother.

The party headed south—over the same road, biographers remind us, that his mistress had traveled when she had been dispatched two years before. They hit a military blockade and made it only as far as the town of Ostia. One day in Ostia, Augustine was looking out a window that overlooked a garden (many events in his life take place in gardens), and he was talking with his mother. Monica clearly had a sense by this time that death was coming to her. She was fifty-six.

Augustine describes their conversation, saying that together they experienced "the very highest delight of the earthly senses, in the very purest material light . . . in respect of the sweetness of that light." But in the intimacy between mother and son, they began talking about God, and they "did by degrees pass through all things bodily, even the very heaven when sun and moon and stars shine upon the earth." From these material things "we came to our own minds and went beyond them into the realm of pure spirit."

In describing their talk, Augustine includes a long sentence that is hard to parse, but it includes, in some translations, the word "hushed" over and over—the tumult of the flesh was hushed, the waters and the air were hushed, all dreams and shallow visions were hushed, tongues were hushed, everything that passes away was hushed, the self was hushed in moving beyond the self into a sort of silence. Mother or son makes an exclamation: "We did not make ourselves, he who made us never passes away." But after saying this, that voice, too, is hushed. And "He who made them, He alone speaks, not through men or women, but by himself." And Augustine and Monica heard God's word "not through any tongue of flesh, or Angels' voices, not sound of thunder, nor in the dark riddle of similitude," but they heard "his very Self." And they sighed after a moment of pure understanding.

Augustine is describing here a perfect moment of elevation: hushed . . . hushed . . . hushed . . . hushed. All the clamors of the world slip into silence. Then a desire to praise the creator comes over them, but then even that praise is hushed amid the kenosis, the self-emptying. And then comes the infusing vision of eternal wisdom, what Augustine calls the "glad hidden depths." One imagines mother and son lost in joy in this climactic encounter. After the years of tears and anger, control and escape, rupture and reconciliation, pursuit and manipulation, friendship and fighting, they finally achieve some sort of outward-facing union. They come together and dissolve together in contemplation of what they both now love.

Monica tells him, "Son, for mine own part I have no further delight in any thing in this life. . . . One thing there was for which I desired to linger for a while in this life, that I might see thee a Catholic Christian before I died. My God has done this for me more than abundantly."

TO BE HEALED IS to be broken open. The proper course is outward. C. S. Lewis observed that if you enter a party consciously trying to make a good impression, you probably won't end up making one. That happens only when you are thinking about the other people in the room. If you begin an art project by trying to be original, you probably won't be original.

And so it is with tranquillity. If you set out trying to achieve inner peace and a sense of holiness, you won't get it. That happens only obliquely, when your attention is a focused on something external. That happens only as a byproduct of a state of self-forgetfulness, when your energies are focused on something large.

For Augustine, that's the crucial change. Knowledge is not enough for tranquillity and goodness, because it doesn't contain the motivation to be good. Only love impels action. We don't become better because we acquire new information. We become better because we acquire better loves. We don't become what we know. Education is a process of love formation. When you go to a school, it should offer you new things to love.

A few days later, Monica came down with her fatal illness, which took only nine days to carry her off. She told Augustine that it was no longer important for her to be buried back in Africa, because no place was far from God. She told him that in all their tribulations she had never heard him utter a sharp word to her.

At the moment of her death, Augustine bent over and closed her eyes. "An innumerable sorrow flowed up into my heart and would have overflowed in tears." At that moment, Augustine, not even now fully renouncing classical Stoicism, felt he should exercise self-command and not give in to weeping. "But my eyes, under the mind's strong constraint, held back their flow and I stood dry-eyed. In that struggle it went very hard with me. . . . Because I had now lost the great comfort of her, my soul was wounded and my very life torn asunder, for it had been one life—made of hers and mine together."

Augustine's friends gathered around him, while he still tried to repress his grief: "For I was very much ashamed that these human emotions could have such power over me. . . . I felt a new grief at my grief and so was afflicted by a double sorrow."

Augustine went to take a bath and soothe his self-division, then fell asleep and awoke feeling better. "And then, little by little, I began to recover my former feeling about Your handmaid, remembering how loving and devout was her conversation with me, of which I was thus suddenly deprived. And I found solace in weeping in Your sight both about her and for her, about myself and for myself."

MONICA HAD ENTERED A world in which the Roman Empire dominated Europe and a rationalist philosophy dominated thinking. In his writing, Augustine uses her as an example of faith against pure rationalism, of spiritual relentlessness against worldly ambition. He would spend the rest of his life as a bishop fighting and preaching and writing, fighting and arguing. He achieved the immortality he sought in his youth, but he did it in an unexpected way. He started with the belief that he could control his own life. He had to renounce that, to sink down into a posture of openness and surrender. Then, after that retreat, he was open enough to receive grace, to feel gratitude and rise upward. This is life with an advance-retreat-advance shape. Life, death, and resurrection. Moving down to dependence to gain immeasurable height.

CHAPTER 9

SELF-EXAMINATION

SAMUEL JOHNSON WAS BORN IN LICHFIELD, ENGLAND, IN 1709. HIS father was an unsuccessful bookseller. His mother was an uneducated woman who nonetheless thought she had married beneath her. "My father and mother had not much happiness from each other," Johnson would remember. "They seldom conversed; for my father could not bear to talk of his affairs; and my mother, being unacquainted with books, could not talk of anything else. . . . Of business she had no distinct conception; and therefore her discourse was composed only of complaint, fear, and suspicion."[1]

Johnson was a frail infant who surprised everybody by living through the ordeal of birth. He was immediately handed over to a wet nurse whose milk infected him with tuberculosis of the lymph nodes, which made him permanently blind in one eye, with poor vision in the other, and deaf in one ear. He later developed smallpox, which left his face permanently scarred. His doctors, in an attempt to relieve his disease, made an incision, without anesthesia, in his left arm. They kept the wound open with horsehair for six years, periodically discharging the fluids they associated with disease. They also cut into his neck glands. The operation was botched and Johnson went through life with deep scars running down the left side of his face from his ear to his jaw. Physically, he was large, ugly, scarred, and ogrelike.

He fought vehemently against his maladies. One day, as a child, he was walking home from school but could not see the gutter in the street, and feared tripping on it. He got down on all fours and crawled along the street, peering closely at the curb so that he could measure his step. When a teacher offered to give him a hand, he became enraged and furiously beat her away.

All his life, Johnson was suspicious of the self-indulgence that he believed the chronically ill were prone to. "Disease produces much selfishness," he wrote toward the end of his life. "A man in pain is looking after ease." He responded to his illness, Walter Jackson Bate notes, with "a powerful sense of self demand, a feeling of complete personal responsibility. . . . What is of special interest to us now is how quickly as a small child—in discovering the physical differences between himself and others—he began groping his way to the independence and defiant disregard for physical limitations that he was always to maintain."[2]

Johnson's education was thorough and severe. He went to a school that trained him in the classical curriculum that was the core of Western education from the Renaissance until the twentieth century— Ovid, Virgil, Horace, the Athenians. He learned Latin and Greek. When he was lazy he was beaten. His teachers would have the boys lean over their chairs and then they'd swing at them with a rod. "And this I do to save you from the gallows," they'd say.[3] Later in life, Johnson would have some complaints about the beatings. But he believed the rod was still kinder than psychological pressure and emotional manipulation—the sort of suasion many parents use today.

Johnson's most important education was self-administered. Though he never warmed to his elderly father, he read through his father's stock of books, devouring travel books, romances, and histories, with a special taste for daring tales of chivalry. He read vividly. At age nine he was reading *Hamlet* when he came upon the ghost scene. He ran frantically out into the street, terrified and desperate to be reminded of the living world. His memory was tenacious. He could read a prayer once or twice and recite it for the rest of his life. He seems to have remembered everything he read, bringing obscure authors into conversations decades after encountering them. When he was a small boy, his father would parade him before dinner parties and force him to recite for the admiring crowd. Young Sam was disgusted by his father's vanity.

When Johnson was nineteen, his mother came into a small legacy, which was enough to pay for a single year at Oxford. Johnson promptly made the least of the opportunity. He came to Oxford fully aware of his ability, burning with ambition, panting, as he would later put it, for a name and the "pleasing hope of endless fame." But, accustomed to his independent autodidactic life and feeling financially and socially inferior to many of the students around him, he was incapable of playing by Oxford rules. Instead of submitting to the torpid system, he battled against it, reacting to the slightest touch of authority with rude aggression. "I was mad and violent," he would later recall. "It was bitterness which they mistook for frolic. I was miserably poor, and I thought to fight my way by my literature and my wit; so I disregarded all power and all authority."[4]

Johnson was recognized as a brilliant student, winning praise for his translation into Latin of a poem by Alexander Pope; Pope himself said he couldn't tell which was better, the Latin version or the original. But he was also rebellious, rude, and lazy. He told his tutor that he had neglected to attend lectures because he preferred to go sledding. He worked in a stop-and-start pattern that he would use all his life. He would sit in complete indolence for days, staring at a clock face but unable even to tell the time, and then he would rise to a feverish level of activity and fire off an assignment in a single masterful draft just before it was due.

Johnson became a Christian at Oxford, after a fashion. He sat down one day with the theological book by William Law titled *A Serious Call to a Devout and Holy Life,* expecting, he wrote, "to find it a dull book (as such books generally are) and perhaps to laugh at it. But I found Law quite an overmatch for me, and this was the first occasion of my thinking in earnest of religion, after I became capable of rational inquiry." Law's book, like Johnson's later moral writing, is concrete and practical. He invents characters to construct satirical portraits of types who neglect their spiritual interests. He emphasized that worldly pursuits fail to fill the heart. Christianity didn't really change Johnson, but it made him more of what he already was—extremely suspicious of self-indulgence, rigorous in his moral demands of himself.

Aware of his own mental abilities, he fixed his attention all his life on the biblical parable of the talents, and the lesson that the "wicked and slothful servant" who has not fully used the talents that have been bestowed upon him will be cast "into outer darkness, where there shall be weeping and gnashing of teeth." Johnson's God was a rigorous God more than a loving or healing God. Johnson would spend his life with a sense of being perpetually judged, aware of his inadequacy, fearing his own damnation.

After that one year at Oxford, Johnson's money ran out, and he returned to Lichfield in disgrace. He suffered what seems to have been a bout of severe depression. As his chronicler, James Boswell, would write, "He felt himself overwhelmed with a horrible hypochondria, with perpetual irritation, fretfulness, and impatience; and with a dejection, gloom and despair, which made existence misery."[5]

Johnson took thirty-two-mile hikes to occupy himself. He may have contemplated suicide. He seemed completely incapable of controlling his body movements. He developed a series of tics and gestures that look to many modern experts like Tourette's syndrome. He would twist his hands, rock back and forth, roll his head in a strange and compulsive manner. He would emit a bizarre whistling sound and display symptoms of obsessive compulsive disorder, tapping his cane in odd rhythms as he walked down the street, counting the number of steps it took him to enter a room and then reentering if the number wasn't right. To dine with him was a challenge. He ate like a wild animal, devouring huge quantities of food in messy haste, spewing it over his notoriously slovenly clothing. The novelist Fanny Burney would write, "[He] has a face most ugly, a person the most awkward, & manners the most singular that ever were, or ever can be seen. He has almost perpetual convulsive motions, either of his hands, lips, feet, knees and sometimes all together."[6] Strangers would see him in a tavern and mistake him for a village idiot, or somebody with a debilitating mental affliction. He would then astonish them by unfurling full paragraphs studded with erudition and classical allusion. He seemed to enjoy this effect.

Johnson's misery continued for years. He tried to teach, but a man with his tics was bound to generate more ridicule than respect from his students. The school he started, one historian noted, was "perhaps the most unsuccessful private school in the history of education." He married Elizabeth Porter when he was twenty-six and she was forty-six, in what many thought an odd pairing. Biographers have never known what to make of Porter, whom he called Tetty. Was she beautiful or haggard? Was she philosophical or frivolous? She, to her credit, saw a sign of the future greatness beneath the rough exterior, and he, to his credit, would remain loyal to her throughout his life. He was a very tender and grateful lover, with a great capacity for empathy and affection, but they spent many of those years apart, leading separate lives. It was her money that furnished the capital to start the school, and much of it was lost.

Until his late twenties, his life had been a steady calamity. On March 2, 1737, Johnson set off for London with his former pupil David Garrick (who would go on to become one of the most famous actors in British history). Johnson settled near Grub Street and began scratching out a living as a freelance writer. He wrote on any subject and across genres: poetry, drama, political essays, literary criticism, gossip items, casual essays, and on and on. The life of a Grub Street hack was hand-to-mouth, chaotic, disheveled, and frequently miserable. One poet, Samuel Boyse, pawned all his clothing and sat on his bed naked but for his blanket. He cut a hole in it large enough to stick his arm through and wrote poems on sheets of paper balanced on his knee. When he was writing a book, he would pawn the first few pages to raise money to pay for food so he could complete the next ones.[7] Johnson never quite sank to that low state, but much of the time, especially in the early years, he barely scraped by.

During this time, though, Johnson performed one of the most amazing feats in the history of journalism. In 1738, the House of Commons passed a law that it would be a "breach of privilege" to publish parliamentary speeches. *The Gentleman's Magazine* decided to publish thinly veiled fictional accounts of the speeches, to let the public know what was going on. For two and a half years, Johnson was the sole author, though he set foot in Parliament only once. A source would tell him who spoke and in what order, what general positions they took and the arguments they made. Johnson would then make up eloquent speeches, as they might have been given. These speeches were so well written that the speakers themselves did not disavow them. They were taken as authentic transcripts for at least the next twenty years. As late as 1899, they were still appearing in anthologies of the world's best oratory, credited to the alleged speakers and not to

Johnson.[8] Once, overhearing the company at a dinner party raving over the brilliance of a speech by William Pitt the Elder, Johnson interrupted, "That speech I wrote in a garret in Exeter Street."[9]

Johnson was living a life, familiar to us now but more unusual in his own day, in which he was thrown continually back on himself. Without a settled trade, like farming or teaching, separated from the rootedness of extended family life, he was compelled to live as a sort of freelancer according to his wits. His entire destiny—his financial security, his standing in his community, his friendships, his opinions and meaning as a person—were determined by the ideas that flashed through his mind.

The Germans have a word for this condition: *Zerrissenheit*—loosely, "falling-to-pieces-ness." This is the loss of internal coherence that can come from living a multitasking, pulled-in-a-hundred-directions existence. This is what Kierkegaard called "the dizziness of freedom." When the external constraints are loosened, when a person can do what he wants, when there are a thousand choices and distractions, then life can lose coherence and direction if there isn't a strong internal structure.

Johnson's internal fragmentation was exacerbated by his own nature. "Everything about his character and manners was forcible and violent," Boswell observed—the way he spoke, ate, read, loved, and lived. Moreover, many of his qualities were at odds with one another. Plagued by tics and mannerisms, he could not fully control his own body. Plagued by depression and instability, he could not fully control his own mind. He was an intensely social person who warned all his life against the perils of solitude, but he was stuck in a literary profession that required long stretches of private time for composition. He effectively lived a bachelor's life, but he had an enormously strong sexual drive and struggled all his life with what he regarded as his "polluting thoughts." He had a short attention span. "I have read few books through," he confessed; "they are generally so repulsive I cannot."[10]

Imagination

HE WAS ALSO PLAGUED BY HIS OWN IMAGINATION. WE IN POST-ROMANTIC times tend to regard the imagination as an innocent, childlike faculty that provides us with creativity and sweet visions. Johnson saw the imagination as something to be feared as much as treasured. It was at its worst in the middle of the night. In those dark hours his imagination would plague him, introducing nighttime terrors, jealousies, feelings of worthlessness, and vain hopes and fantasies of superficial praise and admiration. The imagination, in Johnson's darker view, offers up ideal visions of experiences like marriage, which then leave us disappointed when the visions don't come true. It is responsible for hypochondria and the other anxieties that exist only in our heads. It invites us to make envious comparisons, imagining scenes in which we triumph over our rivals. The imagination simplifies our endless desires and causes us to fantasize that they can be fulfilled. It robs us of much of the enjoyment of our achievements by compelling us to think upon the things left undone. It distracts us from the pleasures of the moment by leaping forward to unattained future possibilities.

Johnson was always impressed, puzzled, and terrified by the runaway nature of the mind. We are all a bit like Don Quixote, he observed, fighting villains of our own imagining, living within ideas of our own concoction rather than in reality as it actually is. Johnson's brain was perpetually on the move, at odds with itself. As he wrote in one of his Adventurer essays, "We have less reason to be surprised or offended when we find others differ from us in opinions because we very often differ from ourselves."

Johnson did not just surrender to these mental demons; he fought them. He was combative, with others and with himself. When an editor accused him of wasting time, Johnson, a large and powerful man, pushed the man over and put his foot on his neck. "He was insolent and I beat him, and he was a blockhead and I told of it."

His diaries are rife with self-criticism and vows to organize his time better. From 1738: "Oh lord, enable me . . . in redeeming the time which I have spent in Sloth." From 1757: "Almighty God. Enable me to shake off sloth." From 1769: "I purpose to rise and hope to rise . . . at eight, and by degrees at six."[11]

At those moments when he succeeded in conquering indolence and put pen to paper, his output was torrential. He could produce twelve thousand words, or thirty book pages, in a sitting. In these bursts, he'd write eighteen hundred words an hour, or thirty words a minute.[12] Sometimes the copy boy would be standing at his elbow and would take each page to the printer as it was done so he could not go back and revise.

His modern biographer, Walter Jackson Bate, usefully reminds us that though Johnson's output as a freelancer astounds for its quantity and quality, for the first two decades not a single piece of it went out under his own name. This was partly his decision, and partly the rules of the Grub Street press at the time. Even into middle age, he had done nothing that he felt proud of, or that he thought made anything close to full use of his talents. He was little known and also anxiety-riddled and emotionally torn. His life, as he put it, had been "radically wretched."

The familiar picture we have of Johnson comes from Boswell's magisterial *Life of Johnson*. Boswell was an epicurean and an acolyte and knew Johnson only in his old age. Boswell's Johnson is anything but wretched. He is joyful, witty, complete, and compelling. In Boswell's account we find a man who has achieved some integration. But this was a construction. Through writing and mental effort he constructed a coherent worldview. He brought himself to some coherence without simplification. He became trustworthy and dependable.

Johnson also used his writing to try to serve and elevate his readers. "It is always a writer's duty to make the world better," Johnson once wrote, and by maturity he had found a way.

Humanism

HOW DID HE DO THIS? WELL, HE DID NOT DO IT ALONE ANY MORE THAN ANY of us does. Much of our character talk today is individualistic, like all our talk, but character is formed in community. Johnson happened to come to maturity at a time when Britain was home to a phenomenally talented group of writers, painters, artists, and intellectuals, ranging from Adam Smith to Joshua Reynolds to Edmund Burke. Each raised the standards of excellence for the others.

These were humanists, their knowledge derived from their deep reading of the great canonical texts of Western civilization. They were heroic, but they practiced an intellectual form of heroism, not a military one. They tried to see the world clearly, resisting the self-deceptions caused by the vanity and perversities in their own nature. They sought a sort of practical, moral wisdom that would give them inner integrity and purpose.

Johnson was the ultimate representative of the type. Johnson, as biographer Jeffrey Meyers put it, was "a mass of contradictions: lazy and energetic, aggressive and tender, melancholic and humorous, commonsensical and irrational, comforted yet tormented by religion."[13] He fought these impulses within himself, as James Boswell put it, like a Roman gladiator in the Colosseum. He fought "the wild beasts of the Arena, ready to be let out upon him. After a conflict, he drove them back into their dens; but not killing them, they were still assailing him." All his life he combined the intellectual toughness of Achilles with the compassionate faith of a rabbi, priest, or mullah.

JOHNSON PROCESSED THE WORLD in the only way he could: with his (barely functioning) eye, with his conversation, and with his pen. Writers are not exactly known for their superlative moral character, but Johnson more or less wrote himself to virtue.

He did his work in the tavern and café. Johnson—gross, disheveled, and ugly—was an astonishingly convivial man. He also thought by talking, uttering a relentless barrage of moral maxims and witticisms, a cross between Martin Luther and Oscar Wilde. "There is no arguing with Johnson," the novelist and playwright Oliver Goldsmith once said, "for when his pistol misses fire, he knocks you down with the butt end of it." Johnson would use whatever argument came to hand and often switched sides in a debate entirely if he thought it would make the controversy more enjoyable. Many of his most famous sayings feel as if they either emerged spontaneously during a tavern conversation or were polished to give the appearance of spontaneity: "Patriotism is the last refuge of a scoundrel. . . . A decent provision for the poor is the true test of civilization. . . . When a man knows he is to be hanged in a fortnight it concentrates his mind wonderfully. . . . When a man is tired of London he is tired of life."

His literary style had the to-and-fro structure of good conversation. He'd make a point, then balance it with a counterpoint, which in turn would be balanced by yet another counterpoint. The maxims above, which everybody quotes, give a false air of certainty to Johnson's views. His common conversational style was to raise a topic—say, card playing—list the virtues and vices associated with it, and then come down tentatively on one side. Writing of marriage, he displays his tendency to see every good linked with a bad: "I drew upon a page of my pocket book a scheme of all female virtues and vices, with the vices which border upon every virtue, and the virtues which are allied to every vice. I considered that wit was sarcastic, and magnanimity imperious; that avarice was economical and ignorance obsequious."

Johnson was a fervent dualist, believing that only tensions, paradoxes, and ironies could capture the complexity of real life. He was not a theorist, so he was comfortable with antitheses, things that didn't seem to go together but in fact do. As the literary critic Paul Fussell observed, the *buts* and *yets* that dotted his prose became the substance of his writing, part of his sense that to grasp anything you have to look at it from many vantage points, seeing all its contradictory parts. [14]

One certainly gets the sense that he spent a lot of time just hanging out, engaging in the sort of stupid small adventures groups of friends get into when they are just passing the time. Told that someone had drowned in a certain stretch of river, Johnson proceeded to jump right into it to see if he could survive. Told that a gun could explode if loaded with too much shot, Johnson immediately put seven balls in the barrel of one and fired it into a wall.

He threw himself into London life. He interviewed prostitutes. He slept in parks with poets. He did not believe knowledge was best pursued as a solitary venture. He wrote, "Happiness is not found in self contemplation; it is perceived only when it is reflected from another." He sought self-knowledge obliquely, testing his observations against the reality of a world he could see concretely in front of him. "I look upon every day to be lost in which I do not make a new acquaintance," he observed. He dreaded solitude. He was always the last one to leave the pub, preferring walking the streets throughout the night with his dissolute friend Richard Savage to going home to the loneliness of his haunted chambers.

"The true state of every nation," he observed, "is the state of common life. The manners of a people are not to be found in schools of learning or the palaces of greatness." Johnson socialized with people at every level. Late in life he took vagabonds into his house. He also entertained and insulted lords. After Johnson had arduously completed his great dictionary, Lord Chesterfield belatedly tried to take credit as its patron. Johnson rebuked him with one of the greatest epistolary acts of revolt ever written, which climaxed with the passage:

> Is not a patron, my lord, one who looks with unconcern on a man struggling for life in the water, and, when he has reached ground, encumbers him with help? The notice which you have been pleased to take of my labors, had it been early, had been kind; but it has been delayed till I am indifferent, and cannot enjoy it; till I am solitary, and cannot impart it; till I am known, and do not want it.

Absolute Honesty

JOHNSON DID NOT BELIEVE THAT THE PRIMARY HUMAN PROBLEMS CAN BE solved by politics or by rearranging social conditions. He is, after all, the author of the famous couplet "How small, of all that human hearts endure, / That part which laws and kings can cause or cure." Nor was he a metaphysician or a philosopher. He liked science but thought it a secondary concern. He discounted those who led lives of pedantic research surrounded by "learned dust," and he had a deep distrust of intellectual systems that tried to explain all existence in one logical structure. He let his interests roam over the whole surface of life, wherever his natural interests took him, making connections as a generalist, from one field to another. Johnson endorsed the notion that "He who can talk only on one subject, or act only in one department, is seldom wanted, and perhaps never wished for, while the man of general knowledge can often benefit and always please."[15]

He was not mystical. He built his philosophy low to the ground, from reading history and literature and from direct observation—focusing relentlessly on what he would call "the living world." As Paul Fussell observed, he confuted all determinism. He rejected the notion that behavior is shaped by impersonal iron forces. He always focused with his searing eye on the particularity of each individual. Ralph Waldo Emerson would later observe that "Souls are not saved in bundles."[16] Johnson fervently believed in each individual's mysterious complexity and inherent dignity.

He was, through it all, a moralist, in the best sense of that term. He believed that most problems are moral problems. "The happiness of society depends on virtue," he would write. For him, like other humanists of that age, the essential human act is the act of making strenuous moral decisions. He, like other humanists, believed that literature could be a serious force for moral improvement. Literature gives not only new information but new experiences. It can broaden the range of awareness and be an occasion for evaluation. Literature can also instruct through pleasure.

Today many writers see literature and art only in aesthetic terms, but Johnson saw them as moral enterprises. He hoped to be counted among those writers who give "ardor to virtue and confidence to truth." He added, "It is always a writer's duty to make the world better." As Fussell puts it, "Johnson, then, conceives of writing as something very like a Christian sacrament, defined in the Anglican catechism as 'an outward and visible sign of an inward and spiritual grace given to us.'"

Johnson lived in a world of hack writers, but Johnson did not allow himself to write badly—even though he wrote quickly and for money. Instead, he pursued the ideal of absolute literary honesty. "The first step to greatness is to be honest" was one of Johnson's maxims.

He had a low but sympathetic view of human nature. It was said in Greek times that Demosthenes was not a great orator despite his stammer; he was a great orator *because* he stammered. The deficiency became an incentive to perfect the associated skill. The hero becomes strongest at his weakest point. Johnson was a great moralist because of his deficiencies. He came to understand that he would never defeat them. He came to understand that his story would not be the sort of virtue-conquers-vice story people like to tell. It would be, at best, a virtue-learns-to-live-with-vice story. He wrote that he did not seek cures for his failings, but palliatives. This awareness of permanent struggle made him sympathetic to others' failings. He was a moralist, but a tenderhearted one.

The Compassion of the Wounded Man

IF YOU WANT TO KNOW WHAT VICES PLAGUED SAMUEL JOHNSON, JUST look at the subjects of his essays: guilt, shame, frustration, boredom, and so on. As Bate observes, one fourth of his essays in the Rambler series concern envy. Johnson understood that he was particularly prone to resent other people's success: "The reigning error of mankind is that we are not content with the conditions on which the goods of life are granted."

Johnson's redeeming intellectual virtue was clarity of mind. It gave him his great facility for crystallizing and quotable observations. Most of these reveal a psychological shrewdness about human fallibility:

- A man of genius is but seldom ruined but by himself.
- If you are idle, be not solitary; if you are solitary, be not idle.
- There are people whom one should like very well to drop, but would not wish to be dropped by.
- All censure of self is oblique praise. It is in order to show how much he can spare.
- Man's chief merit consists in resisting the impulses of his nature.
- No place affords a more striking conviction of the vanity of human hopes than a public library.
- Very few can boast of hearts which they dare lay open to themselves.
- Read over your compositions, and wherever you meet with a passage you think is particularly fine, strike it out.
- Every man naturally persuades himself he can keep his resolutions; nor is he convinced of his imbecility but by length of time and frequency of experiment.

Through his moral essays, Johnson was able to impose order on the world, to anchor his experiences in the stability of the truth. He had to still himself in order to achieve an objective perception of the world. When people are depressed, they often feel overcome by a comprehensive and yet hard to pin down sadness. But Johnson jumps directly into the pain, pins it down, dissects it, and partially disarms it. In his essay on sorrow he observes that most passions drive you to their own extinction. Hunger leads to eating and satiety, fear leads to flight, lust leads to sex. But sorrow is an exception. Sorrow doesn't direct you toward its own cure. Sorrow builds upon sorrow.

That's because sorrow is "that state of mind in which our desires are fixed upon the past, without looking forward to the future, an incessant wish that something were otherwise than it has been, a tormenting and harassing want of some enjoyment or possession we have lost." Many try to avoid sorrow by living timid lives. Many try to relieve sorrow by forcing themselves to go to social events. Johnson does not approve of these stratagems. Instead, he advises, "The safe and general antidote against sorrow is employment. . . . Sorrow is a kind of rust of the soul, which every new idea contributes in its passage to scour away. It is the putrefaction of stagnant life and is remedied by exercise and motion."

Johnson also uses his essays as exercises in self-confrontation. "Life is combat to Johnson," Fussell writes, "and the combat is moral."[17] Johnson writes essays directly upon those topics that plague him: despair, pride, hunger for novelty, boredom, gluttony, guilt, and vanity. He is under no illusion that he can lecture himself to virtue. But he can plot and plan ways to train his will. For example, envy was indeed the besetting sin of his early adulthood. He understood his own talents, and also understood that others were succeeding while he failed.

He devised a strategy to defeat the envy in his heart. He said that in general he did not believe that one vice should be cured by another. But envy is such a malignant state of mind that the dominance of almost any other quality is to be preferred. So he chose pride. He told himself that to envy another is to admit one's inferiority, and that it is better to insist on one's superior merit than to succumb to envy. When tempted to envy another, he persuaded himself of his own superior position.

Then, turning in a more biblical direction, he preached charity and mercy. The world is so bursting with sin and sorrow that "there are none to be envied." Everyone has some deep trouble in their lives. Almost no one truly enjoys their own achievements, since their desires are always leaping forward and torturing them with visions of goods unpossessed.

The Stability of the Truth

WHAT JOHNSON SAID OF THE ESSAYIST JOSEPH ADDISON COULD BE applied to himself: "He was a man in whose presence nothing reprehensible was out of danger; quick in observing whatever was wrong or ridiculous and not unwilling to expose it."

Through this process of strenuous observation and examination, Johnson did transform his life. As a young man, he was sickly, depressed, and a failure. By late middle age, not only were his worldly accomplishments nationally admired, but he was acknowledged as a great-souled man. The biographer Percy Hazen Houston explained how a man of such a miserable and painful upbringing could look upon the world with judgments tempered with tolerance and mercy:

The iron had entered his soul, and he approached questions of human conduct in the light of a terrible experience, which enabled him to penetrate into human motives with sureness and understanding. Vividly conscious of the pettiness of our lives and the narrow limits of human knowledge, he was content to leave the mystery of final causes to power higher than his; for God's purposes are inscrutable, and man's aim in this early existence should be to seek laws by which he may prepare himself to meet divine mercy.[18]

Johnson thought hard and came to settled convictions about the complex and flawed world around him. He did it by disciplining himself in the effort to see things as they are. He did it through earnestness, self-criticism, and moral ardor.

Montaigne

JOHNSON'S METHOD OF SELF-FORMATION THROUGH MORAL INQUIRY CAN be illuminated by contrast with another great essayist, the delightful sixteenth-century French writer Michel de Montaigne. As one of my students, Haley Adams, put it, Johnson is like an East Coast rapper— intense, earnest, combative. Montaigne is like a West Coast rapper— equally realistic but also relaxed, mellow, sun-drenched. Montaigne was a greater essayist than Johnson. His masterpieces created and defined the form. And in his way he was just as morally earnest, just as intent on finding a way to understand himself and pursue virtue. But they took different approaches. Johnson sought to reform himself through direct assault and earnest effort. Montaigne was more amused by himself and his foibles, and sought virtue through self-acceptance and sweet gestures of self-improvement.

Montaigne had an upbringing nothing like Johnson's. He grew up on an estate near Bordeaux as the treasured member of a wealthy, established family whose money was ample but not ancient. He was raised gently and nurturingly according to a humanist plan devised by the man he thought the best of all fathers, including being awoken sweetly each morning by the sound of a musical instrument. The upbringing was designed to make him educated, well-rounded, and gentle. He went to a prestigious boarding school and then served as a town counselor and member of the local *parlement*.

Montaigne's situation was comfortable, but his times were not. He was a public servant at a time of a series of religious civil wars, trying to play a mediating role in some of them. In his thirty-eighth year, he retired from public life. His goal was to return to his estate and lead a life of learned leisure. Johnson wrote in the teeming pub life of Grub Street; Montaigne wrote from the seclusion of his own tower library, in a large room decorated with Greek, Roman, and biblical maxims.

His initial goal was to study the ancients (Plutarch, Ovid, Tacitus) and learn from his church (at least in public, he was a Roman Catholic with orthodox views, although, with an earthy rather than an abstract slant of mind, he seemed to draw less wisdom from theology than from history). He thought he might write learned pieces on war and high policy.

But his mind did not allow that. Like Johnson, Montaigne had a midlife suspicion that he had been living wrongly in some fundamental way. Once he retired to a life of contemplation, he discovered that his own mind would not allow tranquillity. He found his mind was fragmented, liquid, and scattershot. He compared his thoughts to the shimmerings of light dancing on the ceiling when sunlight is reflected off a pool of water. His brain was constantly racing off in all directions. When he started to think about himself, all he found was some momentary perception, which was followed by some unrelated perception, which was then followed by another.

Montaigne fell into a depression, and in his suffering he became his own literary subject. "We are, I know not how, double within ourselves," he wrote. The imagination runs away. "I cannot fix my subject. He is always restless, and reels with a natural intoxication. . . . I do not portray being. I portray passing. . . . I must suit my story to the hour, for soon I may change."

Montaigne came to realize how hard it was to control one's own mind, or even one's body. He despaired over even his own penis, "which intrudes so tiresomely when we do not require it and fails us so annoyingly when we need it most." But the penis is not alone in its rebellion. "I ask you to consider whether there is a single part of our bodies that does not often refuse to work at our will, and does not often operate in defiance of it."

Writing, then, was an act of self-integration. Montaigne's theory was that much of the fanaticism and violence he saw around him was caused by the panic and uncertainty people feel because they can't grasp the elusiveness within themselves. The push for worldly splendor and eternal glory are futile efforts by people who are seeking external means to achieve internal tranquillity and friendship with themselves. As he put it, "Every man rushes elsewhere into the future, because no man has arrived at himself." Montaigne would use his essays to arrive at himself. He would, through writing, create a viewpoint and a prose style that would impose order and equanimity on the fragmented self inside.

Both Johnson and Montaigne were seeking deep self-awareness, but they went about it by different methods. Johnson described other people and the outer world, hoping to define himself obliquely. Sometimes he would write a biography of someone else, but so many of his own traits peeped through that his portrait seems like an autobiography in disguise. Montaigne started from the other end. He described himself, and his responses to things, and through self-examination hoped to define the nature that all men and women share, observing, "Each man bears within himself the entire form of man's estate."

Johnson's essays sound authoritative, but Montaigne's are written in a style that is modest, provisional, and tentative. They were not organized formally. They do not follow a clear logical structure; they accrete. He would make a point, and if some related point came to him months later, he'd scrawl it in the margins for inclusion in the final edition. That haphazard method disguised the seriousness of his enterprise. He made it look easy, but he did not take his mission lightly. He understood how original his project was: completely honest self-revelation, and through that, a vision of the moral life. He understood he was trying to create a new method of character formation and implying a new type of hero, a hero of ruthlessly honest but sympathetic self-understanding. The manner was carefree, but the task was arduous: "We must really strain our soul to be aware of our own fallibility." The idea was not simply to expand his knowledge of himself, or to play around in his own mind, or to expose himself for the sake of fame or attention or success. His goal was to confront himself in order to lead a coherent and disciplined life: "Greatness of the soul is not so much pressing upward and forward as knowing how to set oneself in order and circumscribe oneself."

Montaigne sought to address his moral problems through self-knowledge and self-reform. He argued that this sort of self-confrontation imposes even harsher demands than those placed on an Alexander the Great or a Socrates. Those figures operate in public and are rewarded with glory and renown. The solitary seeker after honest self-knowledge works in private. Other people seek the approval of the crowd; Montaigne sought self-respect. "Every one can play his part in the farce, and act an honest role on the stage. But to be disciplined within, in one's own breast, where all is permissible and all is concealed. That is the point."

Montaigne cut short a successful career because he felt the struggle for internal depth and self-respect was more important. He did it by bravely facing the truth about himself. Even during the act of self-confrontation he created an attitude of equipoise that has charmed readers throughout the centuries since. He was willing to face unpleasant truths about himself without getting defensive or trying to rationalize them away. Most of the time his own deficiencies just made him smile.

He had, in the first place, a humble but secure view of himself. He admits that he is a small and uncharismatic man. If he rides around with his staff, people can't tell who is master and who is servant. If he has a poor memory, he will tell you. If he is bad at chess and other games, he will tell you. If he has a small penis, he will tell you. If he is decaying with age, he will tell you.

Like most people, he observes, he's a bit venal: "Let anyone search his heart and we will find that our inward wishes are for the most part born and nourished at the expense of others." He notes that most of the things we struggle for are ephemeral and fragile. A philosopher can cultivate the greatest mind in history, but one bite from a rabid dog could turn him into a raving idiot. Montaigne is the author of the take-you-down-a-peg saying that "on the loftiest throne in the world we are still only sitting on our own rump." He argues that "if others examined themselves attentively, as I do, they would find themselves, as I do, full of inanity and nonsense. Get rid of it I cannot without getting rid of myself. We are all steeped in it, one as much as another; but those who are aware of it are a little better off—though I don't know." As Sarah Bakewell observes in her superb book on the man, *How to Live,* that final coda "though I don't know" is pure Montaigne.

One day, one of his servants, who was riding behind him, took off at full gallop and crashed right into Montaigne and his horse. Montaigne was thrown ten paces behind his horse and lay unconscious, spread on the ground, as if dead. His terrified servants began carrying his lifeless form back to the castle. As they did, he began to come to. His servants later told him how he had behaved—gasping for air, scratching furiously at his chest, ripping at his clothes as if to free himself, apparently in agony. Inside, though, the mental scene was quite different. "I felt infinite sweetness and repose," he recalled, and took pleasure in "growing languid and letting myself go." He had the sensation of being gently carried aloft on a magic carpet.

What a difference, Montaigne later reflected, between the outward appearance and the inner experience. How astonishing. One sanguine lesson he drew is that nobody has to bother learning how to die: "If you don't know how to die, don't worry; Nature will tell you what to do on the spot, fully and adequately. She will do the job perfectly for you; don't bother your head about it."[19]

It's almost as if Montaigne's temperament could be reduced to an equation: a low but accurate view of one's own nature plus a capacity for wonder and astonishment at the bizarreness of creation equals a calming spirit of equipoise. He was, as Bakewell puts it, "liberated to lightheartedness."[20] He seemed to maintain an even keel, neither surrendering to exuberance when things were going well nor falling into despair when they weren't. He created a prose style that embodied graceful nonchalance and then tried to become as cool as his writing. "I seek only to grow indifferent and relaxed," he writes at one point, not entirely convincingly. "I avoid subjecting myself to obligation, he observes (or advises). In essay after essay you can practically see him trying to will himself into easy self-acceptance: "I may wish on the whole, to be otherwise; I may condemn my general character, and implore God to reform me throughout, and to excuse my natural weakness. But I should not, I think, give the name of repentance to this, any more than I should to my dissatisfaction at not being an angel or Cato. My actions are controlled and shaped to what I am and to my condition of life. I can do no better." He gave himself a moderating slogan: "I hold back."

He's a slow reader, so he focuses on just a few books. He's a little lazy, so he learns to relax. (Johnson gave himself fervent self-improvement sermons, but Montaigne would not. Johnson was filled with moral sternness; Montaigne was not.) Montaigne's mind naturally wanders, so he takes advantage and learns to see things from multiple perspectives. Every flaw comes with its own compensation.

The ardent and the self-demanding have never admired Montaigne. They find his emotional register too narrow, his aspirations too modest, his settledness too bland. They have trouble refuting him (he doesn't write in traditional logical structures, so it's hard to find the *there* there to refute), but they conclude that his pervasive skepticism and self-acceptance just lead to self-satisfaction, even a tinge of nihilism. They dismiss him as the master of emotional distance and conflict avoidance.

There's some truth to that view, as Montaigne, of course, would have been the first to admit: "A painful notion takes hold of me; I find it quicker to change it than subdue it. I substitute a contrary one for it, or, if I cannot, at all events a different one. Variation always solaces, dissolves and dissipates. If I cannot combat it, I escape it; and in fleeing I dodge. I am tricky."

Montaigne's example teaches that if you have realistically low expectations, you'll end up pleased in most circumstances. But he is not merely a mellow fellow, a sixteenth-century beach bum with an estate. He sometimes pretends to nonchalance, and he often hides his earnest intent, but he does have a higher vision of the good life and the good society. It is not based on ultimate salvation or ultimate justice, as more ambitious souls would prefer, but on friendship.

His essay on friendship is one of the most moving pieces he produced. It was written to celebrate the bond he shared with his dear friend Étienne de la Boetie, who died about five years into their relationship. They were both writers and thinkers. As we would say nowadays, they were genuine soul mates.

Everything in such a friendship is held in common—will, thoughts, opinions, property, families, children, honor, life. "Our souls travelled so unitedly together, they felt so strong an affection for one another and with this same affection saw in the very depths of each other's hearts, that not only did I know his as well as my own, but I should certainly have trusted myself more freely to him than to myself." If you were to construct a perfect society, he concludes, this sort of friendship would be at its peak.

Two Styles of Goodness

BOTH MONTAIGNE AND JOHNSON WERE BRILLIANT ESSAYISTS, MASTERS OF shifting perspective. Both were humanists in their way, heroically trying to use literature to find the great truths they believed the human mind is capable of comprehending but also doing so with a sense of humility, compassion, and charity. Both tried to pin down the chaos of existence in prose and create a sense of internal order and discipline. But Johnson is all emotional extremes; Montaigne is emotionally moderate. Johnson issues stern self-demands; Montaigne aims at nonchalance and ironic self-acceptance. Johnson is about struggle and suffering, Montaigne is a more genial character, wryly amused by the foibles of the world. Johnson investigated the world to become his desired self; Montaigne investigated himself to see the world. Johnson is a demanding moralist in a sensual, competitive city. He's trying to fire moral ardor and get ambitious bourgeois people to focus on ultimate truths. Montaigne is a calming presence in a country filled with civil war and religious zealotry. Johnson tried to lift people up to emulate heroes. Montaigne feared that those who try to rise above what is realistically human end up sinking into the subhuman. In search of purity they end up burning people at the stake.

We can each of us decide if we are a little more like Montaigne or a little more like Johnson, or which master we can learn from on which occasion. For my part I'd say that Johnson, through arduous effort, built a superior greatness. He was more a creature of the active world. Montaigne's equipoise grew in part from the fact that he grew up rich, with a secure title, and could retire from the messiness of history to the comfort of his estate. Most important, Johnson understood that it takes some hard pressure to sculpt a character. The material is resistant. There has to be some pushing, some sharp cutting, and hacking. It has to be done in confrontation with the intense events of the real world, not in retreat from them. Montaigne had such a genial nature, maybe he could be shaped through gentle observation. Most of us will end up mediocre and self-forgiving if we try to do that.

Industry

IN 1746, JOHNSON SIGNED A CONTRACT TO CREATE AN ENGLISH DICTIONary. Just as he was slowly bringing order to his own internal life, he would also bring order to his language. The French Academy had embarked on a similar project in the previous century. It had taken forty scholars fifty-five years to complete the task. Johnson and six clerks completed their task in eight. He defined 42,000 words and included roughly 116,000 illustrative quotations to show how the words were used. He culled an additional hundred thousand quotations that he ended up not using.

Johnson would pore over all the English literature he could get his hands on, marking the word usage and the usable quotations. He would have these copied onto slips of paper and then collate them in a vast organizational structure. The work was tedious, but Johnson saw a virtue in the tedium. He thought the dictionary would be good for the country and calming to himself. He entered the work, he wrote, "with the pleasing hope that, if it was low, it likewise would be safe. I was drawn forward with the prospect of employment, which, though not splendid, would be useful, and which, though it could not make my life envied, would keep it innocent; which would awaken no passion, engage me in no contention, nor throw in my way any temptation to disturb the quiet of others by censure, or my own by flattery."[21]

While Johnson was working on the dictionary, his wife, Tetty, died. She had suffered from poor health and she drank more and more as the years went by. One day she was upstairs sick in bed when there was a knock on the door. A maid answered and told the visitor that Tetty was ill. It turned out the man was Tetty's grown son from her first marriage. He had become estranged from her when she married Johnson and had not seen her in all the years since. When Tetty heard a few moments later that her son had been at the door, she threw on some clothes and rushed down to find him. But he had left, and she would never see him again.

Johnson was hit hard by her passing. His journals are filled with vows to honor her memory in one way or another. "Enable me to begin and perfect that reformation which I promised her. . . . I kept this day as the anniversary of my Tetty's death with prayer & tears. . . . Resolved . . . to consult my resolves on Tetty's coffin. . . . Thought on Tetty, dear poor Tetty, with my eyes full."

The dictionary made Johnson famous and, if never rich, at least financially secure. He emerged as one of the great figures of British literary life. He spent his days, as usual, in cafés and taverns. He was in the Club, a group of men who met together regularly to dine and discuss. It was probably the single greatest collection of intellectual and artistic friends in British history, and maybe beyond. Its members included not only Johnson but the statesman Edmund Burke, the economist Adam Smith, the painter Joshua Reynolds, the actor (and Johnson's former pupil) David Garrick, the novelist and playwright Oliver Goldsmith, and the historian Edward Gibbon.

Johnson socialized with the lords and intellectuals but spent his domestic life with the down and out. His home was perpetually occupied by a strange collection of indigents and the marginalized. A former slave lived with him, as did an impoverished doctor and a blind poetess. One night he found a prostitute lying ill and exhausted on the street. He put her on his back, brought her home, and gave her a place to live. The beneficiaries of his mercy fought with each other and with him, and they made the home a crowded, fractious place, but Johnson was loath to turn them out.

He also did amazing amounts of writing for friends. The man who said "no man but a blockhead ever wrote except for money" composed thousands of pages for free. An eighty-two-year-old former physician had spent years trying to come up with a more accurate way to determine longitude while at sea. He was now dying, his work having come to nothing. Johnson, feeling compassion for the man, studied up on navigation and the man's theories on it and wrote a book, which he put out under the man's name, titled *An Account of an Attempt to Ascertain the Longitude of the Sea,* just to give him the sense at the end of his life that his ideas would live on. Another friend, a twenty-nine-year-old man named Robert Chambers, was elected to a professorship of law at Oxford. Chambers, sadly, was neither a noted legal mind nor a good writer. Johnson agreed to help him out by ghostwriting his law lectures. Johnson wrote sixty separate lectures for him stretching over sixteen hundred pages.

Johnson worked feverishly nearly until his death. Between the ages of sixty-eight and seventy-two he wrote his *Lives of the Poets,* fifty-two biographies covering 378,000 words, at a time when age seventy really was elderly. He never achieved the equanimity that seems to have marked Montaigne's mature years, or the calmness and reserve he admired in others. He lived all his life with periodic feelings of despair, depression, shame, masochism, and guilt. In old age he asked a friend to hold a padlock for him that could be used if he should go insane and require physical restraint.

Nonetheless, there is an unmistakable largeness to Johnson's character in his final few years. Late in life, with his companion and biographer Boswell, he became one of the most famous conversationalists of all time. He could unfurl long paragraphs of repartee on almost any subject and for almost any occasion. These observations didn't just arise spontaneously. They were the product of a lifetime of mental labor.

He also built a consistent point of view. It began with an awareness of the constant presence of egotism, self-centeredness, and self-deception. But it was fueled by his own rebel spirit. From childhood and university days up through adult life he had a deep instinct to revolt against authority. He turned that rebellious spirit against his own nature. He turned it against evil, interior and exterior. He used it as fuel to propel him into self-combat.

Self-combat was his path to redemption. He defined a different type of courage, the courage of honesty (Montaigne had it, too). He believed that the expressive powers of literature, if used with utter moral sincerity, could conquer demons. Truth was his bondage breaker. As Bate puts it, "Johnson time and again walks up to almost every anxiety and fear the human heart can feel. As he puts his hands directly upon it and looks at it closely, the lion's skin falls off, and we often find beneath it only a donkey, maybe only a frame of wood. That is why we so often find ourselves laughing as we read what he has to say. We laugh partly through sheer relief."[22]

Everything was a moral contest for Johnson, a chance to improve, to degrade or repent. His conversation, even when uproarious, was meant to be improving. When he was an old man he recalled an episode in his youth. His father had asked him to man the family bookstall in the market square of a town called Uttoxeter. Johnson, feeling superior to his father, had refused. Now elderly, feeling the lingering shame, he made a special trip to the market square of Uttoxeter and stood on the spot where his father's stall had been. As he later recalled:

> Pride was the source of that refusal, and the remembrance of it was painful. A few years ago I desired to atone for this fault. I went to Uttoxeter in very bad weather and stood for a considerable time bareheaded in the rain. . . . In contrition I stood, and I hope that the penance was expiatory.

Johnson never triumphed, but he integrated, he built a more stable whole than would have seemed possible from his fragmented nature. As Adam Gopnick wrote in *The New Yorker* in 2012, "He was his own whale, and brought himself home."

Finally, when Johnson was seventy-five, death approached. He had a powerful fear of damnation. He put a text on his watch, "The night cometh," to remind himself to commit no sins that would lead to a bad final judgment. Nonetheless it hung passionately upon his mind. Boswell records an exchange with a friend:

> Johnson: I am afraid I may be one of those who shall be damned (looking dismally).
> Dr. Adams: What do you mean by damned?
> Johnson: (passionately and loudly). Sent to Hell, Sir, and punished everlastingly.

IN HIS FINAL WEEK his doctor told him he would surely die soon. He asked to be taken off the opium so he would not meet God "in a state of idiocy." When his doctor made some incisions in his legs to drain fluid, Johnson cried out, "Deeper, deeper; I want length of life, and you are afraid to give me pain, which I do not value." Later Johnson got some scissors and plunged them into his own legs in a further attempt to drain them. His pronouncement in the face of death was of a piece with his manner in life: "I will be conquered; I will not capitulate."

Johnson stands now as an example of humane wisdom. From his scattered youth, his diverse faculties cohered into a single faculty—a mode of seeing and judging the world that was as much emotional as intellectual. Especially toward the end of his life, it becomes hard to categorize his writing. His journalism rose to the level of literature; his biographies contained ethics; his theology was filled with practical advice. He became a universal thinker.

The foundation of it all was his tremendous capacity for sympathy. His life story begins with physical suffering. As a teenager and young man he was one of the world's outcasts, disfigured by fate. He seems never to have shaken that vulnerability, but he succeeded in turning his handicaps and limitations into advantages through sheer hard work. For a man who continually castigated himself for his sloth, his capacity for labor was enormous.

He wrestled, really wrestled with matters that were of real importance, matters of his very being. "To strive with difficulties, and to conquer them, is the highest human felicity," he wrote in one of his essays. "The next is to strive and deserve to conquer; but he whose life has passed without contest, and who can boast neither success nor merit can survey himself only as a useless filler of existence."

That wrestling was undertaken on behalf of an unblinking honesty. The Victorian writer John Ruskin wrote, "The more I think of it I find this conclusion more impressed upon me—that the greatest thing a human soul ever does in this world is to *see* something, and tell what it *saw* in a plain way. Hundreds of people can talk for one who can think, but thousands can think for one who can see."

Johnson's genius for epigram and for pithy observation emerged also out of his extraordinary sensitivity to the world around him. It was nurtured, too, by his skepticism about himself—his ability to doubt his motives, see through his rationalizations, laugh at his vanities, and understand that he was just as foolish as others were.

After his death, the nation mourned. A reaction from William Gerard Hamilton is the most often quoted and most accurately captures the achievement of the man and the void his death created: "He has made a chasm, which not only nothing can fill up, but which nothing has a tendency to fill up. Johnson is dead. Let us go with the next best: There is nobody; no man can be said to put you in mind of Johnson."

CHAPTER 10

THE BIG ME

IN JANUARY 1969, TWO GREAT QUARTERBACKS FACED EACH OTHER from opposite sidelines in Super Bowl III. Both Johnny Unitas and Joe Namath were raised in the steel towns of western Pennsylvania. But they had grown up a decade apart and lived in different moral cultures.

Unitas grew up in the old culture of self-effacement and self-defeat. His father died when he was five and his mother took over the family coal delivery business, supervising its one driver. Unitas went to a strict Catholic school in the old tradition. The teachers were morally demanding and could be harsh and cruel. The domineering Father Barry would hand out report cards personally, flipping them at one boy after another, remarking cruelly, "You'll make a good truck driver some day. You'll be digging ditches." The prophecies terrified the boys.[1]

Football players in Western Pennsylvania gloried in their ability to endure pain.[2] Unitas weighed 145 pounds while playing quarterback for his high school team, and he took a beating during every game. He went to church before every game, deferred to the authority of his coaches, and lived a football-obsessed life.[3] Turned down by Notre Dame, Unitas then played quarterback at a basketball school, the University of Louisville. He had a brief tryout with the Pittsburgh Steelers but was cut. He was back working on a construction gang, playing semipro football, when he got a long-shot call from the Baltimore

Colts. He made the team and spent many of his early years with the Colts steadily losing.

Unitas was not an overnight sensation in the NFL, but he was steadily ripening, honing his skills and making his teammates better. When his pro career looked secure, he bought a split-level house in Towson, Maryland, and also took a job with the Columbia Container Corporation that paid him $125 a week throughout the year.[4] He was a deliberately unglamorous figure with his black high-top sneakers, bowed legs, stooped shoulders, and a crew cut above his rough face. If you look at photos of him traveling with the team you see a guy who looks like a 1950s insurance salesman, with his white short-sleeved button-down shirt and narrow black tie. He and his buddies would sit on the buses and planes, dressed almost exactly the same, haircuts the same, playing bridge.

He was unflamboyant and understated. "I always figured being a little dull was part of being a pro. Win or lose, I never walked off a football field without first thinking of something boring to say to [the press]," he would say later. He was loyal to his organization and to his teammates. In the huddle he'd rip into his receivers for screwing up plays and running the wrong routes. "I'll never throw to you again if you don't learn the plays," he'd bark. Then, after the game, he'd lie to the reporter: "My fault, I overthrew him" was his standard line.

Unitas was confident in his football abilities but unprepossessing in the way he went about his job. Steve Sabol of NFL Films captured some of his manner: "It's always been my job to glorify the game. I'm such a romantic anyway. I've always looked at football in dramaturgical terms. It wasn't the score; it was the struggle, and what kind of music could we use? But when I met Unitas I realized he was the antithesis of all that. Football to him was no different than a plumber putting in a pipe. He was an honest workman doing an honest job. Everything was a shrug of the shoulders. He was so unromantic that he was romantic, in the end."[5] Unitas, like Joe DiMaggio in baseball, came to embody a particular way of being a sports hero in the age of self-effacement.

Namath, who grew up in the same area but a half generation later, lived in a different moral universe. Joe Namath was the flamboyant star, with white shoes and flowing hair, brashly guaranteeing victory. Broadway Joe was outrageously entertaining and fun to be around.

He made himself the center of attention, a spectacle off the field as much as on it, with $5,000 fur coats, long sideburns, and playboy manners. He didn't care what others thought of him, or at least said he didn't. "Some people don't like this image I got myself, being a swinger," Namath told Jimmy Breslin in a famous 1969 piece, "Namath All Night," for *New York* magazine. "But I'm not institutional. I swing. If it's good or bad, I don't know, but it's what I like."

Namath grew up in Unitas's shadow in poor Western Pennsylvania, but into a different way of being. His parents divorced when he was seven and he rebelled against his immigrant family by being cool, hanging around the pool hall and adopting a James Dean leather-jacketed swagger.

Namath's football talents were flamboyantly obvious. He was one of the most highly recruited players in the country that year. He wanted to go to college in Maryland, thinking it was in the South, but his SATs weren't high enough. So he went to the University of Alabama, where he went on to become one of the nation's best collegiate quarterbacks. He was given a gigantic signing bonus to play with the New York Jets and was immediately making much more than any of his teammates.

He cultivated a personal brand that was bigger than the team. He was not just a football star but a lifestyle star. He paid a fine so he could wear a Fu Manchu mustache on the field. He starred in pantyhose commercials, challenging old-fashioned notions of masculinity. He famously had six-inch shag carpets in his bachelor pad, and he popularized the use of the word "foxes" for women. He wrote an autobiography titled *I Can't Wait Until Tomorrow 'Cause I Get Better Looking Every Day*. This is not a title Johnny Unitas would have chosen.

Namath came to stardom at a time when New Journalism was breaking the mold of the old reporting. Namath was the perfect subject. Without a reticent bone in his body, he'd bring reporters along as he worked his way through bottles of scotch the night before games. He openly bragged about what a great athlete he was, how good-looking he was. He cultivated a brashly honest style. "Joe! Joe! You're the most beautiful thing in the world!" he shouted to himself in the bathroom mirror of the Copacabana one night in 1966, as a reporter from *The Saturday Evening Post* tagged along.[6]

Fiercely independent, he did not want to make a deep commitment to any woman. He created an early version of what we would now call the hook-up culture. "I don't like to date so much as I just like to kind of, you know, run into something, man," he told a reporter for *Sports Illustrated* in 1966. He embodied the autonomy ethos that was beginning to sweep through the country. "I believe in letting a guy live the way he wants to if he doesn't hurt anyone. I feel that everything I do is okay for me and doesn't affect anybody else, including the girls I go out with. Look, man, I live and let live. I like everybody."[7]

Namath heralded a new mode for being a professional athlete—a mode of personal branding, lavish endorsements, in which the star expressed his own vibrant personality and outshone the team.

Cultural Change

CULTURES CHANGE IN WAYS THAT ARE BOTH SUPERFICIAL AND PROFOUND. When the essayist Joseph Epstein was young, he observed that when you went into the drugstore the cigarettes were in the open shelves and the condoms were behind the counter. But now when you go to the drugstore, the condoms are in the open shelves and the cigarettes are behind the counter.

The conventional view of the shift from the humility of Unitas to the brash flamboyance of Namath is that it happened in the late 1960s. The conventional story goes something like this. First there was the Greatest Generation, whose members were self-sacrificing, self-effacing, and community-minded. Then along came the 1960s and the Baby Boomers, who were narcissistic, self-expressive, selfish, and morally lax.

But this story doesn't fit the facts. What really happened goes like this: Starting in biblical times there was a tradition of moral realism, the "crooked-timber" school of humanity. This tradition, or worldview, put tremendous emphasis on sin and human weakness. This view of humanity was captured in the figure of Moses, the meekest of men who nonetheless led a people, and by biblical figures like David, who were great heroes, but deeply flawed. This biblical metaphysic was later expressed by Christian thinkers such as Augustine, with his emphasis on sin, his rejection of worldly success, his belief in the necessity of grace, of surrendering oneself to God's unmerited love. This moral realism then found expression in humanists like Samuel Johnson, Michel de Montaigne, and George Eliot, who emphasized how little we can know, how hard it is to know ourselves, and how hard we have to work on the long road to virtue. "We are all of us born in moral stupidity, taking the world as an udder to feed our supreme selves," Eliot wrote.[8] It was also embodied, in different ways and at different times, in the thought of Dante, Hume, Burke, Reinhold Niebuhr, and Isaiah Berlin. All of these thinkers take a limited view of our individual powers of reason. They are suspicious of abstract thinking and pride. They emphasize the limitations in our individual natures.

Some of these limitations are epistemological: reason is weak and the world is complex. We cannot really grasp the complexity of the world or the full truth about ourselves. Some of these limitations are moral: There are bugs in our souls that lead us toward selfishness and pride, that tempt us to put lower loves over higher loves. Some of the limitations are psychological: We are divided within ourselves, and many of the most urgent motions of our minds are unconscious and only dimly recognized by ourselves. Some of them are social: We are not self-completing creatures. To thrive we have to throw ourselves into a state of dependence—on others, on institutions, on the divine. The place that limitation occupies in the "crooked timber" school is immense.

Around the eighteenth century, moral realism found a rival in moral romanticism. While moral realists placed emphasis on inner weakness, moral romantics like Jean-Jacques Rousseau placed emphasis on our inner goodness. The realists distrusted the self and trusted institutions and customs outside the self; the romantics trusted the self and distrusted the conventions of the outer world. The realists believed in cultivation, civilization, and artifice; the romanticists believed in nature, the individual, and sincerity.

For a while, these two traditions lived side by side in society, in creative tension and conversation. Except in artistic circles, realism had the upper hand. If you grew up in early twentieth century America, you grew up with the vocabulary and categories of moral realism, translated into a practical secular or religious idiom. Perkins grew up with the vocabulary of vocation, the need to suppress parts of yourself so you can be an instrument in a larger cause. Eisenhower grew up with the vocabulary of self-defeat. Day learned as a young woman the vocabulary of simplicity, poverty, and surrender. Marshall learned institutional thinking, the need to give oneself to organizations that transcend a lifetime. Randolph and Rustin learned reticence and the logic of self-discipline, the need to distrust oneself even while waging a noble crusade. These people didn't know they were exemplifying parts of the realist tradition. This ethos was just in the air they breathed and the way they were raised.

But then moral realism collapsed. Its vocabulary and ways of thinking were forgotten or shoved off into the margins of society. Realism and romanticism slipped out of balance. A moral vocabulary was lost, and along with it a methodology for the formation of souls. This shift did not happen during the 1960s and 1970s, though that period was a great romantic flowering. It happened earlier, in the late 1940s and 1950s. It was the Greatest Generation that abandoned realism.

By the fall of 1945, people around the world had endured sixteen years of deprivation—first during the Depression, then during the war. They were ready to let loose, to relax, to enjoy. Consumption and advertising took off as people rushed to the stores to buy things that would make life easier and more fun. People in the postwar years wanted to escape from the shackles of self-restraint and all those gloomy subjects like sin and depravity. They were ready to put the horrors of the Holocaust and the war behind them.

People right after the war were ready to read any book that offered a more upbeat and positive vision of life and its possibilities. In 1946, Rabbi Joshua L. Liebman published a book titled *Peace of Mind* that urged people to engrave a new morality on their hearts, one based on setting aside the idea that you should repress any part of yourself. Instead, thou shalt "love thyself properly . . . thou shalt not be afraid of thy hidden impulses . . . respect thyself . . . trust thyself." Liebman had an infinite faith in the infinite goodness of men and women. "I believe that man is infinitely potential, and that given the proper guidance there is hardly a task he cannot perform or a degree of mastery in work and love he cannot attain."[9] He struck a chord. His book remained on the top of the *New York Times* bestseller list for an astounding fifty-eight weeks.

That same year, Benjamin Spock came out with his famous baby book. That book was complex and is often unfairly maligned, but it did, especially in early editions, express a notably rosy view of human nature. Spock said that if your child steals something, you should give him as a present something similar to the item that he stole. That will show that you care for your child and that "he should have his heart's desire if it is reasonable."[10]

In 1949, Harry Overstreet published a wildly popular book titled *The Mature Mind,* which pushed the point a little further. Overstreet argued that those like Saint Augustine who emphasized human sinfulness had "denied to our species the healthy blessing of self-respect."[11] This emphasis on internal weakness encouraged people to "distrust himself and malign himself."

Then, in 1952, Norman Vincent Peale came out with the mother of all optimistic books, *The Power of Positive Thinking,* urging readers to cast negative thoughts from mind and pep-talk themselves into greatness. That book rested atop the *Times* list for an astounding ninety-eight weeks.

Then came humanistic psychology led by people like Carl Rogers, the most influential psychologist of the twentieth century. The humanistic psychologists shifted away from Freud's darker conception of the unconscious and promoted a sky-high estimation of human nature. The primary psychological problem, he argued, is that people don't love themselves enough, and so therapists unleashed a great wave of self-loving. "Man's behavior is exquisitely rational," Rogers wrote, "moving with subtle and ordered complexity toward the goal his organism is endeavoring to achieve."[12] The words that best describe human nature, he continued, are "positive, forward moving, constructive, realistic and trustworthy." People don't need to combat themselves, they only need to open up, to liberate their inner selves, so that their internalized drive to self-actualize can take over. Self-love, self-praise, and self-acceptance are the paths to happiness. To the extent that a person "can be freely in touch with his valuing process in himself, he will behave in ways that are self-enhancing."[13]

Humanistic psychology has shaped nearly every school, nearly every curriculum, nearly every HR department, nearly every self-help book. Soon there were "IALAC" posters on school walls every-where—I AM LOVABLE AND CAPABLE. The self-esteem movement was born. Our modern conversation lives in this romantic vision.

The Age of Self-Esteem

THE SHIFT FROM ONE MORAL CULTURE TO ANOTHER IS NOT A CRUDE STORY of decline, from noble restraint to self-indulgent decadence. Each moral climate is a collective response to the problems of the moment. People in the Victorian era were faced with a decline in religious faith and adopted a strict character morality as a way to compensate. People in the 1950s and 1960s confronted a different set of problems. When people shift from one moral ecology to another, they are making a trade-off in response to changing circumstances. Since legitimate truths sit in tension with one another, one moral climate will put more emphasis here and less emphasis there, for better or worse. Certain virtues are cultivated, certain beliefs go too far, and certain important truths and moral virtues are accidentally forgotten.

The shift in the 1950s and 1960s to a culture that put more emphasis on pride and self-esteem had many positive effects; it helped correct some deep social injustices. Up until those years, many social groups, notably women, minorities, and the poor, had received messages of inferiority and humiliation. They were taught to think too lowly of themselves. The culture of self-esteem encouraged members of these oppressed groups to believe in themselves, to raise their sights and aspirations.

For example, many women had been taught to lead lives so committed to subservience and service that it led to self-abnegation. Katharine Meyer Graham's life illustrates why so many people embraced the shift from self-effacement to self-expression.

Katharine Meyer grew up in a wealthy publishing family in Washington, D.C. She attended the Madeira School, a progressive but genteel private school in which young ladies were raised amid mottoes such as "Function in disaster. Finish in style." At home, she was thoroughly dominated by a father who was awkward and distant and by a mother who demanded Stepford Wife perfection: "I think we all felt we somehow hadn't lived up to what she expected or wanted of us, and the insecurities and lack of self-confidence she bred were long lasting," she would write years later in her superb memoir.[14]

Girls were expected to be quiet, reserved, and correct, and Katharine grew up painfully self-conscious. "Had I said the right thing? Had I worn the right clothes? Was I attractive? These questions were unsettling and self-absorbing, even overwhelming at times."

In 1940, Katharine married a charming, witty, mercurial man named Philip Graham, who had a subtle or not so subtle way of belittling her views and abilities. "I increasingly saw my role as the tail to his kite—and the more I felt overshadowed, the more it became a reality."[15] Graham had a series of affairs, which Katharine discovered and was devastated by.

Graham, who suffered from depression, committed suicide on August 3, 1963. Six weeks later, Katharine was elected president of the Washington Post Company. At first she saw herself as a bridge between her dead husband and her children who would eventually inherit it. But she shut her eyes, took a step as manager, took another step, and found she could do the job.

Over the next few decades the surrounding culture encouraged Katharine to assert herself and to develop the full use of her capacities. The year she took over the *Post,* Betty Friedan published *The Feminine Mystique,* which embraced Carl Rogers's humanistic psychology. Gloria Steinem later wrote a bestselling book, *Revolution from Within: A Book of Self-Esteem*. Dr. Joyce Brothers, a prominent advice columnist at the time, put the ethos bluntly: "Put yourself first—at least some of the time. Society has brainwashed women into believing that their husbands' and children's needs should always be given priority over their own. Society has never impressed on women as it has on men the human necessity of putting yourself first. I am not advocating selfishness. I'm talking about the basics of life. You have to decide how many children you want, what kind of friends you want, what kind of relationships you want with your family."[16]

The emphasis on self-actualization and self-esteem gave millions of women a language to articulate and cultivate self-assertion, strength, and identity. Graham eventually became one of the most admired and powerful publishing executives in the world. She built the *Post* into a major and highly profitable national newspaper. She stood up to the Nixon White House and storm of abuse during the Watergate crisis, maintaining steadfast support for Bob Woodward, Carl Bernstein, and the rest of the journalists who broke that story. She never fully overcame her insecurities, but she did learn to project a formidable image. Her memoir is a masterwork, understated but also honest and authoritative, without a hint of self-pity or false sentiment.

Katharine Graham, like many women and members of minority groups, needed a higher and more accurate self-image—needed to move from Little Me to Big Me.

Authenticity

THE UNDERLYING ASSUMPTIONS ABOUT HUMAN NATURE AND THE SHAPE OF human life were altered by this shift to the Big Me. If you were born at any time over the last sixty years, you were probably born into what the philosopher Charles Taylor has called "the culture of authenticity." This mindset is based on the romantic idea that each of us has a Golden Figure in the core of our self. There is an innately good True Self, which can be trusted, consulted, and gotten in touch with. Your personal feelings are the best guide for what is right and wrong.

In this ethos, the self is to be trusted, not doubted. Your desires are like inner oracles for what is right and true. You know you are doing the right thing when you feel good inside. The valid rules of life are those you make or accept for yourself and that feel right to you.

"Our moral salvation," Taylor writes, describing this culture, "comes from recovering authentic moral contact with ourselves." It is important to stay true to that pure inner voice and not follow the conformities of a corrupting world. As Taylor puts it, "There is a certain way of being that is my way. I am called to live my life in this way and not in imitation of anyone else's. . . . If I am not, I miss the point of my life. I miss what being human is for me."[17]

From an older tradition of self-combat we move to self-liberation and self-expression. Moral authority is no longer found in some external objective good; it is found in each person's unique original self. Greater emphasis is put on personal feelings as a guide to what is right and wrong. I know I am doing right because I feel harmonious inside. Something is going wrong, on the other hand, when I feel my autonomy is being threatened, when I feel I am not being true to myself.

In this ethos, sin is not found in your individual self; it is found in the external structures of society—in racism, inequality, and oppression. To improve yourself, you have to be taught to love yourself, to be true to yourself, not to doubt yourself and struggle against yourself. As one of the characters in one of the *High School Musical* movies sings, "The answers are all inside of me / All I've got to do is believe."

Status Updates

THIS INTELLECTUAL AND CULTURAL SHIFT TOWARD THE BIG ME WAS REIN-forced by economic and technological changes. All of us today live in a technological culture. I'm not a big believer that social media have had a ruinous effect on the culture, as many technophobes fear. There is no evidence to support the idea that technology has induced people to live in a fake online world while renouncing the real one. But information technology has had three effects on the moral ecology that have inflated the Big Me Adam I side of our natures and diminished the humbler Adam II.

First, communications have become faster and busier. It is harder to attend to the soft, still voices that come from the depths. Throughout human history, people have found that they are most aware of their depths when they are on retreats, during moments of separation and stillness, during moments of quiet communion. They have found that they need time, long periods of stillness, before the external Adam quiets and the internal Adam can be heard. These moments of stillness and quiet are just more rare today. We reach for the smartphone.

Second, social media allow a more self-referential information environment. People have more tools and occasions to construct a culture, a mental environment tailored specifically for themselves. Modern information technology allows families to sit together in a room, each absorbed in a different show, movie, or game in the privacy of their own screen. Instead of being a peripheral star in the mass-media world of the Ed Sullivan show, each individual can be the sun at the center of his or her own media solar system, creating a network of programs, apps, and pages oriented around their own needs. A Yahoo advertising campaign vowed, "Now the Internet has a personality—It's You!" Earthlink's slogan was "Earthlink revolves around you."

Third, social media encourages a broadcasting personality. Our natural bent is to seek social approval and fear exclusion. Social networking technology allows us to spend our time engaged in a hyper-competitive struggle for attention, for victories in the currency of "likes." People are given more occasions to be self-promoters, to embrace the characteristics of celebrity, to manage their own image, to Snapchat out their selfies in ways that they hope will impress and please the world. This technology creates a culture in which people turn into little brand managers, using Facebook, Twitter, text messages, and Instagram to create a falsely upbeat, slightly overexuberant, external self that can be famous first in a small sphere and then, with luck, in a large one. The manager of this self measures success by the flow of responses it gets. The social media maven spends his or her time creating a self-caricature, a much happier and more photogenic version of real life. People subtly start comparing themselves to other people's highlight reels, and of course they feel inferior.

The Soul of Man Under Meritocracy

THE PURIFICATION OF THE MERITOCRACY HAS ALSO REINFORCED THE IDEA that each of us is wonderful inside. It has also encouraged self-aggrandizing tendencies. If you have lived through the last sixty or seventy years, you are the product of a more competitive meritocracy. You have, like me, spent your life trying to make something of yourself, trying to have an impact, trying to be reasonably successful in this world. That's meant a lot of competition and a lot of emphasis on individual achievement—doing reasonably well in school, getting into the right college, landing the right job, moving toward success and status.

This competitive pressure meant that we all have to spend more time, energy, and attention on the external Adam I climb toward success and we have less time, energy, and attention to devote to the internal world of Adam II.

I've found in myself, and I think I've observed in others, a certain meritocratic mentality, which is based on the self-trusting, self-puffing insights of the Romantic tradition, but which is also depoeticized and despiritualized. If moral realists saw the self as a wilderness to be tamed, and if people in the New Age 1970s saw the self as an Eden to be actualized, people living in a high-pressure meritocracy are more likely to see the self as a resource base to be cultivated. The self is less likely to be seen as the seat of the soul, or as the repository of some transcendent spirit. Instead, the self is a vessel of human capital. It is a series of talents to be cultivated efficiently and prudently. The self is defined by its tasks and accomplishments. The self is about talent, not character.

This meritocratic mentality was beautifully captured in Dr. Seuss's 1990 book *Oh, the Places You'll Go!,* the fifth-biggest bestseller in the history of the *New York Times* list and still a popular graduation present.

The book is about a boy who is reminded that he has all these amazing talents and gifts, and ultimate freedom to choose his life: "You have brains in your head. You have feet in your shoes. You can steer yourself any direction you choose." The boy is reminded that his life is about fulfilling his own desires. "You're on your own. And you know what you know. And YOU are the guy who'll decide where to go." The challenges the boy faces in life are mostly external. And the life goals he pursues are all Adam I life goals. "Fame! You'll be famous as famous can be, / With the whole wide world watching you win on TV." The ultimate goal in this life is success, to have an impact on the external world. "And will you succeed? / Yes! You will indeed / 98 and ¾ percent guaranteed."[18] And the main character in this success story is YOU. That little word appears in this very short book ninety times.

In this book, the boy is completely autonomous. He is free to choose exactly as he individually wishes. He is reminded how wonderful he is. He is not weighted down by any internal weakness. He proves his merit through work and ascent.

The meritocracy liberates enormous energies, and ranks people in ways good and bad. But it also has a subtle effect on character, culture, and values. Any hypercompetitive system built upon merit is going to encourage people to think a lot about themselves and the cultivation of their own skills. Work becomes the defining feature of a life, especially as you begin to get social invitations because you happen to inhabit a certain job. Subtly, softly, but pervasively, this system instills a certain utilitarian calculus in us all. The meritocracy subtly encourages an instrumental ethos in which each occasion—a party, a dinner—and each acquaintance becomes an opportunity to advance your status and professional life project. People are more likely to think in commercial categories—to speak about opportunity costs, scalability, human capital, cost-benefit analysis, even when it comes to how they spend their private time.

The meaning of the word "character" changes. It is used less to describe traits like selflessness, generosity, self-sacrifice, and other qualities that sometimes make worldly success less likely. It is instead used to describe traits like self-control, grit, resilience, and tenacity, qualities that make worldly success more likely.

The meritocratic system wants you to be big about yourself—to puff yourself, to be completely sure of yourself, to believe that you deserve a lot and to get what you think you deserve (so long as it is good). The meritocracy wants you to assert and advertise yourself. It wants you to display and exaggerate your achievements. The achievement machine rewards you if you can demonstrate superiority—if with a thousand little gestures, conversational types, and styles of dress you can demonstrate that you are a bit smarter, hipper, more accomplished, sophisticated, famous, plugged in, and fashion-forward than the people around you. It encourages narrowing. It encourages you to become a shrewd animal.

The shrewd animal has streamlined his inner humanity to make his ascent more aerodynamic. He carefully manages his time and his emotional commitments. Things once done in a poetic frame of mind, such as going to college, meeting a potential lover, or bonding with an employer, are now done in a more professional frame of mind. Is this person, opportunity, or experience of use to me? There just isn't time to get carried away by love and passion. There is a cost to making a soul-deep commitment to one mission or one love. If you commit to one big thing you will close off options toward other big things. You will be plagued by a Fear of Missing Out.

The shift from the Little Me culture to the Big Me culture was not illegitimate, but it went too far. The realist tradition that emphasized limitation and moral struggle was inadvertently marginalized and left by the side of the road, first by the romantic flowering of positive psychology, then by the self-branding ethos of social media, finally by the competitive pressures of the meritocracy. We are left with a moral ecology that builds up the exterior Adam I muscles but ignores the internal Adam II ones, and that creates an imbalance. It's a culture in which people are defined by their external abilities and achievements, in which a cult of busyness develops as everybody frantically tells each other how overcommitted they are. As my student Andrew Reeves once put it, it cultivates an unrealistic expectation that life will happen on a linear progression, a natural upward slope toward success. It encourages people to "satisfice," to get by on talent and just enough commitment to get the job done on time, without full soul commitment to any task.

This tradition tells you *how* to do the things that will propel you to the top, but it doesn't encourage you to ask yourself *why* you are doing them. It offers little guidance on how to choose among different career paths and different vocations, how to determine which will be morally highest and best. It encourages people to become approval-seeking machines, to measure their lives by external praise—if people like you and accord you status, then you must be doing something right. The meritocracy contains its own cultural contradictions. It encourages people to make the most of their capacities, but it leads to the shriveling of the moral faculties that are necessary if you are going to figure out how to point your life in a meaningful direction.

Conditional Love

LET ME JUST DESCRIBE ONE WAY THE MERITOCRACY'S UTILITARIAN, INstrumentalist mindset can, in some cases, distort a sacred bond: parenthood.

There are two great defining features of child rearing today. First, children are now praised to an unprecedented degree. Dorothy Parker quipped that American children aren't raised, they are incited—they are given food, shelter, and applause. That's much more true today. Children are incessantly told how special they are. In 1966, only about 19 percent of high school students graduated with an A or A- average. By 2013, 53 percent of students graduated with that average, according to UCLA surveys of incoming college freshmen. Young people are surrounded by so much praise that they develop sky-high aspirations for themselves. According to an Ernst & Young survey, 65 percent of college students expect to become millionaires.[19]

The second defining feature is that children are honed to an unprecedented degree. Parents, at least in the more educated, affluent classes, spend much more time than in past generations grooming their children, investing in their skills, and driving them to practices and rehearsals. As Richard Murnane of Harvard found, parents with college degrees invest $5,700 more per year per child on out-of-school enrichment activities than they did in 1978.[20]

These two great trends—greater praise and greater honing—combine in interesting ways. Children are bathed in love, but it is often directional love. Parents shower their kids with affection, but it is not simple affection, it is meritocratic affection—it is intermingled with the desire to help their children achieve worldly success.

Some parents unconsciously shape their expressions of love to steer their children toward behavior they think will lead to achievement and happiness. Parents glow with extra fervor when their child studies hard, practices hard, wins first place, gets into a prestigious college, or joins the honor society (in today's schools, the word "honor" means earning top grades). Parental love becomes merit-based. It is not simply "I love you." It is "I love you when you stay on my balance beam. I shower you with praise and care when you're on my beam."

Parents in the 1950s were much more likely to say they expected their children to be obedient than parents today, who tell pollsters they want their children to think for themselves. But this desire for obedience hasn't vanished, it's just gone underground—from the straightforward system of rules and lectures, reward and punishment, to the semihidden world of approval or disapproval.

Lurking in the shadows of merit-based love is the possibility that it may be withdrawn if the child disappoints. Parents would deny this, but the wolf of conditional love is lurking here. This shadowy presence of conditional love produces fear, the fear that there is no utterly safe love; there is no completely secure place where young people can be utterly honest and themselves.

On the one hand, relationships between parents and children may be closer than ever before. Parents and children, even college-age children, communicate constantly. With only quiet qualms young people have accepted the vast achievement system that surrounds them. They submit to it because they long for the approval they get from the adults they love.

But the whole situation is more fraught than it appears at first glance. Some children assume that this merit-tangled love is the natural order of the universe. The tiny blips of approval and disapproval are built into the fabric of communication so deep that it is below the level of awareness. Enormous internal pressure is generated by the growing assumption that it is necessary to behave in a certain way to be worthy of another's love. Underneath, the children are terrified that the deepest relationship they know will be lost.

Some parents unconsciously regard their children as something like an art project, to be crafted through mental and emotional engineering. There is some parental narcissism here, the insistence that your children go to colleges and lead lives that will give the parents status and pleasure. Children who are uncertain of their parents' love develop a voracious hunger for it. This conditional love is like acid that dissolves children's internal criteria, their capacity to make their own decisions about their own interests, careers, marriages, and life in general.

The parental relationship is supposed to be built upon unconditional love—a gift that cannot be bought and cannot be earned. It sits outside the logic of meritocracy and is the closest humans come to grace. But in these cases the pressure to succeed in the Adam I world has infected a relationship that should be operating by a different logic, the moral logic of Adam II. The result is holes in the hearts of many children across this society.

The Age of the Selfie

THIS CULTURAL, TECHNOLOGICAL, AND MERITOCRATIC ENVIRONMENT HASN'T made us a race of depraved barbarians. But it has made us less morally articulate. Many of us have instincts about right and wrong, about how goodness and character are built, but everything is fuzzy. Many of us have no clear idea how to build character, no rigorous way to think about such things. We are clear about external, professional things but unclear about internal, moral ones. What the Victorians were to sex, we are to morality: everything is covered in euphemism.

This shift in culture has changed us. In the first place, it has made us a bit more materialistic. College students now say they put more value on money and career success. Every year, researchers from UCLA survey a nationwide sample of college freshmen to gauge their values and what they want out of life. In 1966, 80 percent of freshmen said that they were strongly motivated to develop a meaningful philosophy of life. Today, less than half of them say that. In 1966, 42 percent said that becoming rich was an important life goal. By 1990, 74 percent agreed with that statement. Financial security, once seen as a middling value, is now tied as students' top goal. In 1966, in other words, students felt it was important to at least present themselves as philosophical and meaning-driven people. By 1990, they no longer felt the need to present themselves that way. They felt it perfectly acceptable to say they were primarily interested in money.[21]

We live in a more individualistic society. If you humbly believe that you are not individually strong enough to defeat your own weaknesses, then you know you must be dependent on redemptive assistance from outside. But if you proudly believe the truest answers can be found in the real you, the voice inside, then you are less likely to become engaged with others. Sure enough, there has been a steady decline in intimacy. Decades ago, people typically told pollsters that they had four or five close friends, people to whom they could tell everything. Now the common answer is two or three, and the number of people with no confidants has doubled. Thirty-five percent of older adults report being chronically lonely, up from 20 percent a decade ago.[22] At the same time, social trust has declined. Surveys ask, "Generally speaking, would you say that most people can be trusted or that you can't be too careful in dealing with people?" In the early 1960s, significant majorities said that people can generally be trusted. But in the 1990s the distrusters had a 20-percentage-point margin over the trusters, and those margins have increased in the years since.[23]

People have become less empathetic—or at least they display less empathy in how they describe themselves. A University of Michigan study found that today's college students score 40 percent lower than their predecessors in the 1970s in their ability to understand what another person is feeling. The biggest drop came in the years after 2000.[24]

Public language has also become demoralized. Google ngrams measure word usage across media. Google scans the contents of books and publications going back decades. You can type in a word and see, over the years, which words have been used more frequently and which less frequently. Over the past few decades there has been a sharp rise in the usage of individualist words and phrases like "self" and "personalized," "I come first" and "I can do it myself," and a sharp decline in community words like "community," "share," "united," and "common good."[25] The use of words having to do with economics and business has increased, while the language of morality and character building is in decline.[26] Usage of words like "character," "conscience," and "virtue" all declined over the course of the twentieth century.[27] Usage of the word "bravery" has declined by 66 percent over the course of the twentieth century. "Gratitude" is down 49 percent. "Humbleness" is down 52 percent and "kindness" is down 56 percent.

This dwindling of the Adam II lexicon has further contributed to moral inarticulateness. In this age of moral autonomy, each individual is told to come up with his or her own worldview. If your name is Aristotle, maybe you can do that. But if it isn't, you probably can't. For his 2011 book *Lost in Transition,* Christian Smith of Notre Dame studied the moral lives of American college students. He asked them to describe a moral dilemma they had recently faced. Two thirds of the young people either couldn't describe a moral problem or described problems that are not moral at all. For example, one said his most recent moral dilemma arose when he pulled in to a parking space and didn't have enough quarters for the meter.

"Not many of them have previously given much or any thought to many of the kinds of questions about morality that we asked," Smith and his coauthors wrote. They didn't understand that a moral dilemma arises when two legitimate moral values clash. Their default position was that moral choices are just a question of what feels right inside, whether it arouses a comfortable emotion. One student uttered this typical response: "I mean, I guess what makes something right is how I feel about it. But different people feel different ways, so I couldn't speak on behalf of anyone else as to what's right and wrong."[28]

If you believe that the ultimate oracle is the True Self inside, then of course you become emotivist—you make moral judgments on the basis of the feelings that burble up. Of course you become a relativist. One True Self has no basis to judge or argue with another True Self. Of course you become an individualist, since the ultimate arbiter is the authentic self within and not any community standard or external horizon of significance without. Of course you lose contact with the moral vocabulary that is needed to think about these questions. Of course the inner life becomes more level—instead of inspiring peaks and despairing abysses, ethical decision making is just gentle rolling foothills, nothing to get too hepped up about.

The mental space that was once occupied by moral struggle has gradually become occupied by the struggle to achieve. Morality has been displaced by utility. Adam II has been displaced by Adam I.

The Wrong Life

IN 1886, LEO TOLSTOY PUBLISHED HIS FAMOUS NOVELLA *THE DEATH OF IVAN Ilyich*. The central character is a successful lawyer and magistrate who one day is hanging curtains in his fancy new house when he falls awkwardly on his side. He thinks nothing of it at first, but then he develops an odd taste in his mouth and grows ill. Eventually he realizes that at age forty-five he is dying.

Ilyich had lived a productive upwardly mobile life. Tolstoy tells us he was "capable, cheerful, good-natured and sociable, though strict in the fulfillment of what he considered to be his duty: and he considered his duty to be what was so considered by those in authority."[29] In other words, he was a successful product of the moral ecology and social status system of his time. He had a good job and a fine reputation. His marriage was cold, but he spent less time with his family and regarded this as normal.

Ilyich tries to go back to his former way of thinking, but the onrushing presence of death thrusts new thoughts into his head. He thinks back on his childhood with special fondness, but the more he thinks about his adulthood, the less satisfactory it seems. He had rushed into marriage almost as an accident. He had been preoccupied with money year after year. His career triumphs now seem trivial.

"Maybe I did not live as I ought to have done?" he suddenly asks himself.[30]

The whole story plays with notions of up and down. The higher he goes externally, the farther he sinks internally. He begins to experience the life he had led as "a stone falling downward with increasing velocity."[31]

It occurs to him that he had felt small, scarcely noticeable impulses to struggle against what was thought good and proper by society. But he had not really attended to them. He now realizes that "his professional duties and the whole arrangement of his life and of his family and all his social and official interests, might all have been false. He tried to defend those things to himself and suddenly felt the weakness of what he was defending. There was nothing to defend."[32]

Tolstoy probably goes overboard in renouncing Ivan's Adam I life. It had not all been false and worthless. But he starkly paints the portrait of a man without an inner world until the occasion of his death. In those final hours the man finally gets a glimpse of what he should have known all along: "He fell through the hole and there at the bottom was a light. . . . At that very moment Ivan Ilyich fell through and caught sight of the light, and it was revealed to him that though his life had not been what it should have been, this could still be rectified. He asked himself, 'What is the right thing?' and grew still, listening."

Many of us are in Ivan Ilyich's position, recognizing that the social system we are part of pushes us to live out one sort of insufficient external life. But we have what Ilyich did not have: time to rectify it. The question is how.

The answer must be to stand against, at least in part, the prevailing winds of culture. The answer must be to join a counterculture. To live a decent life, to build up the soul, it's probably necessary to declare that the forces that encourage the Big Me, while necessary and liberating in many ways, have gone too far. We are out of balance. It's probably necessary to have one foot in the world of achievement but another foot in a counterculture that is in tension with the achievement ethos. It's probably necessary to reassert a balance between Adam I and Adam II and to understand that if anything, Adam II is more important than Adam I.

The Humility Code
—

EACH SOCIETY CREATES ITS OWN MORAL ECOLOGY. A MORAL ECOLOGY IS a set of norms, assumptions, beliefs, and habits of behavior and an institutionalized set of moral demands that emerge organically. Our moral ecology encourages us to be a certain sort of person. When you behave consistently with your society's moral ecology, people smile at you, and you are encouraged to continue acting in that way. The moral ecology of a given moment is never unanimous; there are always rebels, critics, and outsiders. But each moral climate is a collective response to the problems of the moment and it shapes the people who live within it.

Over the past several decades we have built a moral ecology around the Big Me, around the belief in a golden figure inside. This has led to a rise in narcissism and self-aggrandizement. This has encouraged us to focus on the external Adam I side of our natures and ignore the inner world of Adam II.

To restore the balance, to rediscover Adam II, to cultivate the eulogy virtues, it's probably necessary to revive and follow what we accidentally left behind: the counter-tradition of moral realism, or what I've been calling the crooked-timber school. It's probably necessary to build a moral ecology based on the ideas of this school, to follow its answers to the most important questions: Toward what should I orient my life? Who am I and what is my nature? How do I mold my nature to make it gradually better day by day? What virtues are the most important to cultivate and what weaknesses should I fear the most? How can I raise my children with a true sense of who they are and a practical set of ideas about how to travel the long road to character?

So far the propositions that define the crooked-timber tradition have been scattered across the many chapters that make up this book. I thought it might be useful to draw them together and recapitulate them here in one list, even if presenting them in numbered-list form does tend to simplify them and make them seem cruder than they are. Together these propositions form a Humility Code, a coherent image of what to live for and how to live. These are the general propositions that form this Humility Code:

1. We don't live for happiness, we live for holiness. Day to day we seek out pleasure, but deep down, human beings are endowed with moral imagination. All human beings seek to lead lives not just of pleasure, but of purpose, righteousness, and virtue. As John Stuart Mill put it, people have a responsibility to become more moral over time. The best life is oriented around the increasing excellence of the soul and is nourished by moral joy, the quiet sense of gratitude and tranquillity that comes as a byproduct of successful moral struggle. The meaningful life is the same eternal thing, the combination of some set of ideals and some man or woman's struggle for those ideals. Life is essentially a moral drama, not a hedonistic one.

2. Proposition one defines the goal of life. The long road to character begins with an accurate understanding of our nature, and the core of that understanding is that we are flawed creatures. We have an innate tendency toward selfishness and overconfidence. We have a tendency to see ourselves as the center of the universe, as if everything revolves around us. We resolve to do one thing but end up doing the opposite. We know what is deep and important in life, but we still pursue the things that are shallow and vain. Furthermore, we overestimate our own strength and rationalize our own failures. We know less than we think we do. We give in to short-term desires even when we know we shouldn't. We imagine that spiritual and moral needs can be solved through status and material things.

3. Although we are flawed creatures, we are also splendidly endowed. We are divided within ourselves, both fearfully and wonderfully made. We do sin, but we also have the capacity to recognize sin, to feel ashamed of sin, and to overcome sin. We are both weak and strong, bound and free, blind and far-seeing. We thus have the capacity to struggle with ourselves. There is something heroic about a person in struggle with herself, strained on the rack of conscience, suffering torments, yet staying alive and growing stronger, sacrificing a worldly success for the sake of an inner victory.

4. In the struggle against your own weakness, humility is the

greatest virtue. Humility is having an accurate assessment of your own nature and your own place in the cosmos. Humility is awareness that you are an underdog in the struggle against your own weakness. Humility is an awareness that your individual talents alone are inadequate to the tasks that have been assigned to you. Humility reminds you that you are not the center of the universe, but you serve a larger order.

5. Pride is the central vice. Pride is a problem in the sensory apparatus. Pride blinds us to the reality of our divided nature. Pride blinds us to our own weaknesses and misleads us into thinking we are better than we are. Pride makes us more certain and closed-minded than we should be. Pride makes it hard for us to be vulnerable before those whose love we need. Pride makes coldheartedness and cruelty possible. Because of pride we try to prove we are better than those around us. Pride deludes us into thinking that we are the authors of our own lives.

6. Once the necessities for survival are satisfied, the struggle against sin and for virtue is the central drama of life. No external conflict is as consequential or as dramatic as the inner campaign against our own deficiencies. This struggle against, say, selfishness or prejudice or insecurity gives meaning and shape to life. It is more important than the external journey up the ladder of success. This struggle against sin is the great challenge, so that life is not futile or absurd. It is possible to fight this battle well or badly, humorlessly or with cheerful spirit. Contending with weakness often means choosing what parts of yourself to develop and what parts not to develop. The purpose of the struggle against sin and weakness is not to "win," because that is not possible; it is to get better at waging it. It doesn't matter if you work at a hedge fund or a charity serving the poor. There are heroes and schmucks in both worlds. The most important thing is whether you are willing to engage in this struggle.

7. Character is built in the course of your inner confrontation. Character is a set of dispositions, desires, and habits that are slowly engraved during the struggle against your own

weakness. You become more disciplined, considerate, and loving through a thousand small acts of self-control, sharing, service, friendship, and refined enjoyment. If you make disciplined, caring choices, you are slowly engraving certain tendencies into your mind. You are making it more likely that you will desire the right things and execute the right actions. If you make selfish, cruel, or disorganized choices, then you are slowly turning this core thing inside yourself into something that is degraded, inconstant, or fragmented. You can do harm to this core thing with nothing more than ignoble thoughts, even if you are not harming anyone else. You can elevate this core thing with an act of restraint nobody sees. If you don't develop a coherent character in this way, life will fall to pieces sooner or later. You will become a slave to your passions. But if you do behave with habitual self-discipline, you will become constant and dependable.

8. The things that lead us astray are short term—lust, fear, vanity, gluttony. The things we call character endure over the long term—courage, honesty, humility. People with character are capable of a long obedience in the same direction, of staying attached to people and causes and callings consistently through thick and thin. People with character also have scope. They are not infinitely flexible, free-floating, and solitary. They are anchored by permanent attachments to important things. In the realm of the intellect, they have a set of permanent convictions about fundamental truths. In the realm of emotion, they are enmeshed in a web of unconditional loves. In the realm of action, they have a permanent commitment to tasks that cannot be completed in a single lifetime.

9. No person can achieve self-mastery on his or her own. Individual will, reason, compassion, and character are not strong enough to consistently defeat selfishness, pride, greed, and self-deception. Everybody needs redemptive assistance from outside—from God, family, friends, ancestors, rules, traditions, institutions, and exemplars. If you are to prosper in the confrontation with yourself, you have to put yourself in a state of affection. You have to draw on something outside

yourself to cope with the forces inside yourself. You have to draw from a cultural tradition that educates the heart, that encourages certain values, that teaches us what to feel in certain circumstances. We wage our struggles in conjunction with others waging theirs, and the boundaries between us are indistinct.

10. We are all ultimately saved by grace. The struggle against weakness often has a U shape. You are living your life and then you get knocked off course—either by an overwhelming love, or by failure, illness, loss of employment, or twist of fate. The shape is advance-retreat-advance. In retreat, you admit your need and surrender your crown. You open up space that others might fill. And grace floods in. It may come in the form of love from friends and family, in the assistance of an unexpected stranger, or from God. But the message is the same. You are accepted. You don't flail about in desperation, because hands are holding you up. You don't have to struggle for a place, because you are embraced and accepted. You just have to accept the fact that you are accepted. Gratitude fills the soul, and with it the desire to serve and give back.

11. Defeating weakness often means quieting the self. Only by quieting the self, by muting the sound of your own ego, can you see the world clearly. Only by quieting the self can you be open to the external sources of strengths you will need. Only by stilling the sensitive ego can you react with equipoise to the ups and downs of the campaign. The struggle against weakness thus requires the habits of self-effacement—reticence, modesty, obedience to some larger thing—and a capacity for reverence and admiration.

12. Wisdom starts with epistemological modesty. The world is immeasurably complex and the private stock of reason is small. We are generally not capable of understanding the complex web of causes that drive events. We are not even capable of grasping the unconscious depths of our own minds. We should be skeptical of abstract reasoning or of trying to apply universal rules across different contexts. But over the centuries, our ancestors built up a general bank of

practical wisdom, traditions, habits, manners, moral sentiments, and practices. The humble person thus has an acute
historical consciousness. She is the grateful inheritor of the
tacit wisdom of her kind, the grammar of conduct and the
store of untaught feelings that are ready for use in case of
emergency, that offer practical tips on how to behave in different situations, and that encourage habits that cohere into
virtues. The humble person understands that experience is a
better teacher than pure reason. He understands that wisdom is not knowledge. Wisdom emerges out of a collection
of intellectual virtues. It is knowing how to behave when
perfect knowledge is lacking.

13. No good life is possible unless it is organized around a vocation. If you try to use your work to serve yourself, you'll
find your ambitions and expectations will forever run ahead
and you'll never be satisfied. If you try to serve the community, you'll always wonder if people appreciate you enough.
But if you serve work that is intrinsically compelling and
focus just on being excellent at that, you will wind up serving yourself and the community obliquely. A vocation is
not found by looking within and finding your passion. It is
found by looking without and asking what life is asking of
us. What problem is addressed by an activity you intrinsically enjoy?

14. The best leader tries to lead along the grain of human nature
rather than go against it. He realizes that he, like the people
he leads, is likely to be sometimes selfish, narrow-minded,
and self-deceiving. Therefore he prefers arrangements that
are low and steady to those that are lofty and heroic. As long
as the foundations of an institution are sound, he prefers
change that is constant, gradual, and incremental to change
that is radical and sudden. He understands that public life is
a contest between partial truths and legitimate contesting
interests. The goal of leadership is to find a just balance between competing values and competing goals. He seeks to
be a trimmer, to shift weight one way or another as circumstances change, in order to keep the boat moving steadily
forward on an even keel. He understands that in politics and

business the lows are lower than the highs are high. The downside risk caused by bad decisions is larger than the upside benefits that accrue from good ones. Therefore the wise leader is a steward for his organization and tries to pass it along in slightly better condition than he found it.

15. The person who successfully struggles against weakness and sin may or may not become rich and famous, but that person will become mature. Maturity is not based on talent or any of the mental or physical gifts that help you ace an IQ test or run fast or move gracefully. It is not comparative. It is earned not by being better than other people at something, but by being better than you used to be. It is earned by being dependable in times of testing, straight in times of temptation. Maturity does not glitter. It is not built on the traits that make people celebrities. A mature person possesses a settled unity of purpose. The mature person has moved from fragmentation to centeredness, has achieved a state in which the restlessness is over, the confusion about the meaning and purpose of life is calmed. The mature person can make decisions without relying on the negative and positive reactions from admirers or detractors because the mature person has steady criteria to determine what is right. That person has said a multitude of noes for the sake of a few overwhelming yeses.

Modes of Living

THE CHARACTERS IN THIS BOOK FOLLOWED MANY DIFFERENT COURSES and had many different traits. Some, like Augustine and Johnson, were quite introspective. Others, like Eisenhower and Randolph, were not. Some, like Perkins, were willing to soil their hands in politics in order to get things done. Others, like Day, wanted not only to do good but to be good, to live a life that was as pure as possible. Some of these figures, like Johnson and Day, were very hard on themselves. They felt the need to arduously attack their own weaknesses. Others, like Montaigne, accepted themselves and had a lighter and more relaxed attitude toward life, trusting in nature to take care of life's essential problems. Some, like Ida Eisenhower, Philip Randolph, and Perkins, were private people, a little detached and emotionally reticent. Others, like Augustine and Rustin, exposed themselves emotionally. Some, like Day, were saved by religion, while others, like Eliot, were harmed by religion or were, like Marshall, not religious. Some, like Augustine, surrendered agency and let grace flood in. Others, like Johnson, took control of life and built their soul through effort.

Even within the tradition of moral realism, there are many differences of temperament, technique, tactics, and taste. Two people who both subscribe to the "crooked timber" view may approach specific questions in different ways. Should you stay in your suffering or move on from it as soon as possible? Should you keep a journal to maximize self-awareness, or does that just lead to paralyzing self-consciousness and self-indulgence? Should you be reticent or expressive? Should you take control of your own life or surrender it to God's grace?

Even within the same moral ecology, there's a lot of room for each person to chart a unique path. But each of the lives in this book started with a deep vulnerability, and undertook a lifelong effort to transcend that vulnerability. Johnson was fragmented and storm-tossed. Rustin was hollow and promiscuous. Marshall was a fearful boy. Eliot was desperate for affection. And yet each person was redeemed by that weakness. Each person struggled against that weakness and used that problem to grow a beautiful strength. Each person traveled down into the valley of humility in order to ascend to the heights of tranquillity and self-respect.

Stumblers

THE GOOD NEWS OF THIS BOOK IS THAT IT IS OKAY TO BE FLAWED, SINCE everyone is. Sin and limitation are woven through our lives. We are all stumblers, and the beauty and meaning of life are in the stumbling—in recognizing the stumbling and trying to become more graceful as the years go by.

The stumbler scuffs through life, a little off balance here and there, sometimes lurching, sometimes falling to her knees. But the stumbler faces her imperfect nature, her mistakes and weaknesses, with unvarnished honesty, with the opposite of squeamishness. She is sometimes ashamed of the perversities in her nature—the selfishness, the self-deceit, the occasional desire to put lower loves above higher ones.

But humility offers self-understanding. When we acknowledge that we screw up, and feel the gravity of our limitations, we find ourselves challenged and stretched with a serious foe to overcome and transcend.

The stumbler is made whole by this struggle. Each weakness becomes a chance to wage a campaign that organizes and gives meaning to life and makes you a better person. We lean on each other as we struggle against sin. We depend on each other for the forgiveness of sin. The stumbler has an outstretched arm, ready to receive and offer care. He is vulnerable enough to need affection and is generous enough to give affection at full volume. If we were without sin, we could be solitary Atlases, but the stumbler requires a community. His friends are there with conversation and advice. His ancestors have left him diverse models that he can emulate and measure himself by.

From the smallness of her own life, the stumbler commits herself to ideas and faiths that are nobler than any individual ever could be. She doesn't always live up to her convictions or follow her resolutions. But she repents and is redeemed and tries again, a process that gives dignity to her failing. The victories follow the same arc: from defeat to recognition to redemption. Down into the valley of vision and then up into the highlands of attachment. The humble path to the beautiful life.

Each struggle leaves a residue. A person who has gone through these struggles seems more substantial and deep. And by a magic alchemy these victories turn weakness into joy. The stumbler doesn't aim for joy. Joy is a byproduct experienced by people who are aiming for something else. But it comes.

There's joy in a life filled with interdependence with others, in a life filled with gratitude, reverence, and admiration. There's joy in freely chosen obedience to people, ideas, and commitments greater than oneself. There's joy in that feeling of acceptance, the knowledge that though you don't deserve their love, others do love you; they have admitted you into their lives. There's an aesthetic joy we feel in morally good action, which makes all other joys seem paltry and easy to forsake.

People do get better at living, at least if they are willing to humble themselves and learn. Over time they stumble less, and eventually they achieve moments of catharsis when outer ambition comes into balance with inner aspiration, when there is a unity of effort between Adam I and Adam II, when there is that ultimate tranquillity and that feeling of flow—when moral nature and external skills are united in one defining effort.

Joy is not produced because others praise you. Joy emanates unbidden and unforced. Joy comes as a gift when you least expect it. At those fleeting moments you know why you were put here and what truth you serve. You may not feel giddy at those moments, you may not hear the orchestra's delirious swell or see flashes of crimson and gold, but you will feel a satisfaction, a silence, a peace—a hush. Those moments are the blessings and the signs of a beautiful life.

Newport Community
Learning & Libraries

ACKNOWLEDGMENTS

ANNE C. SNYDER WAS THERE WHEN THIS BOOK WAS BORN AND walked with me through the first three years of its writing. This was first conceived as a book about cognition and decision making. Under Anne's influence, it became a book about morality and inner life. She led dozens of discussions about the material, assigned me reading from her own bank of knowledge, challenged the superficiality of my thinking in memo after memo, and transformed the project. While I was never able to match the lyricism of her prose, or the sensitivity of her observations, I have certainly stolen many of her ideas and admired the gracious and morally rigorous way she lives her life. If there are any important points in this book, they probably come from Anne.

April Lawson came in for the final eighteen months of this effort. She is the editor of my newspaper column and brought that same astounding judgment to this manuscript. I may come to understand many things about life, but I will never understand how one so young can possess so much mature and considered wisdom, can understand so much about other people's lives, and can offer such bold and useful suggestions.

Campbell Schnebly-Swanson was a student of mine at Yale who helped with the final research, fact checking, and thinking. She is a tornado of insights, judgments, and enthusiasms. Her reactions sharpened this text, and her research infuses these pages. I wait with a sort of awed anticipation to see what kind of mark she leaves on the world.

For three years, I have taught a course at Yale University loosely based on some of the ideas here. My students there have wrestled with this topic alongside of me, and offered immeasurable insights, both in the classroom and at the bar of The Study Hotel. They've made the first two days of every week unbelievably fun. I'd especially like to thank my Yale colleagues Jim Levinsohn, John Gaddis, Charles Hill, and Paul Kennedy for welcoming me into their midst. Another Yale professor, Bryan Garsten, read a large chunk of the manuscript and helped clarify and deepen the thinking here. Large faculty groups at Yale and at Wheaton College heard me out and offered feedback and advice.

Will Murphy and I have worked on two books now for Random House. He is as supportive an editor as it is possible to imagine. I am the rare author who has nothing but good things to say about his publishing house. I've been fortunate to be writing for an enthusiastic, professional, and supportive team, especially London King, this book's lead publicist, who is as good at her job as anyone I've worked with. Cheryl Miller helped me early on to conceive the project and select the characters. Catherine Katz and Lauren Davis filled in with vital research and advice.

Many friends deserve my gratitude, acknowledgment, and devotion. Blair Miller read through everything, hunted for a less-than-awful title, encouraged me when that was needed, and offered advice and wisdom, large and small. Blair is an astonishing judge and connector of people and ideas. She did her best to help me tie the larger moral issues to the problems people face in the real world every day. In her own work, Blair serves the world, and the poorest people in the world, in a way that is practical and also idealistic, dignified but also joyful. She encouraged me to try to make this book of use to people, to make it not just a philosophical or sociological ramble, but an act of service.

My parents, Michael and Lois Brooks, are still my best and toughest editors. Pete Wehner tirelessly offered counsel and advice. Yuval Levin is much younger than me but has become an intellectual mentor. Kirsten Powers read crucial parts and provided moral and emotional support throughout. Carol Quillen, the president of Davidson College, has helped me understand Augustine, and much else, much better. An ecumenical group of clergy and lay people helped carry me through a crucial time in my life, including: Stuart and Celia McAlpine, David Wolpe, Meir Soloveichik, Tim Keller, and Jerry Root. My agents, Glen Hartley and Lynn Chu, have been friends since college and will remain so through life.

Life has its vicissitudes and unexpected turns. My ex-wife, Sarah, has done and continues to do an amazing job raising our three children. Those children, Joshua, Naomi, and Aaron, are now spread around the globe, and exemplify the traits of character that any parent dreams of: courage, creativity, honesty, fortitude, and loving kindness. They don't really need this book, but I hope they profit from it.

NOTES

CHAPTER 1: THE SHIFT

1. Wilfred M. McClay, *The Masterless: Self and Society in Modern America* (University of North Carolina Press, 1993), 226.
2. Alonzo L. Hamby, "A Wartime Consigliere," review of David L. Roll, *The Hopkins Touch: Harry Hopkins and the Forging of the Alliance to Defeat Hitler* (Oxford University Press, 2012), *Wall Street Journal,* December 29, 2012.
3. David Frum, *How We Got Here: The 70's, the Decade That Brought You Modern Life (for Better or Worse)* (Basic Books, 2000), 103.
4. Jean M. Twenge and W. Keith Campbell, *The Narcissism Epidemic: Living in the Age of Entitlement* (Simon & Schuster, 2009), 13.
5. "How Young People View Their Lives, Futures and Politics: A Portrait of 'Generation Next.'" The Pew Research Center For The People & The Press (January 9, 2007).
6. Elizabeth Gilbert, *Eat, Pray, Love: One Woman's Search for Everything* (Penguin, 2006), 64.
7. James Davison Hunter, *The Death of Character: Moral Education in an Age Without Good or Evil* (Basic Books, 2000), 103.
8. Twenge and Campbell, *Narcissism,* 248.
9. C. J. Mahaney, *Humility: True Greatness* (Multnomah, 2005), 70.
10. Daniel Kahneman, *Thinking, Fast and Slow* (Farrar, Straus and Giroux, 2011), 201.
11. Harry Emerson Fosdick, *On Being a Real Person* (Harper and Brothers, 1943), 25.
12. Thomas Merton, *The Seven Storey Mountain* (Harcourt, 1998), 92.
13. Henry Fairlie, *The Seven Deadly Sins Today* (New Republic Books, 1978), 30.

CHAPTER 2: THE SUMMONED SELF

1. David Von Drehle, *Triangle: The Fire That Changed America* (Atlantic Monthly Press, 2003), 195.
2. Frances Perkins, "The Triangle Factory Fire," lecture, Cornell University online archives. http://trianglefire.ilr.cornell.edu/primary/lectures/francesperkinslecture.html.

3. Von Drehle, *Triangle,* 158.

4. George Martin, *Madam Secretary: Frances Perkins; A Biography of America's First Woman Cabinet Member* (Houghton Mifflin, 1976), 85.

5. Von Drehle, *Triangle,* 138.

6. Von Drehle, *Triangle,* 130.

7. Von Drehle, *Triangle,* 152.

8. Von Drehle, *Triangle,* 146.

9. Perkins, "Triangle Fire" lecture.

10. Naomi Pasachoff, *Frances Perkins: Champion of the New Deal* (Oxford University Press, 1999), 30.

11. Viktor Frankl, *Man's Search for Meaning* (Beacon, 1992), 85.

12. Frankl, *Man's Search for Meaning,* 99.

13. Frankl, *Man's Search for Meaning,* 104.

14. Frankl, *Man's Search for Meaning,* 98.

15. Mark R. Schwehn and Dorothy C. Bass, eds., *Leading Lives That Matter: What We Should Do and Who We Should Be* (Eerdmans, 2006), 35.

16. Kirstin Downey, *The Woman Behind the New Deal: The Life of Frances Perkins, FDR's Secretary of Labor and His Moral Conscience* (Nan Talese, 2008), 8.

17. Downey, *Woman Behind the New Deal,* 5.

18. Martin, *Madam Secretary,* 50.

19. David Hackett Fischer, *Albion's Seed: Four British Folkways in America* (Oxford, 1989), 895.

20. Lillian G. Paschal, "Hazing in Girls' Colleges," *Household Ledger,* 1905.

21. Martin, *Madam Secretary,* 46.

22. Russell Lord, "Madam Secretary," *New Yorker,* September 2, 1933.

23. Mary E. Woolley, "Values of College Training for Women," *Harper's Bazaar,* September 1904.

24. Martin, *Madam Secretary,* 51.

25. Jane Addams, *Twenty Years at Hull House: With Autobiographical Notes* (University of Illinois, 1990), 71.

26. Addams, *Twenty Years at Hull House,* 94.

27. Frances Perkins, "My Recollections of Florence Kelley," *Social Service Review,* vol. 28, no. 1 (March 1954), 12.

28. Martin, *Madam Secretary,* 146.

29. Downey, *Woman Behind the New Deal,* 42.

30. Downey, *Woman Behind the New Deal,* 42.

31. Martin, *Madam Secretary,* 98.

32. Downey, *Woman Behind the New Deal,* 56.

33. Martin, *Madam Secretary,* 125.

34. Downey, *Woman Behind the New Deal,* 66.

35. Martin, *Madam Secretary,* 232.

36. Martin, *Madam Secretary,* 136.

37. Downey, *Woman Behind the New Deal,* 317.

38. Frances Perkins, *The Roosevelt I Knew* (Penguin, 2011), 29.

39. Perkins, "Roosevelt I Knew," 45.

40. Martin, *Madam Secretary,* 206.

41. Martin, *Madam Secretary,* 206.

42. Martin, *Madam Secretary,* 236.

43. Martin, *Madam Secretary,* 237.

44. Perkins, *Roosevelt I Knew,* 156.

45. Downey, *Woman Behind the New Deal,* 284.

46. Downey, *Woman Behind the New Deal,* 279.

47. Martin, *Madam Secretary,* 281.

48. Downey, *Woman Behind the New Deal,* 384.

49. Christopher Breiseth, "The Frances Perkins I Knew," essay, Franklin D. Roosevelt American Heritage Center Museum (Worcester, MA).

50. Martin, *Madam Secretary,* 485.

51. Reinhold Niebuhr, *The Irony of American History* (University of Chicago Press, 2008), 63.

CHAPTER 3: SELF-CONQUEST

1. *The Eisenhower Legacy: Discussions of Presidential Leadership* (Bartleby Press, 1992), 21.

2. Jean Edward Smith, *Eisenhower in War and Peace* (New York: Random House, 2012), 7.

3. Smith, *Eisenhower in War and Peace,* 8.

4. Mark Perry, *Partners in Command: George Marshall and Dwight Eisenhower in War and Peace* (Penguin, 2007), 68.

5. Dwight D. Eisenhower, *At Ease: Stories I Tell to Friends* (Doubleday, 1967), 76.

6. Eisenhower, *At Ease,* 31.

7. Smith, *Eisenhower in War and Peace,* 59.

8. Eisenhower, *At Ease,* 52.

9. Anthony T. Kronman, *The Lost Lawyer: Failing Ideals of the Legal Profession* (Harvard University Press, 1995), 16.

10. Smith, *Eisenhower in War and Peace,* 59.

11. Evan Thomas, *Ike's Bluff: President Eisenhower's Secret Battle to Save the World* (Little, Brown, 2012), 27.

12. Thomas, *Ike's Bluff,* 27.

13. Paul F. Boller, Jr., *Presidential Anecdotes* (Oxford University Press, 1996), 292; Robert J. Donovan, *Eisenhower: The Inside Story* (New York: Harper and Brothers, 1956), 7.

14. Thomas, *Ike's Bluff,* 33.

15. State of the Union message, Washington, D.C., January 10, 1957.

16. Thomas, *Ike's Bluff,* 30.

17. Fred Greenstein, *The Presidential Difference: Leadership Style from Roosevelt to Clinton* (Free Press, 2000), 49.

18. Stephen E. Ambrose, *Eisenhower: Soldier and President* (Simon and Schuster, 1990), 65.

19. Smith, *Eisenhower in War and Peace,* 19.

20. Smith, *Eisenhower in War and Peace,* 48.

21. Eisenhower, *At Ease,* 155.

22. Eisenhower, *At Ease,* 135

23. William Lee Miller, *Two Americans: Truman, Eisenhower, and a Dangerous World* (Vintage, 2012), 78.

24. Thomas, *Ike's Bluff,* 26; John S. D. Eisenhower, *Strictly Personal* (Doubleday, 1974), 292.

25. Smith, *Eisenhower in War and Peace,* 61.

26. Smith, *Eisenhower in War and Peace,* 65.

27. Dwight D. Eisenhower, *Ike's Letters to a Friend, 1941–1958* (University Press of Kansas, 1984), 4.

28. Eisenhower, *At Ease,* 193.

29. Boller, *Presidential Anecdotes,* 290.

30. Eisenhower, *At Ease,* 213.

31. Eisenhower, *At Ease,* 214.

32. Eisenhower, *At Ease*, 228.

33. Smith, *Eisenhower in War and Peace*, 147.

34. Smith, *Eisenhower in War and Peace*, 443.

35. Ambrose, *Eisenhower: Soldier and President*, 440.

36. Thomas, *Ike's Bluff*, 153.

37. Thomas, *Ike's Bluff*, 29.

38. Quoted in Steven J. Rubenzer and Thomas R. Faschingbauer, *Personality, Character, and Leadership in the White House: Psychologists Assess the Presidents* (Potomac Books, 2004), 147.

39. Thomas, *Ike's Bluff*, introduction, 17.

40. Thomas, *Ike's Bluff*, 161.

41. Thomas, *Ike's Bluff*, 161.

42. Smith, *Eisenhower in War and Peace*, 766.

43. Eisenhower, *Ike's Letters to a Friend*, 189, July 22, 1957.

CHAPTER 4: STRUGGLE

1. Dorothy Day, *The Long Loneliness: The Autobiography of the Legendary Catholic Social Activist* (Harper, 1952), 20.

2. Day, *Long Loneliness*, 21.

3. Paul Elie, *The Life You Save May Be Your Own: An American Pilgrimage* (Farrar, Straus and Giroux, 2003), 4.

4. Elie, *Life You Save*, 4.

5. Day, *Long Loneliness*, 24.

6. Day, *Long Loneliness*, 35.

7. Elie, *Life You Save*, 16.

8. Day, *Long Loneliness*, 87.

9. Jim Forest, *All Is Grace: A Biography of Dorothy Day* (Orbis Books, 2011), 47.

10. Elie, *Life You Save*, 31.

11. Forest, *All Is Grace*, 48.

12. Forest, *All Is Grace*, 50.

13. Deborah Kent, *Dorothy Day: Friend to the Forgotten* (Eerdmans Books, 2004), 35.

14. Day, *Long Loneliness*, 79.

15. Day, *Long Loneliness*, 79.

16. Elie, *Life You Save*, 38.

17. Day, *Long Loneliness*, 60.

18. Robert Coles, *Dorothy Day: A Radical Devotion* (Da Capo Press, 1989), 6.

19. Elie, *Life You Save*, 45.

20. Nancy Roberts, *Dorothy Day and the Catholic Worker* (State University of New York Press, 1985), 26.

21. Forest, *All Is Grace*, 62.

22. Day, *Long Loneliness*, 141.

23. Coles, *Radical Devotion*, 52.

24. Coles, *Radical Devotion*, 53.

25. Robert Elsberg, ed., *All the Way to Heaven: The Selected Letters of Dorothy Day* (Marquette University Press, 2010), 23.

26. Roberts, *Dorothy Day*, 26.

27. Day, *Long Loneliness*, 133.

28. William Miller, *Dorothy Day: A Biography* (Harper & Row, 1982), 196.

29. Day, *Long Loneliness*, 165.

30. Forest, *All Is Grace*, 61.

31. Dorothy Day, *The Duty of Delight: The Diaries of Dorothy Day* (Marquette University, 2011), 519.

32. Day, *Long Loneliness*, 182.

33. Day, *Long Loneliness*, 214.

34. Day, *Duty of Delight*, 68.

35. Schwehn and Bass, eds., *Leading Lives That Matter*, 34.

36. Day, *Duty of Delight*, 42.

37. Coles, *Radical Devotion*, 115.

38. Coles, *Radical Devotion*, 120.

39. Day, *Long Loneliness*, 236.

40. Forest, *All Is Grace*, 168.

41. Forest, *All Is Grace*, 178.

42. Forest, *All Is Grace*, 118.

43. Day, *Long Loneliness*, 243.

44. Day, *Long Loneliness*, 285.

45. Day, *Duty of Delight*, 9.

46. Rosalie Riegle Troester, *Voices from the Catholic Worker* (Temple University Press, 1993), 69.

47. Troester, *Voices*, 93.

48. Day, *Duty of Delight*, 287.

49. Day, *Duty of Delight*, 295.

50. Coles, *Radical Devotion*, 16.

CHAPTER 5: SELF-MASTERY

1. Forrest C. Pogue, *George C. Marshall*, 4 vols. (Viking Press, 1964), vol. 1, *Education of a General, 1880–1939*, 35.

2. Ed Cray, *General of the Army: George C. Marshall, Soldier and Statesman* (W. W. Norton, 1990), 20.

3. Cray, *General of the Army*, 25.

4. William Frye, *Marshall: Citizen Soldier* (Bobbs-Merrill, 1947), 32–65.

5. Pogue, *Marshall*, 63.

6. Pogue, *Marshall*, 63.

7. Richard Livingstone, *On Education: The Future in Education and Education for a World Adrift* (Cambridge, 1954), 153.

8. James Davison Hunter, *The Death of Character: Moral Education in an Age Without Good or Evil* (Basic Books, 2000), 19.

9. Leonard Mosley, *Marshall: Hero for Our Times* (Hearst Books, 1982), 13.

10. Mosley, *Hero for Our Times*, 14.

11. Mosley, *Hero for Our Times*, 15.

12. Frye, *Citizen Soldier*, 49.

13. David Hein, "In War for Peace: General George C. Marshall's Core Convictions & Ethical Leadership," *Touchstone*, March, 2013.

14. Mosley, *Hero for Our Times*, Introduction, xiv.

15. Mosley, *Hero for Our Times*, 19.

16. Cray, *General of the Army*, 64.

17. Quoted in Major James R. Hill, "A Comparative Analysis of the Military Leadership Styles of Ernest J. King and Chester W. Nimitz," published master's thesis, General Staff College, Fort Leavenworth, KS, 2008.

18. Mosley, *Hero for Our Times*, 64.

19. Pogue, *Marshall*, 79.

20. Pogue, *Marshall,* 246; Mosley, *Hero for Our Times,* 93.

21. André Comte-Sponville, *A Small Treatise on the Great Virtues: The Uses of Philosophy in Everyday Life* (Macmillan, 2002), 10.

22. Frye, *Citizen Soldier,* 85.

23. Cray, *General of the Army,* 276.

24. Mark Perry, *Partners in Command: George Marshall and Dwight Eisenhower in War and Peace* (Penguin, 2007), 15.

25. Cray, *General of the Army,* 278.

26. Cray, *General of the Army,* 297.

27. Mosley, *Hero for Our Times,* 211.

28. Mosley, *Hero for Our Times,* 292.

29. Dwight D. Eisenhower, *Crusade in Europe* (Doubleday, 1948), 197.

30. Perry, *Partners in Command,* 238.

31. Pogue, *George C. Marshall* (Viking, 1973), vol. 3, *Organizer of Victory, 1943–1945,* 321.

32. Perry, *Partners in Command,* 240.

33. John S. D. Eisenhower, *General Ike: A Personal Reminiscence* (Simon and Schuster, 2003), 99, reproduced in Dwight D. Eisenhower, *Crusade in Europe,* 208.

34. John Eisenhower, *General Ike,* 103.

35. Mosley, *Hero for Our Times,* 341.

36. Mosley, *Hero for Our Times,* prologue, xxi.

37. Frye, *Citizen Soldier,* 372.

38. Robert Faulkner, *The Case for Greatness: Honorable Ambition and Its Critics* (Yale University Press, 2007), 39.

39. Faulkner, *Case for Greatness,* 40.

40. Aristotle, *Nichomachean Ethics* (Focus Publishing, 2002), 70; Faulkner, *Case for Greatness,* 43.

41. Mosley, *Hero for Our Times,* 434.

42. Mosley, *Hero for Our Times,* 522.

43. Mosley, *Hero for Our Times,* 523.

44. Mosley, *Hero for Our Times,* 523.

CHAPTER 6: DIGNITY

1. Cynthia Taylor, *A. Philip Randolph: The Religious Journey of an African American Labor Leader* (New York University Press, 2006), 13.

2. Jervis Anderson, *A. Philip Randolph: A Biographical Portrait* (University of California Press, 1973), 43.

3. Anderson, *Biographical Portrait,* 9.

4. Anderson, *Biographical Portrait,* 10.

5. Anderson, *Biographical Portrait,* 272.

6. Anderson, *Biographical Portrait,* 339.

7. Aaron Wildavsky, *Moses as Political Leader* (Shalem Press, 2005), 45.

8. Irving Kristol, *The Neoconservative Persuasion: Selected Essays, 1942–2009,* edited by Gertrude Himmelfarb (Basic Books, 2011), 71.

9. Murray Kempton, "A. Philip Randolph: The Choice, Mr. President," *New Republic,* July 6, 1963.

10. Anderson, *Biographical Portrait,* 176.

11. Larry Tye, *Rising from the Rails: Pullman Porters and the Making of the Black Middle Class* (Owl Books, 2005), 154.

12. Doris Kearns Goodwin, *No Ordinary Time: Franklin and Eleanor Roosevelt: The Home Front in World War II* (Simon & Schuster, 2013), 251.

13. Paula F. Pfeffer, *A. Philip Randolph: Pioneer of the Civil Rights Movement* (Louisiana State University Press, 1996), 66.

14. Pfeffer, *Pioneer*, 58.

15. John D'Emilio, *Lost Prophet: The Life and Times of Bayard Rustin* (Simon and Schuster, 2003), 11.

16. D'Emilio, *Lost Prophet*, 16.

17. D'Emilio, *Lost Prophet*, 19.

18. Rachel Moston, "Bayard Rustin on His Own Terms," *Haverford Journal,* 2005, 82.

19. Michael G. Long, ed., *I Must Resist: Bayard Rustin's Life in Letters* (City Lights, 2012), 228.

20. Moston, "Bayard Rustin on His Own Terms," 91.

21. D'Emilio, *Lost Prophet*, 77.

22. Long, *I Must Resist*, 50.

23. D'Emilio, *Lost Prophet*, 172.

24. Long, *I Must Resist*, 49.

25. Long, *I Must Resist*, 51.

26. Long, *I Must Resist*, 65.

27. D'Emilio, *Lost Prophet*, 112.

28. D'Emilio, *Lost Prophet*, 159.

29. David L. Chappell, *A Stone of Hope: Prophetic Religion and the Death of Jim Crow* (University of North Carolina Press, 2004), 48.

30. Chappell, *Stone of Hope*, 54.

31. Chappell, *Stone of Hope*, 179.

32. Chappell, *Stone of Hope*, 55.

33. Chappell, *Stone of Hope*, 56.

34. D'Emilio, *Lost Prophet*, 150.

35. Chappell, *Stone of Hope*, 50.

36. Reinhold Niebuhr, *The Irony of American History* (University of Chicago Press, 2008), 5.

37. Niebuhr, *Irony of American History*, 23.

38. D'Emilio, *Lost Prophet*, 349.

39. D'Emilio, *Lost Prophet*, 352.

40. Anderson, *Biographical Portrait*, 332.

CHAPTER 7: LOVE

1. George Eliot, *Daniel Deronda* (Wordsworth, 2003), 15.

2. Kathryn Hughes, *George Eliot: The Last Victorian* (Cooper Square Press, 2001), 16.

3. Hughes, *Last Victorian*, 18.

4. Frederick R. Karl, *George Eliot: Voice of a Century; A Biography* (W. W. Norton, 1995), 36.

5. Karl, *George Eliot: Voice of a Century*, 36.

6. Rebecca Mead, *My Life in Middlemarch* (Crown, 2013), 28.

7. Hughes, *Last Victorian*, 47.

8. Mead, *My Life in Middlemarch*, 66.

9. Mead, *My Life in Middlemarch*, 125.

10. Karl, *Voice of a Century*, 146.

11. Gordon S. Haight, *George Eliot: A Biography* (Oxford University Press, 1968), 133.

12. Brenda Maddox, *George Eliot in Love* (Palgrave Macmillan, 2010), 59.

13. Haight, *George Eliot,* 144.

14. Karl, *Voice of a Century,* 167.

15. Michael Ignatieff, *Isaiah Berlin: A Life* (Henry Holt, 1999), 161.

16. Christian Wiman, *My Bright Abyss: Meditation of a Modern Believer* (Farrar, Straus and Giroux, 2013), 23.

17. William Shakespeare, *Romeo and Juliet,* Act II, Scene I.

18. Karl, *Voice of a Century,* 178.

19. Karl, *Voice of a Century,* 157.

20. Hughes, *Last Victorian,* 186.

21. Mead, *My Life in Middlemarch,* 266.

22. Virginia Woolf, "George Eliot," *The Times Literary Supplement,* November 20, 1919.

23. Barbara Hardy, *George Eliot: A Critic's Biography* (Continuum, 2006), 122.

CHAPTER 8: ORDERED LOVE

1. Peter Brown, *Augustine of Hippo: A Biography* (University of California Press, 2000), 17.

2. Brown, *Augustine of Hippo,* 18.

3. Matthew Arnold, *Culture and Anarchy* (Cambridge University Press, 1993), 130.

4. Arnold, *Culture and Anarchy,* 128.

5. Arnold, *Culture and Anarchy,* 128.

6. Arnold, *Culture and Anarchy,* 132.

7. Brown, *Augustine of Hippo,* 13.

8. Garry Wills, *Saint Augustine* (Penguin, 1999), 7.

9. Brown, *Augustine of Hippo,* 36.

10. Wills, *Saint Augustine,* 26.

11. Brown, *Augustine of Hippo,* 37.

12. Reinhold Niebuhr, *The Nature and Destiny of Man: A Christian Interpretation: Human Nature,* vol. I (Scribner's, 1996), 155.

13. Brown, *Augustine of Hippo,* 173; Augustine, *Confessions,* book 10, section 37.

14. Niebuhr, *Nature and Destiny of Man,* 157.

15. Lewis B. Smedes, *Shame and Grace: Healing the Shame We Don't Deserve* (Random House, 1994), 116.

16. Augustine, *Psalm 122: God Is True Wealth;* Mary Clark, *Augustine of Hippo: Selected Writings* (Paulist Press, 1984), 250.

17. Timothy Keller, *Freedom of Self Forgetfulness* (10Publishing, 2013), 40.

18. Jennifer A. Herdt, *Putting On Virtue: The Legacy of the Splendid Vices* (University of Chicago Press, 2008), 176.

19. Herdt, *Putting On Virtue,* 57.

20. Augustine, *The Works of Saint Augustine: A Translation for the 21st Century* (New City Press, 1992), 131.

21. Paul Tillich, *The Essential Tillich* (Scribner, 1999), 131.

22. Brown, *Augustine of Hippo,* 157.

23. Brown, *Augustine of Hippo,* 157.

CHAPTER 9: SELF-EXAMINATION

1. Jeffrey Meyers, *Samuel Johnson: The Struggle* (Basic Books, 2008), 6.

2. W. Jackson Bate, *Samuel Johnson: A Biography* (Counterpoint, 2009), 8.

3. Bate, *Samuel Johnson*, 31.

4. John Wain, *Samuel Johnson* (Macmillan, 1980), 49.

5. Boswell, *Boswell's Life of Johnson* (Harper, 1889), 74.

6. Meyers, *Samuel Johnson: The Struggle*, 50.

7. Bate, *Samuel Johnson*, 211.

8. Meyers, *Samuel Johnson: The Struggle*, 205.

9. Bate, *Samuel Johnson*, 204.

10. Paul Fussell, *Samuel Johnson and the Life of Writing* (Norton, 1986), 236.

11. Bate, *Samuel Johnson*, 218.

12. Meyers, *Samuel Johnson: The Struggle*, 114.

13. Meyers, *Samuel Johnson: The Struggle*, 2.

14. Fussell, *Johnson and the Life of Writing*, 163.

15. Fussell, *Johnson and the Life of Writing*, 51.

16. Ralph Waldo Emerson, *The Spiritual Emerson: Essential Writings* (Beacon, 2004), 216.

17. Fussell, *Johnson and the Life of Writing*, 147.

18. Percy Hazen Houston, *Doctor Johnson: A Study in Eighteenth Century Humanism* (Cambridge University Press, 1923), 195.

19. Sarah Bakewell, *How to Live: Or a Life of Montaigne in One Question and Twenty Attempts at an Answer* (Other Press, 2010), 21.

20. Bakewell, *How to Live*, 14.

21. Fussell, *Johnson and the Life of Writing*, 185.

22. Bate, *Samuel Johnson*, 4.

CHAPTER 10: THE BIG ME

1. Tom Callahan, *Johnny U: The Life and Times of John Unitas* (Random House, 2007), 16.

2. Michael Novak, *The Joy of Sports: Endzones, Bases, Baskets, Balls, and the Consecration of the American Spirit* (Madison Books, 1976), 241.

3. Callahan, *Johnny U*, 20.

4. Jimmy Breslin, "The Passer Nobody Wanted," *Saturday Evening Post*, November 1, 1958.

5. Callahan, *Johnny U*, 243.

6. John Skow, "Joe, Joe, You're the Most Beautiful Thing in the World," *Saturday Evening Post*, December 3, 1966.

7. Dan Jenkins, "The Sweet Life of Swinging Joe," *Sports Illustrated*, October 17, 1966.

8. George Eliot, *Middlemarch* (Penguin, 2003), 211.

9. Joshua L. Liebman, *Peace of Mind: Insights on Human Nature That Can Change Your Life* (Simon and Schuster, 1946), 56.

10. Benjamin Spock, *The Pocket Book of Baby and Child Care* (Duell, Sloan and Pearce, 1946), 309.

11. Harry A. Overstreet, *The Mature Mind* (Norton, 1949), 261.

12. Carl Ransom Rogers, *On Becoming a Person: A Therapist's View of Psychotherapy* (Harcourt, 1995), 194.

13. Carl Ransom Rogers, *The Carl Rogers Reader* (Houghton Mifflin, 1989), 185.

14. Katharine Graham, *Personal History* (Random House, 1997), 51.

15. Graham, *Personal History*, 231.

16. Eva Illouz, *Saving the Modern Soul: Therapy, Emotions, and the Culture of Self-Help* (University of California Press, 2008), 117.

17. Charles Taylor, *Multiculturalism: Examining the Politics of Recognition* (Princeton University Press, 1994), 30.

18. Dr. Seuss, *Oh, the Places You'll Go!* (Random House, 1990).

19. Ernst & Young Survey, "Sixty-five Per Cent of College Students Think They Will Become Millionaires" (Canada, 2001).

20. Greg Duncan and Richard Murnane, *Whither Opportunity? Rising Inequality, Schools, and Children's Life Chances* (Russell Sage Foundation, 2011), 11.

21. "The American Freshman" Thirty Year Trends, 1966–1996. By Alexander W. Astin, Sarah A. Parrott, William S. Korn, Linda J. Sax. Higher Education Research Institute Graduate School of Education & Information Studies. University of California, Los Angeles. February, 1997.

22. Gretchen Anderson, "Loneliness Among Older Adults: A National Survey of Adults 45+" (AARP Research and Strategic Analysis, 2010).

23. Francis Fukuyama, *The Great Disruption: Human Nature and the Reconstitution of Social Order* (Profile, 1999), 50.

24. Sara Konrath, "Changes in Dispositional Empathy in American College Students Over Time: A Meta-Analysis" (University of Michigan, 2011).

25. Jean M. Twenge, W. Keith Campbell, and Brittany Gentile, "Increases in Individualistic Words and Phrases in American Books, 1960–2008" (2012), PLoS ONE 7(7): e40181, doi:10.1371/journal.pone.0040181.

26. David Brooks, "What Our Words Tell Us," *New York Times,* May 20, 2013.

27. Pelin Kesebir and Selin Kesebir, "The Cultural Salience of Moral Character and Virtue Declined in Twentieth Century America," *Journal of Positive Psychology,* 2012.

28. Christian Smith, Kari Christoffersen, Hilary Davidson, *Lost in Transition: The Dark Side of Emerging Adulthood* (Oxford University Press, 2011), 22.

29. Leo Tolstoy, *The Death of Ivan Ilyich* (White Crow Books, 2010), 20.

30. Tolstoy, *The Death of Ivan Ilyich,* 66.

31. Tolstoy, *The Death of Ivan Ilyich,* 68.

32. Tolstoy, *The Death of Ivan Ilyich,* 71.

PERMISSION CREDITS

GRATEFUL ACKNOWLEDGMENT IS MADE TO THE FOLLOWING
FOR PERMISSION TO REPRINT MATERIAL:

CITY LIGHTS BOOKS: Excerpts from *I Must Resist: Bayard Rustin's Life in Letters,* edited by Michael G. Long, copyright © 2012 by Michael G. Long. Reprinted by permission of City Lights Books.

HARPERCOLLINS PUBLISHERS: Excerpts from *The Long Loneliness* by Dorothy Day, copyright © 1952 by Harper & Row Publishers, Inc., and copyright renewed 1980 by Tamar Teresa Hennessy. Reprinted by permission of HarperCollins Publishers.

HOUGHTON MIFFLIN HARCOURT PUBLISHING COMPANY: Excerpts from *A. Philip Randolph: A Biographical Portrait* by Jervis B. Anderson, copyright © 1972 and copyright renewed 2000 by Jervis B. Anderson; excerpts from *Madam Secretary, Frances Perkins* by George Martin, copyright © 1976 by George Martin. Reprinted by permission of Houghton Mifflin Harcourt Publishing Company. All rights reverved.

DAVE JOLLY: Email from Dave Jolly to David Brooks. Reprinted by permission of Dave Jolly.

NAN A. TALESE, AN IMPRINT OF THE KNOPF DOUBLEDAY PUBLISHING GROUP, A DIVISION OF PENGUIN RANDOM HOUSE LLC: Excerpts from *The Woman Behind the New Deal: The Life of Frances Perkins, FDR's Secretary of Labor and His Moral Conscience* by Kirstin Downey, copyright © 2009 by Kirstin Downey. Reprinted by permission of Nan A. Talese, an imprint of the Knopf Doubleday Publishing Group, a division of Penguin Random House LLC. All rights reserved.

RANDOM HOUSE CHILDREN'S BOOKS, A DIVISION OF PENGUIN RANDOM HOUSE LLC: Excerpt from *Oh, the Places You'll Go!* by Dr. Seuss, TM and copyright © by Dr. Seuss Enterprises L.P., 1990. Reprinted by permission of Random House Children's Books, a division of Penguin Random House LLC. All rights reserved.

RANDOM HOUSE, AN IMPRINT AND DIVISION OF PENGUIN RANDOM HOUSE LLC AND CURTIS BROWN LTD.: "Leap Before You Look" from *W. H. Auden: Collected Poems,* copyright © 1945 and copyright renewed 1973 by W. H. Auden. Print rights throughout the United Kingdom and Commonwealth and digital rights throughout out the world administered by Curtis Brown Ltd. Reprinted by permission of Random House, an imprint and division of Penguin Random House LLC and Curtis Brown Ltd. All rights reserved.

RANDOM HOUSE, AN IMPRINT AND DIVISION OF PENGUIN RANDOM HOUSE LLC: Excerpt from *Eisenhower in War and Peace* by Jean Edward Smith, copyright © 2012 by Jean Edward Smith. Reprinted by permission of Random House, an imprint and division of Penguin Random House LLC. All rights reserved.

CASS SUNSTEIN: Excerpt from a toast given by Leon Wieseltier at the wedding of Cass Sunstein to Samantha Power. Used by permission.

INDEX

ALLEN LANE
an imprint of
PENGUIN BOOKS

Recently Published

Peter Hennessy and James Jinks, *The Silent Deep: The Royal Navy Submarine Service Since 1945*

Sean McMeekin, *The Ottoman Endgame: War, Revolution and the Making of the Modern Middle East, 1908–1923*

Charles Moore, *Margaret Thatcher: The Authorized Biography, Volume Two: Everything She Wants*

Dominic Sandbrook, *The Great British Dream Factory: The Strange History of Our National Imagination*

Larissa MacFarquhar, *Strangers Drowning: Voyages to the Brink of Moral Extremity*

Niall Ferguson, *Kissinger: 1923-1968: The Idealist*

Carlo Rovelli, *Seven Brief Lessons on Physics*

Tim Blanning, *Frederick the Great: King of Prussia*

Ian Kershaw, *To Hell and Back: Europe, 1914–1949*

Pedro Domingos, *The Master Algorithm: How the Quest for the Ultimate Learning Machine Will Remake Our World*

David Wootton, *The Invention of Science: A New History of the Scientific Revolution*

Christopher Tyerman, *How to Plan a Crusade: Reason and Religious War in the Middle Ages*

Andy Beckett, *Promised You A Miracle: UK 80–82*

Carl Watkins, *Stephen: The Reign of Anarchy*

Anne Curry, *Henry V: From Playboy Prince to Warrior King*

John Gillingham, *William II: The Red King*

Roger Knight, *William IV: A King at Sea*

Douglas Hurd, *Elizabeth II: The Steadfast*

Richard Nisbett, *Mindware: Tools for Smart Thinking*

Jochen Bleicken, *Augustus: The Biography*

Paul Mason, *PostCapitalism: A Guide to Our Future*

Frank Wilczek, *A Beautiful Question: Finding Nature's Deep Design*

Roberto Saviano, *Zero Zero Zero*

Owen Hatherley, *Landscapes of Communism: A History Through Buildings*

César Hidalgo, *Why Information Grows: The Evolution of Order, from Atoms to Economies*

Aziz Ansari and Eric Klinenberg, *Modern Romance: An Investigation*

Sudhir Hazareesingh, *How the French Think: An Affectionate Portrait of an Intellectual People*

Steven D. Levitt and Stephen J. Dubner, *When to Rob a Bank: A Rogue Economist's Guide to the World*

Leonard Mlodinow, *The Upright Thinkers: The Human Journey from Living in Trees to Understanding the Cosmos*

Hans Ulrich Obrist, *Lives of the Artists, Lives of the Architects*

Richard H. Thaler, *Misbehaving: The Making of Behavioural Economics*

Sheldon Solomon, Jeff Greenberg and Tom Pyszczynski, *Worm at the Core: On the Role of Death in Life*

Nathaniel Popper, *Digital Gold: The Untold Story of Bitcoin*

Dominic Lieven, *Towards the Flame: Empire, War and the End of Tsarist Russia*

Noel Malcolm, *Agents of Empire: Knights, Corsairs, Jesuits and Spies in the Sixteenth-Century Mediterranean World*

James Rebanks, *The Shepherd's Life: A Tale of the Lake District*

David Brooks, *The Road to Character*

Joseph Stiglitz, *The Great Divide*

Ken Robinson and Lou Aronica, *Creative Schools: Revolutionizing Education from the Ground Up*

Clotaire Rapaille and Andrés Roemer, *Move UP: Why Some Cultures Advances While Others Don't*

Jonathan Keates, *William III and Mary II: Partners in Revolution*

David Womersley, *James II: The Last Catholic King*

Richard Barber, *Henry II: A Prince Among Princes*

Jane Ridley, *Victoria: Queen, Matriarch, Empress*

John Gray, *The Soul of the Marionette: A Short Enquiry into Human Freedom*

Emily Wilson, *Seneca: A Life*

Michael Barber, *How to Run a Government: So That Citizens Benefit and Taxpayers Don't Go Crazy*

Dana Thomas, *Gods and Kings: The Rise and Fall of Alexander McQueen and John Galliano*

Steven Weinberg, *To Explain the World: The Discovery of Modern Science*

Jennifer Jacquet, *Is Shame Necessary?: New Uses for an Old Tool*

Eugene Rogan, *The Fall of the Ottomans: The Great War in the Middle East, 1914-1920*

Norman Doidge, *The Brain's Way of Healing: Stories of Remarkable Recoveries and Discoveries*

John Hooper, *The Italians*

Sven Beckert, *Empire of Cotton: A New History of Global Capitalism*

Mark Kishlansky, *Charles I: An Abbreviated Life*

Philip Ziegler, *George VI: The Dutiful King*

David Cannadine, *George V: The Unexpected King*

Stephen Alford, *Edward VI: The Last Boy King*

John Guy, *Henry VIII: The Quest for Fame*

Robert Tombs, *The English and their History: The First Thirteen Centuries*

Neil MacGregor, *Germany: The Memories of a Nation*

Uwe Tellkamp, *The Tower: A Novel*

Roberto Calasso, *Ardor*

Slavoj Žižek, *Trouble in Paradise: Communism After the End of History*

Francis Pryor, *Home: A Time Traveller's Tales from Britain's Prehistory*

R. F. Foster, *Vivid Faces: The Revolutionary Generation in Ireland, 1890-1923*

Andrew Roberts, *Napoleon the Great*

Shami Chakrabarti, *On Liberty*

Newport Library and
Information Service

03/5/16